Critical Language Awareness

Editor: Norman Fairclough

LONGMAN
London and New York

Longman Group UK Limited,
Longman House, Burnt Mill, Harlow,
Essex CM20 2JE, England
and Associated Companies throughout the world.

Published in the United States of America by Longman Publishing,
New York

First published 1992

British Library Cataloguing in Publication Data
A catalogue record for this book is available from the British Library

Library of Congress Cataloging-in-Publication Data
Critical language awareness / editor, Norman Fairclough.
    p.   cm. -- (Real language series)
Includes bibliographical references (p.) and index.
    ISBN 0–582–06466–X. -- ISBN 0–582–06467–8 (pbk.)
    1. Language awareness.   2. Language and education.
    I. Fairclough, Norman, 1941–   . II. Series.
    P120.L34C75   1992
    306.4'4--dc20
                                                            91–23532
                                                            CIP

Set in 10/12pt Sabon

Produced by Longman Singapore Publishers (Pte⁻) Ltd.
Printed in Singapore

Contents

List of contributors   vii

Acknowledgements   xi

1 Introduction   1
   Norman Fairclough

Part I Language Awareness:
           Critical and Non-critical Approaches   31

   2 The appropriacy of 'appropriateness'   33
     Norman Fairclough

Part II Critical Language Awareness in
            Diverse Educational Contexts   57

   3 Critical literacy awareness in the EFL classroom   59
     Catherine Wallace

   4 Making it work – communicaton skills training
     at a black housing association   93
     Pete Sayers

   5 Principles and practice of CLA in the classroom   117
     Romy Clark

   6 Who's who in academic writing?   141
     Roz Ivanič and John Simpson

   7 The construction of gender in a teenage magazine   174
     Mary Talbot

Part III   Critical Language Awareness in Schools   201

8 English teaching, information technology and
critical language awareness   203
Michael Stubbs

9 'What I've always known but never been told':
euphemisms, school discourse and empowerment   223
Malcolm McKenzie

10 Initial steps towards critical practice in
primary schools   238
Paul Clarke and Nick Smith

11 Critical approaches to language, learning and
pedagogy: a case study   256
Lesley Lancaster and Rhiannan Taylor

12 Whose resource? Minority languages, bilingual
learners and language awareness   285
Arvindh Bhatt and Marilyn Martin-Jones

Part IV   Critical Language Awareness: Perspectives
for Emancipation   303

13 Critical language awareness and emancipatory
discourse   305
Hilary Janks and Roz Ivanič

Index   332

List of Contributors

Arvindh Bhatt is the Advisory Teacher for Community Languages with Leicestershire. He has taught mathematics and Gujarati in British schools. He is a founder member and the chairman of Gujarati Shikshan Sangh. He has served as Chief Examiner for both the Midland Examining Group and for the RSA Diploma in Teaching of Community Languages. He is currently working at Leicester University on a research project to evaluate health promotion for minority ethnic groups.

Romy Clark has worked as a teacher and teacher trainer in ELT for many years, overseas and in the UK. She now works in the Institute for English Language Education at the University of Lancaster. She is responsible for coordinating the university's programme for Communication for Academic Purposes (Study Skills), for native and non native speakers of English. She is currently particularly interested in classroom applications of Critical Language Awareness/Discourse Analysis and the teaching of writing for academic purposes.

Paul Clarke is an advisory teacher for Assessment and Record Keeping in primary schools. His interests include the study of children using story to make sense of their learning, and using self-assessment as a means of curriculum change. He is a part-time student at Lancaster University where he is based in the Department of Linguistics and Modern English Language.

Norman Fairclough is a lecturer in the Department of Linguistics and Modern English Language at the University of Lancaster. His major interests are in critical and interdisciplinary studies of changing discourse practices in relation to social and cultural change. His publications include *Language and power* (Longman, 1989) and *Discourse and social change* (Polity Press, 1991).

Roz Ivanič and John Simpson have worked together intermittently since 1983, learning and researching academic writing. During that time Roz has worked as an adult literacy volunteer tutor, the coordinator of the language support unit at Kingsway College, London, a member of the Lancaster Literacy Research Group and of the Research and Practice in Adult Literacy editorial group. Since 1986 she has been working in the Department of Linguistics and Modern English Language at Lancaster University. In 1983 John was a basic education student; since then he completed the requirements of the Open College of the North West to qualify for higher education, and in 1991 graduated with a B.A. in Social Ethics. This is one of three articles they have co-authored on the subject of writer identity in academic writing.

Hilary Janks obtained degrees in English Literature and Applied Linguistics from the University of the Witwatersrand, South Africa. She is a Senior Lecturer at the University, working in both mother-tongue and second language teacher education. She serves on the the National Education Consultative Committee and helped to formulate the draft proposals for People's English. She is registered as a student at Lancaster University and is presently writing and researching critical language awareness materials for schools.

Lesley Lancaster studied linguistics at University and has been long interested in the relationship between language, learning and classroom practice. She has taught variously at primary, secondary and further education levels, mainly in London and Lancashire. She has also worked at the NFER, part of the time on the APU Language team. At present she works in Shropshire as a member of the Language Advisory Team and is closely involved with the LINC (Language in the National Curriculum) project.

Marilyn Martin-Jones has been teaching Linguistics at Lancaster University since 1983. From 1979 to 1983, she was a member of the Linguistic Minorities Project research team based at the University of London, Institute of Education. She is also joint author of *The other languages of England* (Routledge & Kegan

Paul, 1985). Her main area of research interest is bilingualism, language education policy and minority groups. At present, she is the coordinator of a new research project which is focusing on the classroom role of bilingual support staff in primary schools in the North West of England. She is also working on a book on bilingualism and linguistic minorities.

Malcolm McKenzie is at present Head of English at Maru a Pula Secondary School in Gaborone, Botswana. He has lectured at the tertiary level but his major current interest is to explore ways of introducing critical language teaching and critical thinking skills into the secondary classroom. Recent publications include 'Critical Linguistics and Practical Stylistics: Teaching the People's English Instead of the Queen's English' and 'Letting Lexis Come from the Learner: A Word in the Hand is Worth Two in the Bush'.

Pete Sayers worked for twelve years in Industrial Language Training in Bradford providing training in English as a Second Language, Communication Skills and Equal Opportunities in a wide variety of workplaces. He co-authored *Signing off* a source book of ESL teaching materials for the unemployed, and was a member of national Industrial Language Training (ILT) research group analysing cross-cultural interviewing. He has also published on this topic. He has an MA in Linguistics from Lancaster University where he developed his interest in language and power. He is now the staff development adviser for Bradford University.

John Simpson *see* Roz Ivanič

Nick Smith is currently a specialist support teacher, working in a local authority support service. His interests include the development of language awareness and literacy in the early years of school. He has carried out research into linguistic variation and dialect effects in young children's writing, class activities based around language awareness, and developing literacy with children who have learning difficulties.

Michael Stubbs is Professor of English Linguistics at the University of Trier, West Germany. He was previously Professor of English at the Institute of Education, University of London (1985–90), and Lecturer in Linguistics at the University of Nottingham (1974–85). He has also lectured in Australia, China, India, Japan, USA, Yemen Arab Republic and several European countries. His main publications include: *Discourse analysis* (Blackwell, 1983) and *Educational linguistics* (Blackwell, 1986). He was a member of the Cox Committee, appointed by the Secretary of State for Education to advise on the English curriculum in schools in England and Wales (1988–89). He has been chair of the British Association for Applied Linguistics (1988–91).

Mary Talbot is lecturer in the Department of English Literature at Chester College of Higher Education. She teaches courses on Language Varieties and Language and the Developing Self. She is currently working on a book on fiction as social practice, with particular attention to romance and feminist science fiction.

Rhiannan Taylor was Head of Modern Languages at Madeley Court School in Shropshire. Her interest in language grew from her multilingual family background and led to her studying languages at University. She became a classroom teacher in Liverpool, before moving to Shropshire. She is currently working as Advisory Teacher for Equal Opportunities and completing an MA, specialising in bilingualism and education.

Catherine Wallace is a principal lecturer in EFL/ESL in the Department of English Language Teaching at Ealing College, London. Her major responsibility is as coordinator of an MA course – Language in the Multicultural Community. She is the author of *Learning to read in a multicultural society: the social context of second language literacy* (Prentice-Hall, 1988) and she has a forthcoming publication entitled *Reading* to be published by Oxford University Press in 1991.

Acknowledgements

We are grateful to the following for permission to reproduce copyright material;

Argus Newspapers Ltd for the article 'Ignore the Third World driver at your peril' by Sue Olswang from *Saturday Star* 23.12.89, copyright Saturday Star; Conservative Central Office for the article 'Mother knows best' by Margaret Thatcher from *Onward* April 1954 (pub Conservative Party); European Magazines Ltd for an extract from the article 'The Giraffe-Necked Women of Burma' by Linda Grant from *Marie Claire* magazine, December 1989; Hakuhodo UK Ltd for an advertisement for Citizen watches; Solo Syndication & Literary Agency Ltd for the article 'The blame that Spain must share' by Richard Kay from *Daily Mail* 3.8.89; D C Thomson & Co Ltd for extracts from the article 'Lips Inc!' from *Jackie* magazine 20.9.86, (c) D C Thomson & Co Ltd, 1986.

1 Introduction

Norman Fairclough

This book is a contribution to current debate on the role and nature of 'language awareness' in language education. In recent years, language awareness has been widely advocated as an important part of language education. The chapters in this volume agree with this position, but they also share the view that language awareness programmes and materials have hitherto been insufficiently 'critical'. That is, they have not given sufficient attention to important social aspects of language, especially aspects of the relationship between language and power, which ought to be highlighted in language education.[1]

The term 'language awareness' has been used since the early 1980s to refer specifically to the advocacy by a group of language teachers, educationalists and applied linguists of a new language awareness element in the school curriculum, at the top end of primary school or in the early years of secondary school (Hawkins 1984, NCLE 1985). I shall use the abbreviation 'LA' for this language awareness movement. But the term is also used alongside others such as 'knowledge about language' to designate in a more general way conscious attention to properties of language and language use as an element of language education. Arguments for language awareness in schools in this broader sense occurred before LA (Doughty et al. 1971 is a notable example), and can be found in recent reports on the teaching of English within the national curriculum (DES 1988, DES 1989). This book is concerned with language awareness in the more general sense, and not only in schools but also in other domains of education. But in using the expression 'language awareness' in the title, and in referring to 'critical language awareness' (henceforth CLA) rather than, say, 'critical knowledge of language', we recognise the importance of LA during the past decade in advancing the general case for making knowledge about language a significant element in language education, and doing so partly on the basis of social concerns which overlap to some extent with our own. Much of the discussion of existing work in language awareness in this book focuses upon LA.

The book is in part a critique of existing conceptions of language awareness, but its focus is upon the nature of alternative conceptions, and upon their practical implementation in various educational contexts. Contexts referred to include primary and secondary schools, universities and colleges of higher education. Contributors write both as theorists and as practitioners, with a variety of interests and professional concerns – including language in multicultural education, teaching of English in primary and secondary schools, industrial language training and race awareness training, literacy and adult literacy, language and gender, English as a foreign language, and theoretical interests in critical approaches to language study. The distinction between theory and practice is not however a neat one, since some contributors engage in both. Nor does it simply correspond to the distinction between those working in higher education and those working in other educational spheres: some of the latter make theoretical contributions, and some of the former write primarily as practitioners. I think that the book as a whole achieves an unusually high level of integration between theory and practice, and my hope is that this will make it better able to strengthen critical strands of thinking in current debates about language education.

CLA presupposes and builds upon what is variously called 'critical language study', 'critical linguistics', or 'critical discourse analysis' (see for example Fairclough 1989, Kress 1989, Mey 1985). It also presupposes a critical conception of education and schooling. I shall spell out these presuppositions below, especially the former, which will be new to many readers. But I think that it is vital first of all to situate both critical language study and CLA in their social and historical contexts: I shall argue that the case for critical approaches to language and language education is becoming increasingly persuasive *now*, because of contemporary changes affecting the role of language in social life. I shall also develop the distinction between critical and non-critical approaches to language awareness, and my comments above on the relevance of this book to current debates over language education. The other component of this introduction is a summary of the themes and issues raised by contributors.

Language education in a climate of change

It can hardly be news to anyone that we are living in a period of intense social change. But what is perhaps less obvious is how important language is within the changes that are taking place (Fairclough 1990a). In three ways. First, there are changes in the ways in which power and social control are exercised. There has been a long-term tendency for power relations to be increasingly set up and maintained in the routine workings of particular social practices (e.g. performing one's job, or consulting a doctor), rather than by force. This shift from more explicit to more implicit exercise of power means that the common-sense routines of language practices (e.g. classroom language, or the language of medical consultations) become important in sustaining and reproducing power relations. This has been linked to the salience of ideology in the functioning of power in modern societies (see Thompson 1984, Fairclough 1989).

Second, a significant part of what is changing in contemporary society is precisely language practices – for example, changes in the nature and relative importance of language in various types of work, or changes in ways of talking as part of changes in professional–client relationship. And third, language itself is more and more becoming a target for change, with the achievement of change in language practices being perceived as a significant element in the imposition of change.[1]

It is changes of this sort that make critical approaches to language study of particular contemporary relevance, and make CLA an urgently needed element in language education. CLA is, I believe, coming to be a prerequisite for effective democratic citizenship, and should therefore be seen as an *entitlement* for citizens, especially children developing towards citizenship in the educational system.

Let me give some examples to illustrate the second and third points above. A fundamental and pervasive example of changing language practices as a significant dimension of social change is what is happening to language in places of work. There has been a large-scale restructuring of employment which has led to a larger service sector and a smaller manufacturing sector, and this in itself has major implications for the linguistic demands of work – many more people are having to communicate with 'clients' or 'publics', for example. The quality of the communication is coming to be seen as part of the quality of the service. Even within manufacturing, there is a shift away from isolated work on a production line to team work, and workers are seen as needing more complex 'communicative skills'. One interesting development is that discussions of such skills increasingly highlight abilities in face-to-face interaction, group discussion and decision-making, 'listening skills', and so forth – abilities which have previously been seen (in so far as they have been noticed) as general 'life skills' rather than vocational skills. And of course another new category of skills expected of workers is in communicating with and via computers (see Chapter 8).

Another example of changing language practices which affects people both in their work and as 'clients' is change in the ways in which professional–client interactions are structured. Examples are interactions between doctors and patients, between solicitors and their clients, between teachers and pupils, or between shop assistants and customers. Practice is highly variable, but there does seem to be a tendency towards more informal and more conversational language. Whereas clients were traditionally expected to adapt to the practices imposed by the professions, professionals now seem to be adapting to practices familiar to clients. What this example suggests is that changing language practices are closely tied in with changes in social relationships (between professionals and clients in this instance) and with changing social identities (in this case, both the social identities of professionals and the social identities of their clients).

Notice that both the examples I have given illustrate what is, I think, an important contemporary tendency: for the informal, conversational language associated with face-to-face interaction and group interaction in more private spheres of life to shift into public and institutional spheres. An example which I discuss later in the book (see pp. 44–5) is medical interviews. There is a deep ambivalence about the contemporary 'conversationalisation' of language, as we might call it, in its implications for power:

on the one hand, it goes along with a genuine opening up and democratisation of professional domains, a shift in power towards the client and the consumer. But on the other hand, conversational style provides a strategy for exercising power in more subtle and implicit ways, and many professionals are now trained in such strategies (see Fairclough 1990b). Other areas of what seems like democratisation of language practices are perhaps similarly ambivalent, including greater apparent acceptance of minority languages and non-standard varieties of English in various institutional contexts.

I also suggested above that language itself is becoming a target for change, and change in language practices is coming to be seen as significant in the implementation of more general social and cultural change. Systematic institutional links are being set up between research into existing language practices, redesign of language practices to improve their 'effectiveness', and training of personnel in new language practices. And specialist institutional personnel are being employed to do this work – for example, it is coming to be seen as one aspect of the expertise of management consultants. This more interventionist orientation to language is reflected in how language is pervasively conceptualised in terms of skills or techniques (such as interviewing and counselling) which are designed (and can be redesigned) for particular purposes, and can be applied in various domains and institutions more or less independently of context. I have suggested elsewhere that 'technologisation' of language is a striking feature of contemporary society (Fairclough 1990b).

The process of technologisation is one explanation for the new emphasis upon training in spoken language skills within language education, which seems to be partly motivated by anticipated changes in the demands of work (see Barnes 1988, Fairclough 1990a). Again, training in, for example, interview techniques which underscores the values of informality and client centredness is becoming an increasingly recognised part of the training of managers and professionals, and draws upon the results of (more or less systematic) research into professional interviews. Or again, advertising techniques are a well-established domain of research, design and training. Notice that in the latter two cases technologisation affects not only language, but also non-verbal communication in the case of the former and visual images in the case of the latter, and is often cast in psychological rather than linguistic terms. What is often at issue is the language element in a wider process of technologisation.

These then are some of the ways in which language is involved in contemporary processes of change. One consequence is that language practices are widely problematised: people commonly have problems knowing how to act as professionals, clients, parents, children, managers, employees, colleagues; and part of the problem is not being quite sure how to talk, write, or interpret what others say or write. And interaction between women and men, or between members of different cultures, often aggravates these problems. A rather different sort of problematisation is the unease that people commonly feel about the way language works in politics or the media or advertising. But we all have a relationship to language practices which mixes in various proportions problematisation with naturalisation: even new practices tend to take on the common sense, natural and background properties which the ground rules of social life need to have to a high degree if people are to function. It is this tendency to naturalisation that makes technologising interventions to shape language practices so potentially insidious.

In this context, it is not surprising, I think, that critical approaches to language study have been attracting more interest from linguists and language educators. A critical orientation is called for by the social circumstances we are living in. If power relations are indeed increasingly coming to be exercised implicitly in language, and if language practices are indeed coming to be consciously controlled and inculcated, then a linguistics which contents itself with describing language practices without trying to explain them, and relate them to the social and power relations which underlie them, seems to be missing an important point. And a language education focused upon training in language skills, without a critical component, would seem to be failing in its responsibility to learners. People cannot be effective citizens in a democratic society if their education cuts them off from critical consciousness of key elements within their physical or social environment. If we are committed to education establishing resources for citizenship, critical awareness of the language practices of one's speech community is an entitlement.[2]

Critical language study

A critical view of education and schooling, and a critical approach to language study, are as I suggested earlier presuppositions of CLA. I assume that the development of a critical awareness of the world, and of the possibilities for changing it, ought to be the main objective of all education, including language education, a perspective which is eloquently summed up by Freire:

> Whether it be a raindrop (a raindrop that was about to fall but froze, giving birth to a beautiful icicle), be it a bird that sings, a bus that runs, a violent person on the street, be it a sentence in a newspaper, a political speech, a lover's rejection, be it anything, we must adopt a critical view, that of the person who questions, who doubts, who investigates, and who wants to illuminate the very life we live. (Freire 1985; see also Clark et al. 1988: 32–3)

But the notion of a critical approach to language will be less familiar, and needs more explanation.

Critical language study (CLS henceforth) is not a branch of language study, but an orientation towards language (and maybe in embryo a new theory of language) with implications for various branches. It highlights how language conventions and language practices are invested with power relations and ideological processes which people are often unaware of. It criticises mainstream language study for taking conventions and practices at face value, as objects to be described, in a way which obscures their political and ideological investment. CLS is not new, and in fact one important contribution dates from sixty years ago (Voloshinov 1973, written in the late 1920s), but it has become relatively well known only in the past decade or so (Fowler et al. 1979, Pêcheux 1982, Mey 1985, Fairclough 1989). Important influences have been social theorists such as Pierre Bourdieu, Michel Foucault and Jurgen Habermas, whose work has been relatively language-centred, and theories of discourse which have come to be closely linked with developments in thinking about ideology and the social subject (Foucault 1981, Pêcheux 1982, Henriques et al. 1984). There are various groups and approaches, not all of which identify themselves as 'critical'. The most important one in Britain has been the 'critical linguistics' group (Fowler et al. 1979, Kress & Hodge 1979). The account of CLS below is a personal one, though I think most of it would attract fairly general agreement.

I shall try to characterise CLS as concisely as possible in terms of five theoretical propositions, and a framework for critical analysis of discourse. Needless to say, this account is a highly schematic one, and readers who would like to have a fuller picture should consult some of the material referred to in the last paragraph.

(1) Language use – 'discourse' – shapes and is shaped by society

It is commonplace that use of language is socially determined, and that language varies according to the social situation it is used in. What (1) emphasises is that language use has *effects upon* (other dimensions of) society as well as being shaped by it. It is a two-way, 'dialectical', relationship. From now on I use the term 'discourse' rather than 'language use'.[3]

(2) Discourse helps to constitute (and change) knowledge and its objects, social relations, and social identity

This spells out the effects of discourse upon society – discourse *constitutes* the social. Three dimensions of the social are distinguished – knowledge, social relations, and social identity – and these correspond respectively to three major functions of language: its *ideational* function, its function in representing and signifying the world and our experience; its *relational* function, in constituting and changing social relations; its *identical* function, in constituting and changing social identities. Halliday (1978) collapses the second and third in his *interpersonal* function. In any discourse, these three functions are simultaneously being served – and in any discourse, knowledge, social relations and social identities are simultaneously being constituted or reconstituted.

(3) Discourse is shaped by relations of power, and invested with ideologies

This spells out the effects of society upon discourse. One effect is the way in which particular languages and language varieties are valued or devalued according to the power of their users with the notion of a 'standard' variety legitimising and naturalising particular valuations. It is also helpful to think of these effects as shaping conventions for particular discourse types, such as medical interview genre, which achieve a certain social stability, and which are drawn upon in discourse. (3) suggests that power affects such discourse conventions by 'investing' them ideologically in particular ways. We can think of this in terms of the ideational, relational, and identical meanings built into genres like medical interview: for example, the way medical interviews tend to be organised, in terms of the distribution of 'turns' at talking or in terms of their topics, embodies particular, ideological, assumptions about medical knowledge, relations between doctors and patients, the social identities of doctors and patients.

(4) The shaping of discourse is a stake in power struggles

That is, the processes referred to in (3) are contested. It is clear from (2) why this should be so: if discourse conventions constitute the social in particular ways, then control of these constitutive processes would be a powerful covert mechanism of domination. A particular set of discourse practices and conventions may achieve a high degree of *naturalisation* – they may come to be seen as simply 'there' in a common-sense way, rather than socially put there. This is a measure of the extent to which powerful social forces and groups dominate a society or a particular institution. But dominant practices and conventions may be confronted with alternative or oppositional ones, with different valuations of languages and varieties, or different ideological investments. For example, there are various ways in which medical interviews are conducted these days, including ways favoured by those in an oppositional (or 'alternative') position within medicine, where the interview is less tightly controlled by the doctor, and ideological assumptions about medical knowledge, and doctor–patient relations and social identities, are different.

(5) CLS sets out to show how society and discourse shape each other

In accepting dominant conventions and practices at face value, as just 'data' to be described, mainstream language study can be seen as contributing to the naturalisation effect referred to above – though not of course consciously or deliberately. Social sciences are not neutral or innocent, they stand in particular relationships to dominant or dominated groups and forces, and contribute correspondingly to social struggles. CLS sees itself as a resource for developing the consciousness of particularly those people who are dominated in a linguistic way. Of course, linguistic domination tends to co-occur with other forms of domination. Consciousness is a precondition for the development of new practices and conventions which can contribute to social emancipation – to what one might call emancipatory discourse practices (see Clark et al. 1988, and Chapter 13 by Janks & Ivanič).

The shaping of discourse by society and of society by discourse are on the one hand long-term practices which progressively restructure the sociolinguistic order (Fairclough 1989), but on the other hand processes which affect every instance of discourse. I shall conclude this section with a brief outline of a framework for analysing specific instances of discourse in a way which highlights these processes – for doing 'critical discourse analysis'.

Every discoursal instance has three dimensions: it is a spoken or written language *text*; it is an *interaction* between people, involving processes of producing and interpreting the text; and it is part of a piece of *social action* – and in some cases virtually the whole of it. These dimensions are shown in Figure 1.1 below.

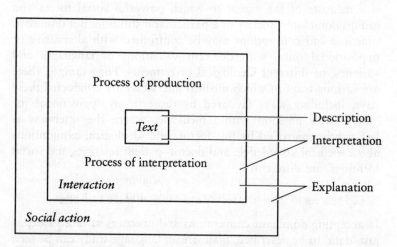

Figure 1.1:   *A three-dimensional view of discourse analysis*

The relationship between social action and text is mediated by interaction: that is, the nature of the interaction, how texts are produced and interpreted, depends upon the social action in which they are embedded; and the nature of the text, its formal and stylistic properties, on the one hand depends upon and constitutes 'traces' of its process of production, and on the other hand constitutes 'cues' for its interpretation. Critical discourse analysis itself also has three dimensions: *description* of the text; *interpretation* of the interaction processes, and their relationship to the text; and *explanation* of how the interaction process relates to the social action. Although attention to formal aspects of the language of texts (within 'description') is an important element of this framework, so too is the emphasis on the need to 'frame' the text and its formal features within the other dimensions of analysis.

In the *interpretation* phase of analysis, the aim is to specify what conventions are being drawn upon, and how. The repertoire of available conventions includes various genres (interview, advertising, lecture) and various discourse types (medical, scientific, legal), including both dominant and oppositional/'alternative' conventions. There are standard, normative ways of using and combining these resources, but they can also be used and combined in creative, innovative ways, and interpretational analysis tries to pinpoint how conventions are used. For example, in the 'alternative' type of medical interview I referred to above, one finds a mixture of conversation, counselling, and a more traditional sort of medical interview – being alternative or oppositional is manifested discoursally in an innovative combination of conventions, which breaks down traditional boundaries between types of discourse practice.

In the *explanation* phase of the analysis, one aim is to explain such properties of the interaction by referring to its social context – by placing the interaction within the matrix of the social action it is a part of. For example, where the social action is conventional and takes place within relatively stable and well-defined social relations and practices, one might expect discourse conventions to be followed in a relatively normative way (as in a traditional medical interview). It is when relations and practices are in flux, and when the social action is perhaps oppositional or in some way problematic, that one might expect innovative combinations of conventions. Explanation is also concerned with assessing the contribution of the discourse to the social action, the effectivity of the discourse in constituting or helping to reconstitute the different dimensions of the social referred to in the second of the five propositions above. And it also aims to specify the ideological and political investment of conventions, and the ideological and political import of particular ways of using and combining them. (See Fairclough 1989 for detailed exemplification of this framework.)

Language awareness: critical and non-critical approaches

Within non-critical approaches to language awareness, I would include the previous work I referred to at the beginning of the introduction: the language awareness movement or LA (Hawkins 1984, NCLE 1985), as well as the Kingman and Cox Reports (DES 1988, DES 1989), and Doughty et al. 1971. In the comparison below, I refer primarily to LA, and then mainly to Hawkins (1984). Critical and non-critical approaches will be compared in terms of: rationale for language awareness; conceptions of language awareness work; the relationship envisaged between language awareness and other elements of language education.

I have constructed a rationale for language awareness work in a critical perspective from my brief analysis above of the way language is implicated in social processes and social relations in the contemporary world: given that power relations work increasingly at an implicit level through language, and given that language practices are increasingly targets for intervention and control, a critical awareness of language is a prerequisite for effective citizenship, and a democratic entitlement.

There is some similarity between the rationale for CLA and part of the rationale for LA, in that the latter attempts like the former to use language education as a resource for tackling social problems which centre around language. But the arguments are cast in very different terms. In Hawkins (1984), this dimension of the rationale for LA refers to social aspects of educational failure (which I discuss below), a lack of understanding of language which impedes parents in supporting the language development of their children, and an endemic 'linguistic parochialism and prejudice' affecting minority languages and non-standard varieties. These are indeed problems which language awareness can help to address, but from a CLA perspective they are just particular points of salience within the much broader contemporary problematisation of language I have been indicating. A fundamental difference between LA and CLA is their assumptions about what language awareness can do for such problems. Within LA, schools seem to be credited with a substantial capacity for contributing to social harmony and integration, and smoothing the workings of the social and sociolinguistic orders. Language awareness work is portrayed as making up for and helping to overcome social problems (e.g. making up for a lack of 'verbal learning tools' in the home, extending access to standard English to children whose homes do not give it to them). In the case of CLA, the argument is that schools dedicated to a critical pedagogy (Freire 1985, Giroux 1983) ought to provide learners with understanding of problems which cannot be resolved just in the schools; and with the resources for engaging if they so wish in the long-term, multifaceted struggles in various social domains (including education) which are necessary to resolve them. I shall suggest below, in discussing the treatment of standard English, that the LA position can in fact have unforeseen detrimental social consequences.

There are a number of other elements in the rationale for LA. I referred above to social aspects of educational failure, and Hawkins refers in this connection to evidence that schools have had the effect of 'widening the gap' between children who get 'verbal learning tools' at home and those who don't (1984: 1). Language awareness work can help all children 'sharpen the tools of verbal learning' (1984: 98). LA is particularly sensitive to the need to improve study skills in the 'difficult transition from primary to secondary school language work, especially the start of foreign language studies and the explosion of concepts and language introduced by the specialist secondary school subjects' (Hawkins 1984: 4). The poor record of British schools in foreign language learning is part of the rationale for LA; there is an emphasis upon developing 'insight into pattern' and 'learning to listen' as conditions for success in foreign language learning. A related educational problem which LA seeks to address is the absence of a coherent approach to language from the child's perspective, including a lack of coordination between different parts of the language curriculum. There is also (NCLE 1985: 23) reference to the particular linguistic demands arising from rapid social change, where 'many more events require interpretation', especially interpretation of linguistic signals.

Although CLA highlights critical awareness of non-transparent aspects of the social functioning of language, that does not imply a lack of concern with issues such as linguistic dimensions of educational failure or inadequacies in foreign language learning. Nor, turning to a comparison of conceptions of language awareness work, does it imply a lack of concern with formal aspects of language, which take up a large proportion of LA materials. I would see the position of CLA rather as claiming that these important issues and dimensions of language awareness ought to be framed within a critical view of language; for example, in describing a framework for critical discourse analysis above I stressed the importance of attending to formal linguistic features of texts, but also stressed the importance of framing such textual analysis within a critical discourse analysis. Having made these points, I shall focus my comparison of conceptions of language awareness work upon views of linguistic variation, and especially the treatment of standard English.

LA, like the Kingman and Cox Reports (DES 1988, DES 1989), takes the position that it is vital for schools to teach pupils standard English, while treating the diversity of languages in the classroom as 'a potential resource of great richness', and recognising that all languages and varieties of languages 'have their rightful and proper place' in children's repertoires and 'each serves good purposes' (Hawkins 1984: 171–5). (See my discussion of the treatment of standard English in the Cox Report later in the book, pp. 35–7.) Standard English and other varieties and languages are presented as differing in conditions of appropriateness. Vigorous arguments are advanced for the *entitlement* of children to education in standard English, especially standard written English, as part of the 'apprenticeship in autonomy' which schools should provide (Hawkins 1984: 65). Stigmatisation of particular varieties or accents is attributed to parochialism or prejudice.

There is no doubt whatsoever that learning standard English does give some learners life chances they would not otherwise have. On the other hand, this view of standard English and language variation misses important issues and can I think have detrimental effects. First, there is an assumption that schools can help iron out the effects of social class and equalise the 'cultural capital' (Bourdieu 1984) of access to prestigious varieties of English. I think this assumption needs cautious handling, because it is easy to exaggerate the capacity of schools for social engineering: the class system is reproduced in many domains, not just education.

Second, there is no recognition in LA work that in passing on prestigious practices and values such as those of standard English *without* developing a critical awareness of them, one is implicitly legitimising them *and* the asymmetrical distribution of cultural capital I have just referred to. Third, portraying standard English and other languages and varieties as differing in conditions of appropriateness is dressing up inequality as diversity: standard English is 'appropriate' in situations which carry social clout, while other varieties are 'appropriate' at the margins. Fourth, attributing the stigmatisation of varieties to individual prejudice papers over the systematic, socially legitimised stigmatisation of varieties. Elevating the standard means demoting other varieties. Again, there is likely to be a mismatch between the liberalism and pluralism of the schools, and the children's experience. It is these mismatches, based upon well-meaning white lies about language variation, that carry the risk of detrimental effects: either they will create delusions, or they will create cynicism and a loss of credibility, or most probably a sequence of the former followed by the latter. I think a CLA position on the treatment of standard English is that one should teach written standard English for pragmatic reasons, but one should also expose learners to views about standard English, including the critical views I have alluded to here. And one should raise with the learners the question of whether and why and how dominant rules of 'appropriateness' might be flouted and challenged (see my Chapter 2 on appropriateness).

At the root of the different conceptions of language awareness work are different conceptions of language, and of sociolinguistic variation. LA is based in a tradition that sees a sociolinguistic order as a given and common-sense reality, effectively a natural domain rather than a naturalised domain, which is 'there' to be described. The question of *why* it is there scarcely arises, and there is certainly not the focus upon sociolinguistic orders being shaped and transformed by relations of power and power struggle, which characterises the critical approach to language study I outlined earlier.

Let me come finally to the relationship envisaged between language awareness and other elements of language education. There is agreement between LA and CLA that, as Hawkins puts it (1984: 73–4), 'awareness' affects 'competence' – or as

I would prefer to put it, awareness affects language capabilities. LA does not, however, set out to build into language education explicit connections between developing awareness and developing capabilities: language awareness work is isolated from other parts of language education as a separate element in the curriculum. By contrast, a central theme in a critical approach is that language awareness should be fully integrated with the development of practice and capabilities.

Figure 1.2 (from Clark et al. 1988) gives one representation of this integration.

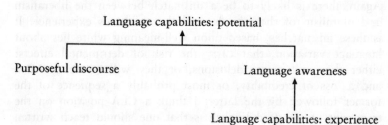

Figure 1.2:   *A model of language learning*

This model incorporates the important principle that critical language awareness should be built from the existing language capabilities and experience of the learner. The experience of the learner can, with the help of the teacher, be made explicit and systematic as a body of knowledge which can be used for discussion and reflection, so that social causes for experiences (e.g. of constraint) can be explored. At the same time, links should constantly be made between work on the development of language awareness and the language practice of the learner. This practice must be 'purposeful'. That is, it must be tied in to the learner's real wishes and needs to communicate with specific real people, because this is the only way for the learner to experience authentically the risks and potential benefits of particular decisions. When critical awareness is linked to such decisions, it broadens their scope to include decisions about whether to flout sociolinguistic conventions or to follow them, whether to conform or not conform (see Chapters five (Clark), six (Ivanič and Simpson) and 13 (Janks and Ivanič). It also allows such decisions to be seen as, in certain circumstances, collective rather than individual ones, associated with the political strategies of groups.

Contributions

The chapters in this volume address a wide range of issues connected with language awareness, referring to diverse educational contexts – primary and secondary schools, colleges of further and higher education and universities. Let me identify some major themes. One is, of course, comparisons between LA and CLA, notably in terms of their treatment of bilingualism and minority languages, their treatment of standard English, and the linguistic and sociolinguistic theories they are based upon. Another important issue is the relationship between CLA and styles of teaching and learning: several chapters argue that the development of CLA ought to go hand-in-hand with the development of critical or 'learner-centred' pedagogy. Some chapters focus upon processes of writing, while others focus upon reading and critical reading practices (linked in one case to 'critical literacy awareness'). A number of these chapters concerned with writing and reading share a focus upon critical awareness of how language relates to social identity: how texts 'position' readers in terms of their social identity, how particular writing practices (e.g. academic writing) entail particular social identities, how attitudes to linguistic practices are underpinned by affective factors (e.g. a sense of linguistic inadequacy on the part of minority groups). Another major theme is the potential of CLA for emancipating and empowering people, and this is also addressed in terms of social identity, e.g. the capacity of groups and individuals to challenge dominant practices in the course of projecting their identities. A final theme is the implications for CLA work of new language practices associated with information technology.

The chapters are grouped in four sections. Part I, Language awareness: critical and non-critical approaches consists of my chapter two, 'The appropriacy of "appropriateness"', which is something of a ground-clearing exercise for CLA, focusing upon views of language variation. It argues that a model of language variation based upon the concept of 'appropriateness' underpins current policy and practice in language education, including non-critical work in language awareness, that this model is a major obstacle to CLA, and that a critique of it is therefore an important undertaking. The first part of the chapter discusses the Cox Report (DES 1989) and prevocational education programmes, arguing that an appropriateness model of variation helps rationalise (a) a policy of teaching standard English while claiming to respect other languages and dialects, and (b) the extension to language of a competence-based model of education, highlighting training in 'language skills'. Crucially, the appropriateness model helps, in the Cox Report for instance, to achieve a compromise between these (respectively conservative and modernising) policy objectives. The second part of the chapter is a critique of the appropriateness model, first on the grounds that it gives a misleading picture of sociolinguistic variation, and second on the grounds that it confuses sociolinguistic realities with ideologies.

Part II deals with CLA in 'other education contexts' – colleges of further and higher education and universities. Catherine Wallace's Chapter three ('Critical literacy awareness in the EFL classroom') describes a procedure for critical reading developed with EFL students in a college of higher education. The author notes the contrast between her own work and a tradition in EFL which avoids contentious texts and sees reading in relatively unproblematic terms. Critical reading is not just a matter of critical responses to texts, it is also a matter of developing critical awareness of literacy. Wallace's procedure is designed to raise three issues: how social groups differ in their reading practices, how particular sorts of texts involve particular processes of production and are designed for particular expected readers, and how contextual factors influence the interpretation of texts. Wallace's method for critical reading stresses the intertextuality of texts – how they relate to other texts, and how they draw upon various genres – and the idea that texts create configurations of discourses which set up 'ideal' reading positions which critical reading should deconstruct. Access to these discourses requires detailed analysis of the language of texts which learners are often ill-equipped to do, though Wallace notes that EFL learners often have better metalinguistic resources for the task than native speakers. Wallace used a variety of methods in her classes, including a critical version of a 'pre-reading, while-reading, post-reading' procedure. Her chapter reports work on three media texts, including one which was interpreted quite differently by different groups according to the linguistic resources and awareness of literacy they were able to bring to it.

Pete Sayers' Chapter four ('Making it work – communications skills training at a black housing association') describes a training course he did for two Asian staff working for a black housing association. This Chapter highlights affective aspects of CLA which have been neglected elsewhere: 'feelings of inadequacy underpin acceptance of dominant ideologies' and dominant linguistic practices, and critical awareness of these ideologies and practices will develop only if these feelings are tackled. I think this raises the important question of how different groups are positioned in different relationships to the linguistic resources of communities; according to Bourdieu (1984), the bourgeoisie are positioned in a relationship of ease and confident control, the petit bourgeoisie in a relationship of anxiety. In the case of the black community, it is assumed by themselves and the white community that they have 'a language problem' – which is often seen to include labouring under the disadvantage of being bilingual! Pete Sayers' strategy was to suggest that maybe white British culture has language problems, or hang-ups, and that responsibility for particular problems may be at least shared. The course focused upon incoming correspondence to the housing association, providing the two Asian learners not only with strategies for processing difficult texts, but also a view of the difficulty as perhaps attributable at least as much to the faults of the writer as to the 'language problem' of the readers. The learners were encouraged to express their feelings, give vent to their frustrations, and laugh at convoluted letters. A similar approach was adopted with spelling. The perception that they had 'a spelling problem' prevented the learners from seeking practical help. They were encouraged to see the spelling system as often 'daft', judgements about the seriousness of spelling errors (especially those made by non-native speakers) as often inequitable. The paper also points to implications of this CLA work for the learners' own writing. It helped them in starting to develop a 'house style' for letters to tenants which accorded with the politics of the housing association, aiming at clarity and sensitivity to the feelings and concerns of tenants.

Chapter five, by Romy Clark, ('Principles and practice of CLA in the classroom') gives an account of a study skills programme which she has developed in a British university, and especially of how the course raises students' consciousness about the writing process. This consciousness-raising work informs and is further informed by collaborative writing workshops and tutorials, and work by the students on real assessment projects within their degree schemes. Clark sees students as aspiring members of an 'academic discourse community' whose conventions they are expected to understand and acquire, though they are often faced with major impediments to doing so. The objective of her study skills course is to 'empower' students by giving them a critical awareness of these conventions – of what you are allowed to say, how you are allowed to say it, and, importantly, what you are allowed to be – what subject positions (social identities) you are allowed to take up in academic writing. The course questions the social origins of these conventions and their effects, and gives students a chance to decide how they feel about them. The course thus provides students with the means for 'emancipation' through the flouting of conventions and the development of forms of non-conventional academic writing, though whether this route is taken is up to the students themselves: a major theme of the paper is that students are faced with the *dilemma*, which they must resolve for themselves, of whether to conform or not conform, whether to lean in the direction of fulfilling obligations or of claiming rights.

Roz Ivanič and John Simpson's Chapter six ('Who's who in academic writing?') shares with Clark's Chapter five a focus upon academic writing and the identity of the writer. The chapter describes co-research between a university teacher and a student now in higher education, into the latter's development as an academic writer. It starts from the assumption that 'writers not only construct their texts but are also constructed by them', and focuses upon a problem of identity: given the overwhelming prestige of 'impersonal', 'objective' academic style, how can a student – this student – project his own identity in his writing, 'find the "I"', show himself as the sort of person he wants to be? 'Finding the "I"' is a matter of responsibility to oneself and to one's readership: it is a way towards truthfulness and clarity. Drawing upon Mary Talbot's ideas (see below and Chapter seven), the authors suggest that writers may be better able to tackle their dilemmas over identity if they become conscious of the 'casts' or 'populations' of identities in the texts they read as well as in their own writing. This is a matter of raising their critical awareness of the standardised conventions of academic writing, and their effects upon identities. The chapter includes an analysis in these terms of three assignments written by John Simpson. The 'population' consists of tutors who set the assignments, the people who wrote what he read, John himself, the people he writes about, and the people who read what he writes. What emerges is a tense relationship between the pressures upon him to conform and his own often cautious and nervous attempts to project his own identity and evolve his own academic style. The authors feel that their research has yielded insight into language and language learning, but also has helped develop the writing of both of them.

Mary Talbot, in Chapter 7, ('The construction of gender in a teenage magazine') takes up again the theme of social identity in language which is dealt with by Clark, and Ivanič and Simpson. Here, however, the focus is upon how a teenage girls' magazine contributes to the construction of feminine social identity. Talbot sees the texts of written media discourse as constructing imaginary identities for readers, often as members of specific 'communities' defined in terms of consumption, which readers may or may not be in a position to contest. She places the question of how readers are constructed within the wider question of what the total 'population' of a text is – the totality of personae or voices represented in a text. A text is seen as a complex and heterogeneous 'tissue of voices', the interactants (writer, reader, but also characters shown as interacting in the text), the characters whose thoughts and words are represented in the text, the subject positions that are set up for interactants in the text. The author discusses a range of textual features (including speech reportage, presupposition, and adjacency pairs) which are clues to text population. Her chapter analyses a 'consumer feature' – a form which mixes editorial material and advertising – dealing with lipstick from the magazine *Jackie*, showing how it constructs an imaginary 'community of lipstick wearers', how it constructs writer and reader as members of a synthetic sisterhood, and how the identity of the writer is constructed as a combination of subject positions – friend, interviewer, historian, advertiser, and so forth. The chapter highlights the importance of a sense of how texts construct identities within CLA, but it also shows the special relevance of that conclusion in the critique of constructions of gender.

Part III is on critical language awareness in schools. Michael Stubbs' Chapter 8 ('English teaching, information technology and critical language awareness') makes the connection between CLA and new language practices associated with the spread of Information Technology (IT). He begins from the statement in the Cox Report (DES 1989), which he helped to write, that most interactions with computers are language experiences. He argues that IT 'can provide a substantial area for work on CLA' within the teaching of English, developing children's awareness of language and its interpretation, new technological contexts in which language is used, and the social implications of these technologies. English teaching 'should be developing to take account of major changes in the ways in which language is used in society'. In fact IT connects with traditional concerns of English teaching in the issues it raises about the creation and interpretation of information. The study of IT 'can contribute to pupils' critical understanding of how messages are conveyed and interpreted in different media' and 'how information can be manipulated'. IT 'is providing a new kind of language environment for children', making it easier to edit and redraft, produce writing with a professional appearance, and (via electronic mail) write for real audiences. IT also has major implications for conceptions of literacy: it may require new competences, favour collaborative writing, radically change conceptions of 'text' and 'author', and have cognitive effects – all of which is of social significance in making possible different relations between texts and people. Stubbs suggests that a syllabus for IT 'should be balanced between the linguistic and the social/cultural, but it should also look directly at the technology' – one cannot discuss social implications without understanding what the machines can and cannot do. English teachers can address 'fundamental issues of how humans and computers *interpret* language', and it is crucial to show that human decisions determine what machines do. Stubbs suggests a number of specific teaching topics, including: computer metaphors for people, and human metaphors for computers, looking at how computers are represented in the media; the validity of psychological terms like *intelligent* applied to computers – whether computers can conduct 'intelligent conversation'; Britain as a databank society, how information is transmitted in modern society and how technologies affect social relations between people. The chapter concludes with a sketch of a framework for researching the educational implications of IT.

Malcolm McKenzie's Chapter 9 ('"What I've always known but never been told": euphemisms, school discourse and empowerment') describes classes he conducted with 15–16 year-old students in an English-medium secondary school in Botswana, aimed at raising critical awareness of the use of euphemism in school reports. The first part of the title ('What I've always known but never been told') indicates McKenzie's view of the significance of euphemism: students know what teachers think of them, yet teachers rarely tell them directly, and perhaps this paradox 'goes to the heart of power relations within many schools'. The choice of topic was influenced by McKenzie's insistence upon the intimate relationship between critical language teaching and a learner-centred pedagogy: critical language teaching should treat classroom practice and classroom content 'like the two wings of a bird', and focus critically upon the discursive practices of the school itself. In so doing, it should 'denaturalise the givens of the language system', show how meaning 'can be deconstructed and reconstructed', and empower students to change aspects of their language and social practice. The learner-centredness of his approach shows in the way the topic was developed through a process of negotiation between students and teacher, relying upon the capacity of the students to generate material. The students' own examples and analyses are a prominent element in the paper, including the writing and rewriting of dummy reports, a student questionnaire for teachers about report writing, and student commentaries upon both. McKenzie concludes that the exercise led to students having 'access to a form of discourse which was no longer strange and unfamiliar', which he sees as 'one kind of empowerment'.

Chapter 10, by Paul Clarke and Nick Smith ('Initial steps towards critical practice in primary schools'), shifts the focus to primary level, exploring possibilities for introducing CLA work into primary schools in the context of constraints imposed by the national curriculum. The authors argue that the case for CLA ought to be incorporated into ongoing debates about 'critical learning' and learners' 'ownership' of their learning processes. Their view of critical learning centres upon the learners becoming aware of the processes they go through in classroom activities, on the basis of which they can discuss and evaluate past activities and come to decisions about the nature of future ones. This assumes that teachers are prepared to hand over substantive decisions to learners. The authors illustrate how developing awareness of learning processes itself has linguistic dimensions and potential for CLA work. For example, learners may produce their own labels for stages and elements of activities, and a discussion of them could raise questions about how different points of view lead to different labels, about how particular labellings 'belong to' particular groups of people, and so forth. Or again, in a multilingual school one aspect of the choices that learners have to make in classroom activities is the choice of which language to use where, and discussion of this can lead to a critical awareness of the different values placed upon different languages by the school. The authors assert that those who wish to develop CLA in schools will now be obliged to do so within the framework of the national curriculum, and they suggest building upon what openings there are for CLA and critical learning in the national curriculum documentation, with a view to constructing a critical dialogue around the national curriculum.

Chapter eleven, by Lesley Lancaster and Rhiannan Taylor of Shropshire County Council's English Advisory Service ('Critical approaches to language, learning and pedagogy: a case study'), gives an evaluation of a language awareness course conceived on critical lines, which took place in the Modern Languages department of a Shropshire secondary school (Madeley Court) in 1987/1988. The chapter opens with a historical account of language awareness work in schools from the 1960s to the National Curriculum, which includes the judgement that recent mainstream work in language awareness is further away than Doughty et al. (1971) from a critical framework. The authors contextualise the Madeley Court experiment within thinking in the county at the time, which was opposed to language teaching in the form of decontextualised exercises, emphasised the considerable amount of knowledge and understanding about language children bring to school, and linked the content of learning with reflection upon the processes of learning and the structures of the classroom. In the latter connection, the authors argue that the process as well as the content of language awareness work ought to be critical.

This entails making the children's language experience central in the learning process, and giving the children the status of 'experts' in the use of language, thereby problematising traditional classroom relations which ascribe expertise exclusively to teachers. In a detailed review of parts of the Madeley Court course, the authors suggest that it succeeded where it did make the children language experts, and failed where it did not. They also explore the difficulties teachers had in giving up some of their expert status and some of their control over the classroom.

Arvindh Bhatt and Marilyn Martin-Jones (Chapter 12) deal with the treatment of minority languages in LA and CLA programmes, focusing upon how minority languages feature in existing language awareness materials. To place this issue in its historical context, they provide an overview of responses to the presence of bilingual learners in the British educational system since the 1960s, and of the position of minority languages in the school curriculum. The treatment of minority languages in LA accords with the displacement of a previously dominant assimilationist 'political grammar' by a pluralist one, in which minority languages are portrayed (usually in rather vague terms) as a 'resource' for learners and teachers. Language awareness materials based upon pluralist assumptions are criticised for being 'colour-blind' about linguistic inequality between minority languages and (standard) English, for attending to random facts about minority languages which are often treated as exotica, and for representing the use of minority languages in a normative way – they are used in 'appropriate', i.e. non-prestigious and marginal, contexts. Bhatt and Martin-Jones are concerned that attention to minority languages in language awareness work might be used as an argument against provision for community language teaching in the mainstream curriculum, advocated by the authors from within a 'critical anti-racist' political grammar. They do, however, see an important role for a critical language awareness, in developing a historical sense of the relationship between minority languages and English, and a critical awareness of the representation of minority languages and their speakers in the media and elsewhere.

Part IV, 'CLA: perspectives for emancipation' contains just one chapter by Hilary Janks and Roz Ivanič (Chapter 13, 'CLA and emancipatory discourse'), which constitutes, I think, an appropriate conclusion to the volume. The chapter asserts the inadequacy of a CLA, which stops at awareness without going on to contest disempowering practices through 'emancipatory discourse' – using language in a way that contributes to greater freedom and respect for all people. Janks and Ivanič tie the concepts of disempowerment and emancipation to the constitution of social identity and subject positions in discourse, and to the possibility of resisting as well as accommodating to the positions that are set up for you. Emancipatory discourse has two dimensions: avoiding the disempowerment of others, and resisting your own disempowerment. The authors see avoiding the disempowerment of others as a matter of being responsible in the ways we speak and write about and to others: CLA can make us aware of how our writing may subject others, or how we may dominate conversation, but it is up to us to act upon that awareness. Resisting disempowerment is a matter of not allowing ourselves to be effaced, 'using language in a way which is true to ourselves and to the group(s) we identify with'. This might involve challenging the domination of the standard variety by using our vernacular for prestigious purposes, challenging the domination of others in interaction, challenging views of the world and subject positions set up in discourse. The choice of whether to conform or challenge is one for the individual to make in the light of the risks and benefits in specific cases, but it is a task for critical educators to ensure learners have the resources for turning awareness into action. The authors discuss in some detail the teaching of writing and the teaching of reading, suggesting a number of classroom activities for each of them. They conclude with an important reminder that when emancipatory practice is 'for real' it can have serious consequences: 'people endanger themselves when they challenge the prevailing power structures. Sometimes they even die.'

Language and education in the 1990s: context and relevance of this book

The 1980s witnessed an intense (and continuing) debate about the nature of language education, particularly in the context of reforms of the school curriculum for English. One element of the debate was the reassertion of the importance of language awareness or knowledge about language in a general sense within language education. Sometimes this took the form of appeals for a return to the 'grammar grind', which has been abandoned in the post-war period. More commonly, there was a search for a more enlightened content for a language awareness syllabus. This is true of the Cox Report and the Kingman Report, and the Cox Report even acknowledges a 'cultural analysis' view of the role of English in the curriculum as 'helping children towards a critical understanding of the world and the cultural environment in which they live'. But these and other influential contributions to the debate remain overwhelmingly committed to a non-critical view of language awareness.

This book presents a radical case for a critical awareness component in the language education curriculum. I believe that it is important for such a position to be a part of the debate. Its relevance is underlined by the increasing prominence within language education through the 1980s and into the 1990s of training in language and communicative skills. I have suggested above that one impetus for competence- or skills-based views of language education has been the changing role of language in work, and new linguistic and communicative demands being placed upon workers. If anything, pressures upon the educational system to subordinate itself to the needs of the economy are likely to increase in the 'workfare' society of the 1990s (Jessop 1990). Language training without language awareness is bound to be language legitimation: that is, it is bound to present problematical and contentious language practices ideologically as simply the way things are done. It is important for the CLA principle summarised in Figure 1.2 above to be set against skills training: the development of the learner's language practice ought to be fully integrated with the development of a critical awareness of language.

Notes

1. In referring to change, one ought in principle to be sensitive to different, overlapping 'periodicities': so, there are aspects of these three dimensions of change which are relatively long-term (e.g. the second in part) and others which are relatively short-term. But all three dimensions of change have, I think, shown a perceptible and significant acceleration in the past decade or so in Britain (with parallel tendencies elsewhere in our increasingly internationalised sociolinguistic order), and it is mainly this recent period of change I have in mind.

2. I take the notion of 'entitlement' to language education from the Kingman and Cox Reports. I think this is a more fundamental entitlement than the one which they highlight – children's entitlement to learn standard English in schools.
3. 'Discourse' is for me rather more than *just* language use: it is language use, whether speech or writing, seen as a type of social practice – that is, having precisely the sort of properties I am talking about here.

References

Barnes D 1988 The politics of oracy. In MacLure M et al. (eds) *Oracy matters*. Open University Press

Bourdieu P 1984 *Distinction. A social critique of the judgement of Taste.* Nice R. (trans). Routledge

Clark R, Fairclough N, Ivanič R, Martin-Jones M 1988 *Critical language awareness*. Centre for Language in Social Life Research Paper, Lancaster University

Department of Education and Science (DES) 1988 *Report of the committee of inquiry into the teaching of English language.* (Kingman Report) HMSO

Department of Education and Science (DES) 1989 *English for ages 5 to 16.* (Cox Report) HMSO

Doughty P, Pearce J, Thornton G 1971 *Language in use.* Edward Arnold

Fairclough N 1989 *Language and power.* Longman

Fairclough N 1990a Critical linguistics, 'New Times' and language education. In Clark R, Fairclough N, Ivanič R, McCleod N, Thomas J (eds) *Language and power: proceedings of the 1989 annual meeting of the British Association for Applied Linguistics.* CILT

Fairclough N 1990b *Technologization of discourse.* Centre for Language in Social Life Research Papers, Lancaster University

Foucault M 1981 The order of discourse. In Young R (ed) *Untying the text.* Routledge

Fowler R, Hodge R, Kress G, Trew T 1979 *Language and control.* Routledge

Freire P 1985 *The politics of education.* Macmillan

Giroux H 1983 *Theory and resistance in education: a pedagogy for the opposition.* Heinemann

Halliday M 1978 *Language as social semiotic.* Edward Arnold

Hawkins E 1984 *Awareness of language: an introduction.* Cambridge University Press

Henriques J, Hollway W, Urwin C, Venn C, Walkerdine V 1984 *Changing the subject: psychology, social regulation and subjectivity.* Methuen

Jessop R 1990 What comes after Thatcherism? *New Statesman and Society* 3: 128, 23 November.

Kress G 1989 *Linguistic processes in sociocultural practice.* Oxford University Press

Kress G, Hodge R 1979 *Language as ideology.* Routledge

Mey J 1985 *Whose language? A study of linguistic pragmatics.* John Benjamins

National Congress on Languages in Education (NCLE) 1985 *Language awareness.* CILT

Pêcheux, M 1982 *Language, semantics and ideology: stating the obvious.* Macmillan

Thompson J B 1984 *Studies in the theory of ideology.* Polity Press

Part I

Language Awareness:
Critical and Non-critical
Approaches

2 The appropriacy of 'appropriateness'

Norman Fairclough

This chapter deals with the concept of 'appropriateness' in language, and the commonplace view that varieties of a language differ in being appropriate for different purposes and different situations. I argue first that many important contributions to recent debate on language education and language awareness depend heavily upon a view of sociolinguistic variation that centres around the concept of appropriateness. The second part of the chapter is a critique of such theories of sociolinguistic variation. I argue that such theories are an ideological obstacle to the development of CLA.

The first part of the chapter will show how central 'appropriateness' has been in recent rethinking of language education and language awareness in Britain. I shall refer mainly to the Cox Report on the teaching of English in schools (DES 1989), but also to language and communication elements in the Certificate of Pre-Vocational Education (FEU 1987). I shall be arguing that theories of appropriateness underpin controversial policies on the teaching of standard English, but also the development of a competence-based 'communication skills' view of language education with a new emphasis on 'oracy' and spoken language education. Indeed, 'appropriateness' is the linchpin of an attempted integration of the two.

The second part of the chapter is a critique of models of language variation based upon 'appropriateness'. I argue that such models incorporate profoundly misleading assumptions about sociolinguistic variation. I also argue that such models derive from a confusion between sociolinguistic realities and political aspirations. In no actual speech community do all members always behave in accordance with a shared sense of which language varieties are appropriate for which contexts and purposes. Yet such a perfectly ordered world is set up as an ideal by those who wish to impose their own social order upon society in the realm of language. So I suggest that appropriateness is an 'ideological' category, which is linked to particular partisan positions within a politics of language – within a struggle between social groups in a speech community for control of (or 'hegemony' over) its sociolinguistic order. And I argue that the critique of appropriateness and models of language variation based upon it, and the development of alternatives, is a central part of making the case for CLA.

'Appropriateness' in language education

The concept of 'appropriateness' has been prominent in recent discussion of the teaching of English in schools, and of pre vocational education (DES 1988, DES 1989, FEU 1987), as well as in language awareness programmes and materials (Hawkins 1985). In this section of the Chapter I want to focus upon two questions. First, how does appropriateness figure within dominant conceptions of language variation? And how in particular does it help to rationalise policies on the teaching of standard English? Second, what is the relationship between appropriateness and competence-based, skills-oriented views of language education? I refer mainly to the Cox Report (DES 1989) but also to prevocational education programmes (FEU 1987).

Appropriateness models of language variation

The following extract is a particularly good example of how appropriateness figures in the Cox Report:

> Pupils working towards level 7 should consider the notion of appropriateness to situation, topic, purpose and language mode and the fact that inappropriate language use can be a source of humour (either intentional or unintentional) or may give the impression that the speaker or writer is pompous or inept or impertinent or rude. Pupils should learn that Standard English is the language of wide

social communication and is particularly likely to be required in public, formal settings. Teaching should cover discussion of the situations in which and purposes for which people might choose to use non-standard varieties rather than Standard English, *e.g. in speech with friends, in a local team or group in television advertising, folk songs, poetry, dialogue in novels or plays.* (6.29, original italics)

I shall discuss in turn three issues raised here: appropriateness and standard English, inappropriateness and normativeness, and appropriateness within language awareness. I shall also discuss a section of the Report which shows rather clearly the limitations of a model of variation based upon appropriateness.

Appropriateness and standard English

Appropriateness is the cornerstone of the Report's policy on the teaching of standard English. The Report argues that children have an 'entitlement' to standard English, and that 'many important opportunities are closed to them' if they do not have access to standard English (4.3, 4.5). The recommendation therefore is that schools should aim to develop pupils' ability to understand and produce both written and spoken standard English (see the Introduction p. 14 for the similar position within non-critical language awareness materials). But this recommendation should be understood in the context of the Report's view of the objectives of the English curriculum and the priority it gives to widening pupils' repertoires of varieties of English and, in the case of bilingual children, their multilingual repertoires (10.13). The 'overriding aim' of the English curriculum is, according to the Report, 'to enable all pupils to develop to the full their ability to use and understand English', in order to maximise the contribution of English to 'the personal development of the individual child' and 'preparation for the adult world' (2.13, 2.14). In pursuit of these objectives, 'teachers should aim to extend the range of varieties of English in which children are competent . . . to enable children to do more with their language' (2.15). The aim is therefore to 'add Standard English to the repertoire, not to replace other dialects or languages' (4.43), and to do so in a way which 'respects the language background of the pupils' (4.36).

But there is an apparent paradox. How is it possible to add without replacing? Is it possible to teach pupils a variety of

English so much more prestigious and powerful than their own dialects or languages, without detriment to the latter? The Cox Report suggests that it is possible, and its argument rests upon the concept of appropriateness: different varieties of English, and different languages, are appropriate for different contexts and purposes, and all varieties have the legitimacy of being appropriate for *some* contexts and purposes. On the face of it, this resolves the paradox. But as soon as appropriate contexts and purposes for varieties other than standard English are listed (see the italicised part of the extract from 6.29 quoted above), it is clear just how fragile this resolution of the paradox is. For these are of course largely in the domain of the private and the quaint, and exclude those public, formal and written domains which have most social prestige. Will children not get the unspoken message that their varieties *may* be 'appropriate', but are pretty marginal and irrelevant? Part of the argument in the second part of this chapter is that the impression of an orderly division of labour between standard English and other varieties cannot in any case be justified.

Inappropriateness and normativeness

Let me turn now to inappropriateness, and the issue of normativeness. Inappropriateness is portrayed in the above extract from the Report on the one hand as a source of humour, and on the other hand as possibly leading to adverse social judgements (that the speaker or writer is 'inept', 'rude', etc.). No good *serious* reasons are given for being inappropriate – it is either a slip-up or a joke. (The Report does not mention the racist or 'classist' nature of much of the humour deriving from inappropriacy.)

The normative and prescriptive nature of the concept of appropriateness becomes particularly clear in discussions of *in*appropriateness. The Report itself ties appropriateness to prescriptivism at one point: 'we need both accurate descriptions of language that are related to situation, purpose and mode (ie whether the language is spoken or written), and prescriptions that take account of context, appropriateness and the expression of meaning' (4.19). But the way in which description and prescription are linked together shows a special characteristic of appropriateness in comparison with other prescriptive concepts such as 'correctness': what is prescribed as appropriate is taken to be in line with descriptively established regularities in the practices of a speech community. This makes the suspect assumption, which I return to in the second part of the chapter, that speech communities are characterised by well-defined varieties clearly distributed among contexts and purposes, so that what is appropriate or inappropriate is a clear-cut matter for all of us. I referred earlier to a further characteristic which distinguishes appropriateness from other prescriptive concepts: it ascribes legitimacy to each and every variety as appropriate in some contexts.

But the theory and language of appropriateness coexists in the Report with a historically earlier theory and language of variation which is normative in a less liberal mode:

> Pupils need to be able to discuss the contexts in which Standard English is *obligatory* and those where its use is *preferable* for social reasons. By and large, the pressures in favour of Standard English will be greater when the language is written, formal and public. Non-standard forms may be much more widely *tolerated* – and, in some cases, *preferred* – when the language is spoken, informal and private. (4.41, my italics)

The appearance of *tolerated* lifts the veil on a tradition of prescriptive bigotry towards non-standard varieties which is largely absent from the Report. The normativeness of this earlier tradition takes the form of prescriptive rules and regulations of a legislative character; *obligatory* and *preferable* belong here, as does *required* in the extract quoted earlier (p. 35). This is in contrast with the normativeness of the appropriateness model, expressed as I have suggested in terms of descriptive rules and regularities. I suggest that the coexistence of these two overlapping normative languages ('discourses' in one sense of that much-used term) in the Report highlights one important role of appropriateness models of language variation: they help to endow prescriptivism with a relatively acceptable face.

Appropriateness within language awareness

The extract from paragraph 6.29 of the Cox Report quoted above refers to the teaching of knowledge about language – to language awareness. The Report proposes that understanding of how language variation is governed by principles of appropriateness should be developed in tandem with capacity to speak and write appropriately, and to assess the speech of writing of others in terms of appropriateness. What I referred to above as the 'suspect assumption' of clear-cut and determinate appropriateness relations between varieties, contexts and purposes is here given the status of knowledge. Suspect (and as I argue later, partisan) assumptions treated as knowledge may reasonably be regarded as ideologies – interpretations and representations from a particular point of view corresponding to particular interests, which are projected as universal. The Cox Report's recommendations on language awareness can in this respect be seen as advocating the teaching of ideological doctrines of language variation in tandem with practices of appropriate use.

I want to conclude this part of the chapter by mentioning one section of the Report where the appropriateness model of language variation is stretched to breaking point: the discussion of relationships between culturally different varieties of interaction associated with different ethnic groups (differences which may be manifest in 'body posture, gesture, preferred distance between speakers, discursive styles, the ways in which politeness is marked or attention to other speakers is signalled'), and between female and male speech styles. The following extract is indicative of the difficulties:

> Whether these characteristic differences are judged positively or negatively will depend on the context and purpose of the task. For example, in some tasks, the more direct way of speaking that is more common to boys will be advantageous; in others, the more tentative approach more frequently found in girls will be more appropriate. (11.15)

Leaving aside the question of whether these characterisations of boys' and girls' speech styles are justifiable, this is an attempt to force these types of variation into an appropriateness model whose inability to accommodate them is thereby exposed. The relationships between the communicative styles of different cultural groups, and between the speech styles of women and the speech styles of men, are relationships of tension, contradiction, and power; the different styles belong to different, divergent and potentially antagonistic repertoires. In trying to accommodate these relationships within an appropriateness model, the Report misconstrues these different styles as alternatives in complementary distribution within a single repertoire. It is indeed the case, in a situation of fluid and shifting gender and ethnic relations such as ours, that these contradictory styles may come to coexist within the repertoires of particular groups and individuals. But such changes are partial and complex, and require a far more sophisticated theoretical framework than a model which flattens variation into a unitary and unidimensional set of complementary options. The need to go beyond an appropriateness model is manifest.

Let me summarise what I have said so far. I have suggested that appropriateness provides an apparent resolution of the paradox that use of standard English is to be taught, while use of other varieties is to be respected; that an appropriateness model of variation is the (relatively) acceptable face of prescriptivism; and that giving an appropriateness view of language variation the status of knowledge in language awareness teaching serves an ideological role. I have also suggested that the attempt to contain ethnicity- and gender-related variation within the appropriacy model over-stretches the model and shows the need to go beyond it.

Appropriateness and skills

Competence-based views of language and language education dominate recent educational thinking – the Kingman Report, the Cox Report – but also (and even more so) the whole range of the prevocational programmes (FEU 1987). But the impact of competence and skills models is much broader than that. There is a general shift towards seeing knowledge operationally, in terms of competence, what people can do; and towards seeing education as training in skills. Indeed the distinction between education and training is coming under increasing pressure, not least from government: according to the former Secretary of State for Trade and Industry Lord Young of Graffham, 'there is no room in a modern world for the old divide between "education" and "training"' (Young 1987). Language competence and skills, communicational competence and skills, come to be items in a list which includes scientific, technological, practical and social competence and skills (FEU 1987).

The development of prevocational education programmes has been a major feature of the 1980s, and these programmes have operated as a powerhouse in developing competence-based systems for many subject areas which have subsequently had a broader influence in primary, secondary and higher education. I shall refer specifically to the syllabus for the Certificate of Pre-Vocational Education (CPVE) to illustrate competence-based views of language education and the way in which they interact with appropriateness models of variation (FEU 1987).

The syllabus is set out as a series of core competences each of which is divided into more specific competences (glossed as 'skills, knowledge and attitudes'). Communication is one of the core competences, whose main aim is 'to develop communication skills as a way of structuring relationships between people in a changing and multicultural society'. It is divided into the five 'aims' of listening, speaking, reading, writing, and communication and interpretation, each of which is further broken down into more specific skills. For example, 'speaking' involves five skills, including: 'talking effectively in a variety of styles and range of contexts – one-to-one/group, familiar/unfamiliar, formal/informal'; 'formulating and conveying requests and instructions clearly and concisely'; 'initiating and sustaining conversations in a range of contexts' (FEU 1987: 30).

Appropriateness figures prominently. For example, 'listening' is glossed as 'to listen and respond appropriately to oral requests and presentations', 'speaking' as 'to talk appropriately in a range of situations'. It also figures under the aim of 'role identification' within the core competence 'social skills': 'distinguishing between appropriate and inappropriate behaviour in a range of personal and situational or organisational roles', 'selecting appropriate behaviour and procedures for achieving a specified goal'.

Competence-based models in education are associated with wider social and cultural tendencies and themes. They incorporate a particular vision of the social subject and of the educability of the subject. They are democratic in their view of subjects: they imply that everyone has the capacity to learn, dependent only upon training. They are simultaneously normalising, and sometimes tightly programmed: they lay down common target behaviours, knowledges and understandings for all learners, sometimes in very precise terms (e.g. the CPVE skills referred to above, or the language skills specified in the Cox Report as attainment targets for ten different levels of attainment). They are at the same time individualising: they focus upon each separate individual as housing a configuration of skills which can be worked upon and improved, and in this respect they connect out to contemporary tendencies for the 'self' to become more autonomous, more 'self-steering' (Rose 1989), and to the contemporary salience of individualism.

And competence-based models are spreading. They have been rapidly 'colonising' many domains of social life in the past decade, perhaps because they seem to fit in well with the values of 'enterprise culture' (Keat & Abercrombie 1990). As the example of CPVE above has shown, competence-based models are certainly prominent in the educational and training initiatives of the 1980s which have been inspired by enterprise culture values. Their success seems to correspond to the changes in the nature of work and corresponding increase in demands upon the communicative and linguistic abilities of workers which I referred to in the Introduction (p.4).

The generalisation of competence models across the curriculum entails the generalisation of assumptions about knowledge, behaviour and learning which make less sense in some parts of the syllabus than in others. For instance, that the domain of knowledge to be taught is well-defined and determinate, and componentially structured into broad competences or skills which are in turn made up of more specific competences and skills; that the relationship between competence and behaviour is a simple relationship of application, and that there is a transparent relationship between domains of behaviour and domains of competence; that competences and skills are freely transferable, so that a competence learnt in one context may be applied in others.

I do not believe that any of these assumptions is valid at least without major qualifications in the case of language, and I would in fact want to argue that the generalisation of a competence model to language is misconceived. There is no space to argue that position in detail here, but what I shall be suggesting shortly is that competence models of language presuppose unacceptable appropriateness models of language variation. One thing which should be noted first, however, is that competence models are not just a recent imposition from outside, from fashions in education, but have their own history within linguistics. They can be traced back to the Chomskyan conception of *linguistic competence* (Chomsky 1965) via Hymes' notion of *communicative competence* (Hymes 1972), which was influential in bringing a competence perspective into language education in the so-called *communicative approach* to the teaching of language, especially English as a foreign language (Candlin 1975). The division of language into the main categories of *skills* (speaking, listening, reading, writing) for pedagogical purposes is a long-established practice in applied linguistics.

Let me turn to the relationship between a competence/skills model and appropriateness. An appropriateness model of language variation facilitates the application of the competence/skills model to language, because it offers a way of squaring the variability of language with the view of language as unitary, normative and determinate practices which people can be trained in. If it is indeed the case that members of a speech community have a shared and well-defined repertoire of language varieties, and if it is indeed the case that each variety can be matched with contexts it is appropriate to with minimal overlap or indeterminacy, then language education can be simply a matter of training people in skills and techniques, increasing their know-how, making them more skilled in language as one might make them more skilled in handling tools. If on the other hand as I suggest below repertoires are plural, variable and often ill-defined, and if the matching of language to context is characterised by indeterminacy, heterogeneity and struggle, how on earth can language education be reduced to skills training? So the rationality of applying the competence/skills model to language depends upon the appropriacy of an appropriateness model of variation, and the concept of appropriateness is therefore of considerable ideological and political significance.

Let me bring the discussion of appropriateness in language education, and the first part of the chapter, to a conclusion. I have been suggesting that appropriateness is a vehicle for other things in recent documents on language education – for policies on the teaching of standard English, and for extending competence models to language. On the one hand, appropriateness helps rationalise a policy of teaching children to understand and produce spoken and written standard English while apparently respecting other dialects and languages. This policy is justified in terms of the 'entitlement' of children to the 'opportunity' which standard English opens up for them. But teaching the appropriate use of standard English inevitably has other effects which the Cox Report remains silent about: it uses the educational system to transmit shared language values (if not practices) based around the hegemony of a particular dialect, but in a way which overcomes on the surface the contemporary dilemma of how to do that while making the politically necessary concessions to liberalism and pluralism. This use of the educational system corresponds to a traditional establishment (or 'Old Right' as Barnes (1988) puts it) agenda. Language standardisation after all is first a matter of hegemony – the hegemony of a particular class extended to the linguistic sector of the cultural domain, manifested as the hegemony of a dialect – and only consequentially a matter of opportunity.

On the other hand, appropriateness helps rationalise the extension to language of a competence-based model of education. Whereas the teaching of the standard is an Old Right priority, teaching language competences and skills is a priority of the modernising New Right (Barnes 1988, Hewitt 1989). It is based upon a planning perspective and the anticipation of new requirements for employees and citizens. It is oriented to a new conception of citizenship, and a sense that modes of hegemony must change in a rapidly changing world. What appropriateness helps to do, in the Cox Report for example, is effect a compromise between these Old Right and New Right perspectives and priorities. It is the linchpin which holds them together in an uneasy, and no doubt temporary, harmony.

Critique of appropriateness models of language variation

What then are the objections to appropriateness models of language variation? There are I think two major lines of objection, which I shall discuss in turn: first, that appropriateness models are based upon presuppositions which misrepresent sociolinguistic variation; and second, that they are ideological in the sense that they portray a political objective as a sociolinguistic reality.

Presuppositions of appropriateness

What image of language variation do appropriateness models give? In one sentence, it is I think an image of clearly distinguished language varieties being used in clearly distinguished contexts, according to clear-cut conventions, which hold for all members of what is assumed to be a homogeneous speech community. Let me spell out more precisely some of the presuppositions about sociolinguistic variation which appropriateness models are based upon:

(1) there is a 1:1, or at least a determinate and well-defined many-to-one, fit between varieties of a language and contexts/purposes they are appropriate for
(2) this determinate fit characterises all parts of the sociolinguistic order
(3) this fit holds for all members of a speech community
(4) the distinction between appropriate and inappropriate language use is clear-cut
(5) varieties of a language, contexts, and purposes, are well-defined and clearly demarcated entities

None of these presuppositions stands up to close scrutiny. In assessing them, it may be helpful to have specific areas of contemporary sociolinguistic variation in mind. I shall refer to two: cross-gender communication in organisations, and medical interviews.

How does a professional woman (in a university or in industry, say) talk appropriately to a senior male colleague, and vice-versa? One need only formulate the question to see that it is difficult to answer in any direct or simple way. A significant feature of the current climate of problematised gender relations is that women and men are often not sure how to talk to each other, and often find themselves in communicative dilemmas. There exist many divergent practices which correspond to some degree, for instance, to different levels of commitment to feminism. And the practices which exist are contested and struggled over, often explicitly, as when people argue for guidelines on non-sexist language use to be adopted by organisations. Any notion of unitary sets of appropriateness conventions for such cross-gender communication would therefore seem to be unsustainable.

Another example, which on the face of it looks more promising for the appropriateness model, is communication between doctors and their patients. But there are problems here too. There are traditional forms of medical interview which are tightly structured around question–answer sequences, with the doctor asking nearly all the questions and the patient being constrained by narrow criteria of medical relevance in answering questions, and with control of the topics raised and the overall course of the interview being firmly in the doctor's hands (Mishler 1984). No doubt one could use an appropriateness model here. The difficulty is that contemporary medical interviews are far more diverse than this suggests. Another form of doctor–patient interview is more like counselling: structured around patient accounts of problems, which are not tightly controlled in terms of medical relevance, but often show criteria of relevance and a communicative style typical of informal conversation. The doctor may exercise minimal control, ask few questions, but show a great deal of empathy with the patient (for examples see Mishler 1984, ten Have 1989, Fairclough forthcoming). Such contrasting forms of interview are in a relationship of tension and conflict, and the choice a doctor makes tends to go along with her or his views of medicine, conception of patients, and so forth. There is no unitary set of appropriate behaviours in medical interviews either.

I now return to the set of presuppositions above. Presupposition (1) specifies a close fit between varieties of a language and contexts/purposes, yet these examples suggest that there may be considerable indeterminacy in that relationship. Moreover, the difference between the two examples suggests that, contrary to presupposition (2), there may be considerable unevenness between different parts of the sociolinguistic order as well as over time in the degree of (in)determinacy of the variety – context/purpose relation: I suspect that most women in organisations have experienced sociolinguistic dilemmas and indeterminacies, whereas traditional medical interview is probably a powerful model still for a great many patients. Presupposition (3) claims that a particular fit between variety and context/purpose will hold for all members of a speech community, but both examples cast doubt upon this in suggesting that different groups of people may have not only different senses of the variety/context/purpose relation but also practices which may come into conflict. Another important aspect of presupposition (3) is that it points to the marginalisation in an appropriateness model of a central characteristic of the contemporary British sociolinguistic order: its multilingualism. There is a plurality of sociolinguistic resources in contemporary

Britain, with widely divergent access to them; not a unitary set of resources used according to shared norms, as appropriacy models suggest. Given the complexity and non-consensual nature of the variety – context/purpose relation, it will evidently not be possible to differentiate appropriate and inappropriate behaviour in a clear-cut way in many instances, and so presupposition (4) becomes problematic.

The final presupposition, that varieties as well as contexts and purposes are well-defined and clearly demarcated, is also problematic, and there seems again to be unevenness between different parts of the sociolinguistic order. A job interview and an informal chat may for example appear on the face of it to be very different varieties, associated with quite different sorts of context and purpose, yet job interviews may sometimes resemble informal chats. We need to recognise that while boundaries between varieties are sometimes carefully policed, in some parts of the sociolinguistic order there are complex mergers and overlaps – interviews in conversational style, information which slides into advertising, written language which is full of features of colloquial speech, and so forth.

I referred in the first section of the chapter to the close relationship in the Cox Report of an appropriateness model of variation and policies on the teaching of standard English. These objections to the five presuppositions apply, of course, to the particular case of variation between standard English and other dialects and languages. Education itself for example is proof that, contra presupposition (1), there is no determinate fit between standard English and particular contexts and purposes: whether and where other varieties are to be used in educational contexts and for educational purposes is a constantly contested issue, a domain of sociolinguistic struggle. This implies that, contra presupposition (3), there are different conceptions in the speech community of where standard and other varieties are appropriate. It is also clear that, contra presupposition (2), the frontier between standard English and other varieties has been less stable and more contested in education than in, say, law or science. Consequently, the presupposition throughout the Cox Report that there is a clear-cut distinction between appropriate and inappropriate uses of standard and other varieties (presupposition (4) above) is not justified.

In short, then, models of language variation based upon the

concept of appropriateness project a misleading and unsustainable image of sociolinguistic practice and how sociolinguistic orders are structured.

Appropriateness as ideology

Levinson gives a critique of conceptions of pragmatics based upon the notion of appropriateness (1983: 24–7), which includes the following three criticisms of the notion itself. They overlap, of course, with the five presuppositions discussed above:

(1) it implies a culturally homogeneous speech community, where-as real speech communities manifest cultural heterogeneity
(2) speakers 'do not always comport themselves in the manner recommended by the prevailing mores – they can be outrageous, and otherwise "inappropriate"'
(3) 'in being grossly inappropriate, one can nevertheless be supremely appropriate', in the sense that speakers exploit (and violate) conventions to communicate particular meanings – ironic meanings, for example

I think Levinson is right about (1) and (3), but that he misses a whole range of further and really more damaging criticisms of appropriateness which are partly but inadequately evoked by (2). Let me develop this by commenting first on (1).

What Levinson has in mind is illustrated by his example of a village in South India 'where there may be say twenty distinct castes' and 'a single honorific particle may have just one meaning (e.g. speaker is inferior to addressee) but have twenty distinct rules for its *appropriate* usage'. Levinson's example sees each caste as a separate and parallel (sub-) speech community within the wider speech community. Thus (1) deals with social *groups* coexisting but not interacting. By contrast (2) deals with *individuals* contesting appropriateness conventions. A very important omission from Levinson's account is *groups contesting conventions*.

What is at issue here is how one sees the relationship between a language and those who speak it in a highly complex modern society such as modern Britain; or rather between the totality of the linguistic resources of a society (which may include many languages) and those who draw upon them. A common view, which Levinson basically subscribes to, acknowledges that linguistic resources are divided – variable – in ways which correspond to the class and other divisions of the society, but sees these divisions in a static way, as a synchronic state. His is a more sophisticated view of variation than what I have been referring to as appropriateness models, but shares with it the property of synchronic idealisation. A different view, which I subscribe to, sees such divisions as constant processes of contestation and struggle between class and other groups, which are struggles over linguistic resources as well as other cultural resources. From this second point of view, seeing a speech community as a static synchronic entity is not only idealising and simplifying, it is also falsifying: it has the effect of making contestation and struggle invisible. Yet contestation and struggle are, I would argue, the absolutely fundamental processes out of which speech communities are shaped and transformed. A 'synchronic state' from this point of view freezes a complex array of processes, and flattens out important distinctions in relative degrees of stability between different parts of such a 'state', distinctions which are connected to the multiplicity of different time-scales or 'periodicities' over which changes occur.

We may call the second perspective 'historical', not just because it is concerned with linguistic change, but more importantly because it sees language as embedded in social history. This in my view is the only properly social way of envisaging language. How then are appropriateness models to be regarded from a historical perspective? In summary, my view is that appropriateness models derive from a confusion between sociolinguistic realities and political projects in the domain of language: social order – e.g. a regulated sociolinguistic order corresponding to the notion of appropriateness in which each variety is neatly attached to its particular context and purpose – is the political objective of the dominant, 'hegemonic', sections of a society in the domain of language as in other domains, but it never has been sociolinguistic reality. Appropriateness models in sociolinguistics or in educational policy documents should therefore be seen as *ideologies*, by which I mean that they are projecting imaginary representations of sociolinguistic reality which correspond to the perspective and partisan interests of one section of society or one section of a particular social institution – its dominant section. Let me develop this view.

I referred above to 'hegemonic' sections of a society. I want to draw upon Gramsci's theory of hegemony as a framework for thinking about power in modern societies (Gramsci 1971). *Hegemony* is to be understood as a form of social domination in which the dominant or *hegemonic* group (actually a dominant class and those associated with it) wins the consent or at least acquiescence of other groups to the practices and ideologies which constitute its domination – ways of operating as a worker or employee, ways of conducting politics, cultural values, ways of speaking and ideologies of language, and so forth. Hegemony is not something that is won once and for all. A hegemonic group may have achieved a relatively stable hegemony in some domains (e.g. the economy and the political system) but not in others (e.g. certain cultural domains). Preserving hegemony requires ongoing struggle, and hegemony is always open to contestation by other social forces to some degree. So a hegemony is as Gramsci said no more than an 'unstable equilibrium', and being hegemonic is never more than a relative and more or less precarious position.

What I want to suggest is that the sociolinguistic order is a domain of hegemonic struggle, and that one dimension of the struggle of a group to establish its hegemony over a domain or institution is a struggle for sociolinguistic hegemony. Parts of the sociolinguistic order may at a given point in time be relatively stable, and may even approximate to the picture conveyed by appropriateness models – well-defined varieties in neat complementary relationships to contrasting functions and contexts, with most people using these varieties 'appropriately' most of the time. But the whole of the sociolinguistic order of a complex society like ours is never like that, and even points of stability become contested and destabilised. In many instances, there are alternative language practices – the example of medical interview given above is a case in point. They may just coexist, but the issue of dominance relationships between them generally arises. And dominance commonly means not the elimination of all but one practice, but the relative marginalisation of non-dominant practices, or the incorporation of non-dominant practices into dominant ones.

Establishing sociolinguistic hegemony means establishing relations of domination and subordination among alternative language practices. For example, the sort of medical interview I described earlier as 'traditional' has long been dominant, and that dominance is part of the hegemony in modern medicine of a professional establishment rooted in a scientific and technological view of medicine as, to put it crudely, mending bodies. That hegemony has in recent decades been under challenge from other groups in the profession committed to wholistic approaches to medicine, and the challenge is partly manifested in the emergence of alternative forms of medical discourse. Notice that I am assuming here relatively 'local' forms of hegemony within particular institutions such as education or medicine. There may be rather complex fits or misfits between hegemonic (class) relations at the societal level, and hegemonic relations among groups (different groups of teachers, administrators, pupils, parents, in the case of education for example) in particular institutions, in relation to sociolinguistic hegemony as in relation to other dimensions of hegemony.

This view of the sociolinguistic order as one terrain of hegemonic struggle will perhaps be surprising to people whose conception of language had been influenced by modern linguistics – one is used to the idea that power relations are enacted within the sociolinguistic conventions of speech community, but these conventions themselves are seen as solid social facts, not as themselves stakes in and outcomes of struggle between social forces. There is an oppositional tradition within linguistics however (Volosinov 1973), as well as a tradition in social theory (Foucault 1984) which recognises a power struggle to control language. According to Foucault, 'as history constantly teaches us, discourse is not simply that which translates struggles or systems of domination, but is the thing for which and by which there is struggle, discourse is the power which is to be seized' (1984: 110). Foucault adds that 'in every society the production of discourse is at once controlled, selected, organised and redistributed by a certain number of procedures whose role is to ward off its powers and its dangers, to gain mastery over its chance events, to evade its ponderous, formidable materiality'. The procedures include 'prohibition': 'we know quite well that we do not have the right to say everything, that we cannot speak of just anything in any circumstances whatsoever, and that not everyone has the right to speak of anything whatever' (1984: 109). What sociolinguists have generally seen – innocently – in terms of a speech community's rules (rules for 'who says what to whom, when and where') is here portrayed by Foucault as the taming and mastery of discourse.

Sociolinguistic hegemony, like other dimensions of hegemony, involves not just shaping practices directly, but also generating theories and doctrines of sociolinguistic practice. Thus one dimension of the developing hegemony of standard English over other varieties was the emergence from the late seventeenth century onwards of 'doctrines of correctness' (Leonard 1925). Doctrines and theories have a double role. First, they help to naturalise hegemonic practices. For example a formulation such as 'language variety x is (not) appropriate in context y' metaphorically expresses a historically specific relationship between people – those who speak the language, those who struggle to impose hegemony and those who contest it – as a timeless relationship between things: between a variety, and a context. It is a case of 'grammatical metaphor' in Halliday's sense (Halliday 1985). It construes what is historical and contingent as natural and necessary. It is also a case of what one might call 'linguistic fetishism' on the model of Marx's famous 'commodity fetishism' (1974: 76–88): constraints which arise from particular social relations are fetishistically attributed to language itself.

Second, doctrines and theories incorporate political projects (in the sense of objectives), especially the 'hegemonic projects' of groups who aspire to hegemony in the domain of language. That is, they project upon the messy and contradictory realities of a sociolinguistic order an idealised and utopian view of what the sociolinguistic order ought to be like from the partisan perspective of a dominant social group. Theories of appropriateness are a case in point. It is certainly not the case that all members of a speech community act in accordance with shared ideas of appropriateness, but it is a natural enough aspiration and project on the part of those trying to impose (their) order upon a society or a social institution. Sometimes the project takes the explicit form of institutional rules and regulations (in schools for example: no speaking in class without teacher's permission, no shouting in the corridors, and so forth), but often it does not.

Doctrines and theories take the common-sense form of language attitudes, and indeed a measure of their hegemony is the extent to which they come to be naturalised as attitudes. It is a strength of ethnographic approaches to linguistic research that the study of the language attitudes of members of a community is seen as an essential complement to and part of the study of their sociolinguistic practices. Practices and attitudes fuel each other. But at the same time there may be striking mismatches between what people do and what they think they (ought to) do, and it is important not to confuse the two in analysis.

'Appropriateness' belongs to the domain of language attitudes: it is one sort of judgement that is made by members of speech communities about language use (Hymes 1972). However, there has been a great deal of slippage between the analysis of language attitudes and the analysis of sociolinguistic practices, and 'appropriateness' has come to be widely used as an analytical concept within the description of the latter. It is common to find linguists writing about what 'is appropriate' in a speech community rather than what is 'judged to be appropriate' (by particular groups). Here are two quite typical examples:

> The development of awareness has a marked effect upon a pupil's ability to cope with the whole range of his work, because he comes to see that many problems are not so much problems in grasping the content of what he studies, but problems of handling the language appropriate to it. (Doughty et al. 1971: 10)

> The next short paragraph seems to be a summary statement of the line to be taken, or of the point at issue, and is generically more appropriate to the discourse convention of an editorial than to that of a newspaper report (Carter 1988: 12).

Such wordings are also common in educational documents, such as the Cox Report cited earlier. They imply the image of a sociolinguistic order based around shared norms of appropriateness, a misrepresentation of sociolinguistic realities as I have argued above. But I have suggested that such an image embodies a hegemonic political project. That is why using 'appropriateness' in this way is ideological: it places the analyst inside the hegemonic project, so to speak; it puts linguistics (sociolinguistics, educational linguistics) in the position of helping to normalise and legitimise a politically partisan representation, and turns a social scientific discipline into a resource for hegemonic struggle. I hasten to add that there is no implication whatsoever of conscious connivance on the part of analysts: the processes whereby people come to be ideologically coopted are generally unconscious ones which none of us are immune to.

Let me now sum up the second part of this chapter. I have criticised appropriateness models of language variation on two connected grounds. First, because they project an idealised image of the sociolinguistic order which is hopelessly at odds with the indeterminacies, unevennesses, diversity, tensions and struggle of real sociolinguistic orders, such as that of modern Britain. Second, because they are ideological. That is, in projecting this idealised image of the sociolinguistic order they are also projecting a hegemonic objective and ideal. This second criticism raises a more general issue: thinking and theorising about language, as Crowley (1989) for example shows in the case of 'history of the language' as a linguistic subdiscipline in Britain, should be open to assessment in its political context – in terms of how it relates to, is shaped by, and helps shape, wider processes of hegemonic struggle.

Conclusion: appropriateness and critical language awareness

Appropriateness models of language variation are widespread, and often have the status of common sense in the theory and practice of language education. They are a major obstacle to the spread of critical language awareness programmes of the sort advocated in this book, which is why the critique of appropriateness is an important issue here. The view of critical language awareness some of us have put forward (Clark et al. 1988) stresses the mutually reinforcing development of critical understanding of the sociolinguistic order, and practice, including the creative practice of probing and shifting existing conventions. Appropriateness models block a critical understanding by ideologically collapsing political projects and actual practices, and they block a creative and critical language practice by foregrounding normativity and training in appropriate behaviour. As we have argued elsewhere (Fairclough & Ivanič 1989), there is a tendency (e.g. in the Kingman and Cox Reports) for creativity in language practice to be ghettoised in parts of the English syllabus dealing with teaching of literature, while non-literary language practice is overwhelmingly construed in terms of appropriateness – 'getting it right'.

This does not mean that the concept of appropriateness has no place in a CLA programme. On the contrary, it is important for learners to scrutinise doctrines of and attitudes towards sociolinguistic practice: they are part of what such a programme should make learners aware of. Judgements on the basis of appropriateness can be assessed in the light of their own socio-linguistic experience, including experience of inequalities between language varieties and constraints upon some of them. Judgements on the basis of appropriateness can also be evaluated in terms of their social genesis and social functions – recall the account in terms of hegemony I gave above. It is also crucially important that learners' own linguistic practice should be informed by estimates of the possibilities, risks and costs of going against dominant judgements of appropriate usage. Learners should for example have a picture of dominant judgements of when standard English is appropriate, but also of how widely such judgements are shared and followed in practice. And they should be encouraged to develop the ability to use standard English in conventional ways when they judge it to be necessary to do so, because they will be disadvantaged if they do not develop that ability. At the same time, they should be encouraged to see their own relationships and struggles as members of various communities as continuous with the relationships and struggles out of which the sociolinguistic practices, doctrines and attitudes of their speech community have been generated. And to see that they contribute through their own practice to the shaping and reshaping of the sociolinguistic order – to reproducing it or transforming it. And to appreciate the possibility, advantages, and risks of critical, creative and emancipatory (see Chapter thirteen) practice as speakers and writers, and as critical readers and listeners, using for example other languages and dialects for the prestigious purposes and contexts where standard English is generally said to be appropriate. Critical language awareness, in other words, should not push learners into oppositional practices which condemn them to disadvantage and marginalisation; it should equip them with the capacities and understanding which are preconditions for meaningful choice and effective citizenship in the domain of language.

Acknowledgement

I would like to thank Romy Clark for her helpful comments on this paper.

References

Barnes D 1988 The politics of oracy. In MacLure M et al. (eds) *Oracy matters*. Open University Press

Candlin C N 1975 *The communicative teaching of English*. Longman

Carter R 1988 Front pages: lexis, style, and newspaper reports. In Ghadessy M (ed) *Registers of written English*. Pinter Publications

Chomsky N 1965 *Aspects of the theory of grammar*. MIT Press

Clark R, Fairclough N, Ivanič R, Martin–Jones M 1988 *Critical Language awareness*. Lancaster University, Centre for Language in Social Life, Working Papers No 1

Crowley T 1989 *The politics of language*. Macmillan

Department of Education and Science (DES) 1988 *Report of the committee of enquiry into the teaching of English language* (Kingman Report) HMSO

Department of Education and Science (DES) 1989 *English for ages 5 to 16* (Cox Report) HMSO

Doughty P, Pearce J, Thornton G 1971 *Language in use*. Edward Arnold

Fairclough N forthcoming Discourse in social change: a conflictual view. To appear in Tollefson J (ed) *Language, power and inequality*. Cambridge University Press

Fairclough N, Ivanič R 1989 Language education or language training? A critique of the Kingman Model of the English language. In Bourne J Bloor T (eds) *The Kingman Report*. Committee for Linguistics In Education (CLIE).

Foucault M 1984 The order of discourse. In Shapiro M (ed) *Language and politics*. Blackwell

Further Education Unit 1987 *Relevance flexibility and competence*. HMSO

Gramsci A 1971 *Selections from the prison notebooks* Hoare Q, Nowell Smith G (eds) Lawrence & Wishart

Halliday M 1985 *An introduction to functional grammar*. Edward Arnold

Hawkins E 1984 *Awareness of language: an introduction*. Cambridge University Press

Hawkins E (ed) 1985 *Awareness of language series*. Cambridge University Press

Hewitt R 1989 The new oracy: another critical glance. Paper delivered to the British Association for Applied Linguistics annual meeting, Lancaster

Hymes D 1972 On communicative competence. In Pride J, Holmes J, *Sociolinguistics*. Penguin

Keat R, Abercrombie N 1990 *Enterprise culture*. Routledge

Leonard S A 1925 *The doctrine of correctness in English language and literature*. University of Wisconsin Press

Levinson S 1983 *Pragmatics*. Cambridge University Press

Marx K 1974 *Capital* v 1. Lawrence & Wishart

Mishler E 1984 *The discourse of medicine*. Ablex

Rose N 1989 Governing the enterprising self. Paper delivered at conference on Values of the Enterprise Culture, Centre for the study of Cultural Values, Lancaster University

ten Have P 1989 The consultation as a genre. In B Torode (ed) *Talk and text as social practice*. Foris

Volosinov V I 1973 *Marxism and the philosophy of language*. Seminar Press

Young, Lord 1987 People, enterprise and jobs. Speech to the National Economic Development Council on its 25th anniversary, 29 April

Part II

*Critical Language Awareness
in Diverse
Educational Contexts*

3 Critical Literacy Awareness in the EFL Classroom

Catherine Wallace

In 1977 the banned Czech writer Sdener Urbanak told me: 'You in the West have a problem. You are unsure when you are being lied to, when you are being tricked. We do not suffer from this: and unlike you, we have acquired the skill of reading between the lines.' In Britain today we need to develop this skill urgently, for as freedom is being gained in the East, it is being lost here.

John Pilger, *The Guardian*, March 1990

I should like to begin by considering the familiar, even hackneyed term which Pilger uses – reading between the lines. If we agree that it is part of effective reading and if it is true that many people do not read in this way, is it possible or desirable for us to attempt as teachers to develop this skill? The expression is usually taken to mean 'drawing inferences' but the nature of these inferences is not always explored – whether for instance, they are part of the author's intended meaning or not; whether we as readers are at liberty to deduce meaning which almost certainly was not intended by the writer. In this chapter I should like to suggest a procedure for reading between the lines or what I shall call critical reading. In doing so I shall draw on models of reading which emphasise the process of reading and the ways in which readers interact with texts. I shall also refer to some of the work which has been done in critical discourse analysis, most recently by Fairclough (1989). This procedure will be discussed in the context of work with some of my own students at Ealing College in West London – where I teach multilingual groups of students, coming from a range of cultural backgrounds. Some are resident in Britain; most plan to return to their own countries on completing their studies.

The interaction between reader and text

Widdowson (1984) one of the first, in the world of English language teaching at least, to talk of reading as an interaction of reader with text, argues that in this interaction a reader can take up an assertive or submissive position. The stance selected depends on the reader's purpose in reading: 'he is free to take up whatever position suits his purpose on the dominance/dependence scale' (p. 91). If the reader is too submissive, Widdowson claims, he may accumulate information without accommodating it into the structure of existing knowledge. If he is too assertive, he may distort the writer's intentions and deny access to new knowledge and experience. In response to Widdowson, I would agree that there are certainly times when our purpose in reading is largely information gathering and we are happy to submit to the undoubted superior knowledge of the writer. However, there are several further important points one might make about the assertive/submissive continuum.

First, there is evidence that some readers – and listeners – are unduly submissive even where they have knowledge of the topic. Andersen, (1988: 151) for instance, quotes the case of a favourable response by a group of experts to a lecture delivered by a specially trained actor which, though based on a genuine paper, was full of non-sequiturs and inconsequential information.

Second, some readers are not in positions where they can readily assert themselves against the power of the text. For instance, children in school may not see assertiveness as an option (cf. for example, Kress 1989). Submission is forced upon them. It is not so much individual choice or even inferior knowledge but the context of learning which imposes submission: the view, not always well-founded, that teacher and text – and test – must know best.

Third, Widdowson is talking largely of propositional knowledge. The reader, he says, may choose to 'assert the primacy of his own conceptual patterns' (1984: 91). There are other grounds on which writers can be challenged. As well as disputing the propositional content of texts one can challenge ideological assumptions. By ideology I mean the common-sense assumptions which help to legitimise existing social relations and differences in power (cf. Fairclough 1989: 2). It is the second territory that I shall deal with below.

Generally, I want to argue that effective reading involves challenging the ideological assumptions as well as propositional knowledge in written texts and that we as teachers may need to guide readers to an awareness of ideological content simply because it is so often presented as 'obvious'. I have in mind the words of Scholes (1985: 16): 'In an age of manipulation when our students are in dire need of critical strength to resist the continuing assaults of all the media, the worst thing we can do is to foster in them an attitude of reverence before texts.' Certainly the risk exists for over-assertive reading and Scholes makes this point. The general tendency, however, 'especially for L2 readers', is an over-deferent stance towards the text. In this chapter I shall suggest some pedagogic approaches which might help readers to resist certain kinds of assaults presented by written texts: to challenge, that is, particular ways of talking about persons, places, events and phenomena and ways of talking to the reader – of positioning her/him in particular ways.

Moreover, critical reading, I shall argue, involves more than a critical response to the text itself. It involves a critical awareness in a broader sense, of what reading itself is, which, in turn, involves a consideration of cross-cultural aspects regarding who reads what and why in what situations.

Critical reading and the EFL classroom

Critical reading has not been generally encouraged in the English as a Foreign Language (EFL) classroom in either the wider or the narrower sense, whether we are talking of those with very limited English language proficiency or of quite advanced learners of English. Students tend not to be invited to draw on their experiences of literacy, or to articulate their understanding of it as a social phenomenon. Reading has been seen to be unproblematic as an activity, simply as what goes on when reader meets text. Texts have not generally been selected for their potential to challenge. They are more frequently seen as either vehicles for linguistic structure, as general interest material usually of a fairly safe, bland kind or as functional survival material for some groups of L2 learners who are given material such as forms or official letters, thus suggesting an assimilationist model of literacy – one which accepts rather than challenges the assumptions as to the future social and occupational roles of second language learners.

One reason given for the conventional avoidance of contentious material has been that learners from cultures other than mainstream British ones might find some material irrelevant and offensive. I think however, that the risk of offence can be overstated. Adult students at least, especially if learning English in an English-speaking country such as the United States or Britain, are more likely to be offended by being patronised, by having texts censored for them. They may not want to be treated as in some way different from other communities of readers, simply by virtue of being a) foreigners and b) in a classroom context. They are likely to want to be in the now famous words of Frank Smith (1983) 'one of the club'.

In short, EFL students are often marginalised as readers; their goals in interacting with written texts are perceived to be primarily those of language learners. What is missing is:

(1) an attempt to place reading activity and written texts in a social context
(2) the use of texts which are provocative
(3) a methodology for interpreting texts which addresses ideological assumptions as well as propositional meaning

The students and data collection

The data I shall draw on comes mainly from one particular class, Class 6, which I teach once a week for two hours. The students, in their twenties and thirties, are on a general English course. They are nearly all women, many with children, mostly from Eastern or Western Europe or Japan. Their general aim is to improve their English; a specific one is to gain the Proficiency examination set by the Cambridge examination board for advanced learners of English. I shall also refer to other groups of students following undergraduate and postgraduate courses and coming from a broader range of linguistic and cultural backgrounds.

Aims and procedure

I wanted to try out a reading course which encouraged learners to look critically, not just at texts themselves, but at the whole practice and process of reading as dependent on social context. Moreover, while I worked largely with Class 6, I also wanted to try out material with other groups in order to establish whether the way texts were read in one particular classroom setting would be different from another. This chapter is therefore divided into two parts: in the first I describe work with a range of texts in a single class; in the second I describe the varying processes of interpretation by several different classes of a single text.

In planning my course for Class 6, my overall pedagogic aim was to help learners to see reading and written texts as problematical – to be critically aware of literacy as a phenomenon and assertive in their interaction with written texts. More specifically, I addressed myself to three questions which saw reading in terms of practices, production and processes. My three questions were:

(1) What reading practices are characteristic of particular social groups, for example, what kind of reading behaviour typifies a particular family or community setting?
(2) How is reading material produced in a particular society, that is how do texts such as newspapers, advertisements, leaflets and public information material come to us in the form they do, who produces them, and how do they come to have the salience they do?
(3) What influences the process of interpreting texts in particular contexts?

Let us take each question in turn in relation to the work done by Class 6.

Reading practices

In beginning with the idea of practices I am talking of the fact that we read as communities of readers as much as individuals. The idea of interpretative communities comes originally from Fish (1980) who applied it to schools of literary critics. However, we can use it in a broader sense, as Carter and Walker (1989: 3) do when they talk of an interpretative community 'within which readers grow up and are educated'. One can extend the notion still further to see the classroom itself as one kind of interpretative community with its own social constraints and literacy experiences. The longer the class is together the more of a community it becomes and the more it begins to share and exchange interpretative resources.

Class 6 came together as strangers, at the beginning of the academic year. They had enrolled initially for only one term on a part-time general English class. As none of us knew each other, it seemed appropriate to start with our own literacy histories. As a way of beginning to think of the part played by literacy in our own lives I used the profiles in the magazine *Marxism Today* of peoples' reading experiences. Here people from a range of professional, political and social backgrounds are asked about the role which reading has played in their lives. These reading histories offered us a framework for thinking about the role of reading in our personal lives and the extent to which this is determined by early family and school experiences. It was possible to transfer these reading histories into the following kind of matrix.

First memories of reading
(what, where, with whom?)

Favourite reading as a child

Favourite reading as an adult

Most important book/s or author/s in your life

Main roles and purposes of reading
(e.g. as parent, professional
for pleasure, religious purposes)

We then took this as a framework to explore the literacy experiences of other individuals and the students brought back into the classroom reading profiles of people they had interviewed. As an extension of this, and relating to our interest in the social as well as individual dimension to reading behaviour, the students then did simple 'family literacy' surveys where people were asked about their reader roles as family members.

Shirley Brice Heath undertook a famous study (Brice Heath 1983) of what she called the 'literacy events' which typified the day-to-day lives of two communities in the United States. Barton, in an ongoing study at Lancaster University, has looked at the kinds of roles which people take on as readers and writers in their own families and communities. Auerbach (1990) describes family literacy practices particularly among language minorities, mainly Hispanic, in Boston USA. Discussion of these studies leads us to consider the ways in which children are influenced by the typical literacy events of the families and communities in which they have been brought up. The students shared their own memories of learning to read, and as many of the students were parents it seemed appropriate to look at children's books – in particular at what their language and content indicated of wider social values.

In surveying reading behaviour and reading material in this way we began to discover, on the one hand, how much can be learned from both about social class membership, education, political views and, on the other hand, how much can be taken for granted assumptions about gender, class and race. One issue, which we discussed, for instance, was the near invisibility of some groups such as oriental people or those with disabilities in the range of children's books we looked at (cf. Wallace 1988 for a fuller discussion).

Production and consumption of reading material

A second stage was to consider how texts come to us in the form they do. The concept of authorship is hazy for beginner readers. How do people come to write books? Can anyone do it? A learner of mine thought that the author's first and surname on the cover of the book were the names of the two figures on the dust-jacket. Experienced L2 readers are aware of authorship but may be less familiar with the whole range of genres to which members of the majority culture have access. I use the term genre here to mean the range of text types from menus to comic strips, which may be either exclusive to a particular culture or, more probably, take on varying formal and semantic characteristics. A Japanese student in Class 6, Yatsuko, brought in an editorial from a Japanese English-language newspaper which, she had observed, was quite different in style and structure to that of a typical British newspaper. Even hazier for many of us is an awareness of the role of publishers and/or proprietors. Many classrooms now encourage

the participation of learners in their own production of material
– in seeing themselves as writers, editors and bookbinders and
distributors, thus gaining an idea of the composing and publishing
process. Very often there is a class newspaper.

This tends to ignore, however, the factors of power in the real
world - what kind of sociopolitical influences affect what gets
published and where and in what form. Does the West as we
are led to believe really have a free press? Pilger, in the article
already quoted, implies not. Where does the news come from?
What is the status of journalists' knowledge? What influence is
brought to bear by publishers and proprietors? Does it matter
that *The Times* and The *Sun* are both owned by the same man?
Finally, who are the intended consumers of texts?

As a way of attempting to address some of these questions in
the classroom context, we first collected a whole range of reading
material – advertisements, bills, letters, and newspapers. This was
the task we used to classify and discuss the texts in class, working
in groups:

(1) Try to classify the texts on each table. Suggested categories
    might be: requests from charities or causes; public information
    leaflets; professional reading material.
(2) When you have worked out five or six broad types of text, try
    to identify the following:

    (a) who produces them? e.g, public bodies, commercial enter-
        prises, local authorities
    (b) for whom are they produced, i.e. who are the consumers
        or the expected readers of the material?
    (c) why has the text been produced?
    (d) is this type of text of interest or relevance to you?
        why/why not?
    (e) choose one text from each category which particularly
        appeals to you, either because of its style or content and
        discuss with other members of your group

Reading Processes

We are familiar with the idea of reading as a psycholinguistic
process whereby during the reading act itself we are continually

predicting and sampling. However reading is also a social process. We read not only as individuals but as members of social groups, as parents, consumers or teachers – one or other of these social identities may be salient on any particular occasion we interact with written language. At the same time, our interpretations of texts are socially determined, dependent partly on previous social experiences and the social context in which we are reading. It follows that reading is not a self-contained activity which takes place in the classroom. Our first language identities and experiences as readers inevitably influence our second language ones.

Equally, texts cannot be understood as self-contained products. And yet in the foreign-language classroom that is frequently the assumption – the text is brought into the classroom, or is reproduced in the textbook, and is then treated to various forms of analysis or followed by exercises. Frequently, the text is shorn of authorship, date and source. It has no history. And yet how a text comes to take the form it does is part of the meaning of a text. We need to know something about 'the historical situation in which it [the text] was composed' (Scholes 1985:21). And, as argued above, we are helped also to know not just about the circumstances of composition but the circumstances of production.

Linked to the notion of history is that of intertextuality – how the text is placed in the context of other texts. One way in which we connect texts is through a recognition of certain kinds of discourse. Let me now say how I interpret the terms 'intertextuality' and 'discourse' in this discussion.

Intertextuality

No text can be interpreted on its own. Texts always exist in relation to other texts. Scholes (1985: 31) claims that 'the object of study is the whole intertextual system that connects one text to another and which finally includes the students' own writing'. Certainly, it is part of the writer's assumption about reader knowledge that there is access to other texts and other genres. Texts can be part of a series – an ongoing topical discussion for instance, or they can relate to each other in terms of genre. Texts can steal from other genres. Fairclough (1989) talks about how some genres or (the term preferred by Fairclough) 'discourse types' have colonised others, advertising being an obvious example. Text A (see the appendix) is an example from an advertisement for a watch.

Discourse

We recognise the influence of two genres in the text A, because we are familiar with the typical discourses of both the language of advertising and the language of romantic fiction suggested by, for example, 'before the night was through'. I am using the term 'discourses' to mean ideologically determined ways of talking or writing about persons, places, events or phenomena. Three major points can be made about discourses as used in this sense: first, discourses are determined by social structure. There are sets of conventions associated with particular social institutions such as courtship and marriage or education which are reflected in conventional ways of talking about them. It follows that discourses are seen as unexceptional – even obvious – both by the writer and by the typical readers of any text. Third, discourses reflect power differential between social groups. There are, for instance, conventionally different ways of talking about those of a different class, race or gender, typified in the text above by the contrast between the assertiveness of the man and the hesitation and silence of the woman.

One of the goals of critical reading is the reconstruction of the discourses within the text. This means looking at the 'obvious' and 'taken for granted' in critical ways so that, for instance, ways of talking about women, blacks and foreigners, which are so commonplace as to be seen as obvious by most readers, are placed under scrutiny.

Closely linked to this notion of discourse is that of the text's ideal or model reader. All texts construct for their reader a reading position. As Eagleton (1983: 84) puts it: 'It is not just that a writer "needs an audience": the language he uses implies one range of possible audiences rather than another.' In other words, the reader is part of the text. One advantage that L2 readers may have is that they are *not* the text's model readers. Simply because they are not part of the intended readership they are in a position to bring fresh and legitimate interpretations to written texts. They are able to exploit their position as outsiders.

Critical reading and the role of language

Critical reading involves us challenging the ideological content of texts as evidenced in their salient discourses. These discourses are indicated through the linguistic choices of the writer. Central to the idea of critical reading is an awareness of the role that language plays in conveying not just a propositional message but an ideological one.

Critical analysis thus involves some explicit understanding of language as a formal system (Fairclough 1989: 241). The means by which discourses are reconstructed from texts is through an analysis of the language itself, from an examination, for instance, of certain kinds of collocation, inclusive and exclusive pronouns and whether nouns function in sentences as agents or patients. One can, for instance, argue the presence of a sexist discourse if, as happens in many children's reading books, boys are actors in events much more frequently than girls, for example in this fairly typical sequence: 'Peter has the red ball. He plays with the boys with the red ball. Jane looks on' (Ladybird Key Words reading scheme, *Things we like*).

Fairly detailed textual analyses have been proposed by Trew (1979) and more recently by Fairclough (1989). These are influenced by Hallidayan grammar. However a difficulty in typical general reading classes, whether of L1 or L2 speakers, is how one might make such models accessible to students and usable by teachers.

I believe it is possible to adapt and select some of the key features of the these descriptions to achieve a workable pedagogy. One advantage which many EFL students tend to have over L1 students is that they know about grammar. They have a metalanguage, a way of talking about texts which native speakers often lack. Some of the traditional terms such as 'pronoun', 'subject and object' and 'active and passive voice' can therefore be drawn upon. It means that this knowledge can be put to use in looking not just at propositional content but ideological assumptions. Rather than just focusing on form for its own sake, as in traditional language and reading exercises, students can do so to adduce evidence for the text's ideological positioning.

In the rest of this chapter I shall talk about a general procedure for critical reading in terms of materials collection and teaching approach with Class 6, concluding with a detailed look at three texts, the first two studied by Class 6 alone, the third discussed and analysed in a range of ways by both Class 6 and three other groups of students.

The selection of texts

The texts selected were all authentic, in the sense of being written for a purpose other than pedagogic and represented a range of genres, such as advertisements, magazine articles and newspaper reports. Students were asked to select texts for the whole class to work with, and part of this procedure involved them giving a reason for their choice of text. I also chose texts myself, especially in the early days. Favourite choices of topic were language, education, topical issues such as the Vietnamese boat people, the poll tax and the role of women.

I supplemented and built on the texts brought in by students by finding texts which dealt with the same topic but from a range of different positions. I also occasionally chose texts with a very clear ideological loading. Our key text, Robbie, described below, is such an example. The fact that the discourses within it are very clearly marked I thought made it a good text with which to begin – moving on later to look at more typical texts and genres with more concealed ideological assumptions and reader positioning.

Methodology

My general aims in terms of methodology were twofold. First, I wanted to avoid approaches which talk of 'finding the right answer' – whether this is seen in terms of the conventional best answer to multiple-choice questions or guessing what 'the teacher has in mind'. I wished to make it clear that a range of interpretations were acceptable but that they would need to be argued through and defended against rival interpretations of the group. This is in line with a broad process view of reading (cf. for instance Alderson and Urquhart 1984) where the means are seen to be as important as the ends. Moreover, even when we did occasionally do traditional 'comprehension' texts which used multiple-choice format questions – as a concession to the imminent Proficiency exam – the questions were critiqued as part of the text. In short, the aim was to encourage reflective critical reading, of any text, whether authentic or selected or adapted with a pedagogic aim.

Second, I wanted to build on a pre-reading/while-reading/post-reading procedure in classroom reading but to add a critical element. Typical pre-reading tasks ask students, for example, to 'give their personal opinion' about the topic. A more critical pre-reading task might be to think of why the topic has been selected in the first place. Similarly, with while-reading: a typical while-reading task is to predict the continuing text. A critical while-reading task would be to consider a whole range of ways of continuing a text, not just the most probable ones. I also encouraged students to see that questions are as important as answers by asking them to generate their own questions of any text rather than reading to find the answers to given questions; also, in the pre-reading part of the lesson, to see this as the opportunity to bring together social attitudinal knowledge as much as propositional knowledge of the genre, topic and discourses represented in the text to be studied.

Specifically, I wanted to build on a framework offered by Kress (cf. Kress 1989:7) to help raise awareness of the ideology of texts. Kress suggests that we ask three simple questions of any text:

(1) Why is this topic being written about?
(2) How is the topic being written about?
(3) What other ways of writing about the topic are there?

I found this helpful as a starting point. In particular 3 is very important in addressing the taken-for-grantedness of certain discourses. Point 3 then was highlighted in dealing with all the texts we considered. However in the light of our claim that the reader is part of the text we might need to add a fourth question:

(4) Who is writing to whom?

Moreover, we frequently need to decide, before we consider why a topic is being written about, what the topic is. This, as with the other questions, is open to interpretation. We might therefore add another question, namely:

(5) What is the topic?

Furthermore, when it comes to exploiting a text in the classroom, different texts lend themselves to different emphases in answering these questions. That is, while 3 is always central, with some texts 4 becomes a more interesting question to address than 2.

I shall take two examples of texts which had in common the fact that they dealt, in very different ways, with the role of women.

The Giraffe-necked Women of Burma (see Text B in Appendix)

This text was chosen from a magazine called *Marie Claire*, brought in by one of the students. Some of the students were able to tell me that this magazine, unlike others of the genre, dealt with social issues and that the model reader was young, liberal and socially aware. The aspect of critical reading which seemed worth highlighting was the discourse about the Burmese women, what ways of talking about these women were selected by the writer (from the range of available options). Because the principle of options is crucial to critical reading approaches, Kress's question – 'What other ways of writing about x are there?' – was central to our discussion. However, if we incorporate this into a pre/while/post-reading classroom procedure, this question can be reformulated as part of pre-reading, namely: What ways of talking about the women are (in principle) available to a writer? Examples could be: the women as actors in their own drama; the women as a tourist attraction; the women as subject to the decisions of men; the tribe (to which the women belong) as subject to the decisions of national government.

The classroom procedure took this pattern:

Pre-reading

What ways are there in which we might write about 'the giraffe-necked women of Burma'?

Why do you think the text was written?
– because of . . . . . e.g. an interest in 'exotica'
– in order to . . . . . inform/persuade/entertain

What is the text about?
Scan pictures, headlines, subheadings to establish the topic.
Describe in a single sentence, e.g. 'the text is a sociological text describing the conflicts between central government and tribal communities'

Choose pre-reading questions which reflect your judgement as to the text's topic, e.g:

(1) role of women: e.g. do women choose to wear the rings?
(2) tribal cultures v. national government: e.g. does the government attempt to stop tribal practices?
(3) women's mutilation of their bodies: e.g. are there other practices carried out by the women?
    can one compare neck elongation to practices in Western cultures, e.g. breast enlargement, ear piercing?

While Reading

How is the material presented? Focusing on the description of the women in the extract below, consider

(1) how far the women or girls take subject position in sentences
(2) if their body parts are seen as part of them or are described as objects, e.g. the difference between 'the rings are placed on the neck' and 'the rings are placed on their necks'

For a Padaung girl, the brass ring procedure begins at the age of ten when the first ring is coiled around the neck by her mother, who recites magic charms which are believed to take away the rigidity of the metal. New rings are added every three years until 21 to 26, or even 28, brass rings encircle the neck. At the same time, the first of the leg spirals is placed between the knees and ankles.

The result is considerably restricted movement. Unable to bend their heads, women have to drink with the aid of a straw and sit with their legs held straight out in front of them. The deformity of the larynx caused by the elongation of the neck affects the women's voices, variously described as sounding 'as if they were speaking up the shaft of a well' by one Victorian observer, or as 'a high-pitched croak' by a German photographer who visited them in the early 1970s.

Despite these restrictions, the women labour in the fields as hard or harder than any other Burmese women, retreating further and further into the jungle to avoid discovery by Government troops, who would force them to abandon their way of life.

(3) the kinds of verbs which describe the women, e.g. active and passive constructions; modal constructions e.g. with 'must', 'have to', 'should'

(4) how far the verbs describe actions, states, and mental processes; the kind of actions and mental processes that are described, e.g. 'work, think, disagree, believe'

Post Reading

To whom is the text addressed?
e.g, – the general public
     – western women
     – women with liberal attitudes

In what other ways could the text have been written?

The final post-reading question echoes the first question, i.e. having reflected initially on what ways in principle the writer could choose to address the topic, the students can be made more aware of which options were and were not taken up.

Mother Knows Best (see Text C in Appendix)

I decided to approach the second text quite differently, by deliberately withdrawing contextual information regarding author, genre and the history of the text, in order to see if the students could reconstruct it by drawing on clues provided by the discourses in the text. I presented chunks of the text in turn (shown by the spacing of the text in the Appendix), after each one of which I asked the students to comment as far as they could on the way in which the language was used to talk about the role of women and marriage. I was also interested to see if they could pick up traces of discourses which, I felt, offered clues to the author's identity, in terms of gender, class and political orientation.

This was the task which was used to see how far information about the text could be progressively built up:

Class 6A   Reconstructing context from text extracts

     After section 1 . . .section 2 . . . .section 3

1. What is the genre?

2. What is the topic?

3. Why was the text written?

4 Who is writing?
   (in terms of gender class nationality and personal traits)

5. To or for whom is he/she writing?

6. What other information is revealed? e.g. time of writing

   After each section pause to ask a question/questions of the author which you feel the text raises.

Only at the end of the text was the introductory section (reproduced at the end of the text in the Appendix) given to the students. It is particularly important in this case as it frames the text and positions the reader to read the text in a particular way, as the journalist who is using the original article signals very clearly her hostility to Thatcher. Indeed a better exercise might have been to compare responses to the text from two groups in the class, one given the uncontextualised version and one the contextualised version.

The Blame that Spain Must Share (see Text D in Appendix)

I should like to conclude with a more detailed study of the way in which a single text was read by diverse groups of students. We came to call this text 'Robbie' and it was introduced first to Class 6. I decided to approach the presentation of the text by beginning with a fragment from the middle of the text and gradually filling out the discourse to see at what point the group would be able to reconstruct likely author, readership and genre. In fact, reaction was immediate and overwhelming especially from the Spanish students in the group. There was disbelief that a mainstream newspaper could produce such an article. We decided to compose a joint response to the *Daily Mail*. One difficulty in doing this was that the world had moved on since the article was published in August 1989. By November there were new discourses in play in the aftermath of the end of the Cold War and The Berlin Wall, relating to a united Europe and changed East–West relations. We decided to use these to make our point. The act of composing the letter, the decision to send it not to the writer of the article, but to the newspaper's editor, an eventual reply from the deputy managing editor – all helped to reveal the role of different participants in the production of texts.

I was interested to know what kind of response the text would receive from groups of students coming to it cold, that is in classes where texts were used primarily for translation purposes and were usually chosen from very different genres such as economics textbooks. The students, all undergraduates ranging from first to final year students and of different nationalities, were asked to write a paragraph commenting on the text. The responses were anonymous and I had originally hoped that it might be possible to identify whether students were British, Spanish or from another European country. Certainly they tended to respond, sometimes very personally, as Spanish or British, but very few challenged the discourses in the text. They did not, that is, respond to the way the language itself was used. Some accepted the author's construct of Robbie without question, e.g. 'It might be very true that Robbie is an average, decent human being at home. . . '. Others responded critically to the propositional content seeing the text as flawed in logic but not questionable in the way phenomena and people were talked about. No-one mentioned the Spanish waiter.

The next group I presented the text to was one where we had talked about language and ideology and the nature of discourse. This group, of lower language ability than the undergraduate students and coming from more diverse and remote cultural backgrounds were able to identify sets of contrasting discourses in the text. Most obvious to us all was the contrast between the Spanish and the British. For instance, the ellipsis in the headline with the deleted prepositional phrase is immediately revealing: *The blame that Spain must share* (with, presumably, Britain). The group also identified a dichotomy between Robbie 1 and Robbie 2. Who was the 'real Robbie' – before or after the fall? Ultimately, we decided, it is possible to see the text in terms of a number of sets of contrasts. Drawing on the lexical and syntactic evidence of the text, they can be expressed as follows:

Robbie 1   v.   Robbie 2
innocence   v.   evil

active   v.   passive
dark   v.   light
urban   v.   rural
Spanish   v.   British

The discourses around what is supposedly 'typically British' centre on a rural scene of pastoral innocence, expressed through, e.g. village, sleepy, Somerset and cricket. Cricket is particularly important, as one student astutely noted. First, it reinforces the picture of peaceful village life. Second, there is a class element. Though there is reason to assume that Robbie is working class, he, that is the 'real' uncorrupted Robbie, aspires to the essentially decent values of any cricket supporter. The choice of 'football' in this text would change the whole impact. Indeed as I write this chapter, the Conservative politician Norman Tebbit has drawn on a cricket discourse to assert that an essential mark of Britishness is support of a British cricket team – thus excluding minorities who support an Indian, West Indian or Pakistani team and, presumably, the rest of us who do not support a cricket team at all.

Finally though, this kind of discussion needs to become more focused by closer engagement with the language itself. With a final group of students who had been introduced to a simple version of Hallidayan grammar (cf. Halliday and Hasan 1989) I formalised our discussion around his categories of field, tenor and mode, relating respectively to the ideational (in Halliday and Hasan, 1989 described as experiential), interpersonal and textual functions of language.

Within the class there were sets of three groups – A, B and C – who focused respectively on field, tenor, and mode and who limited themselves to the first section of the text (reproduced in the Appendix) in which the argument is set out. I offered this framework for them to work with:

A Group to focus on:

Field
Experiential meanings
(How the writer describes what is going on.)

> *participants*:   What/who is talked about?

> *predicates*:   How is X talked about?

i.e. what adjectives or nouns collocate with X?

What verbs (states, actions, mental processes) co-occur with X?

agency: What/who initiates an action?

Effect of the writer's choices?

B group to focus on:

Tenor:

Interpersonal meanings

(How the writer indicates attitude to self, subject and reader.)

mood: What mood is selected: – affirmative?
                                              – imperative?
                                              – interrogative?

modality: What kinds of modal verbs are selected?

person: What personal pronouns are selected?
              How does the writer refer to self, subjects and reader?

Effect of the writer's choices?

C group to focus on:

Mode

Textual meanings

(How the content of the text is organised.)

theme: What information is selected for first position?

voice: When is active or passive voice selected?

cohesive relations: What kinds of connectors are used?

Effect of the writer's choices?

These were the responses:

A. Experiential Meanings

main participants: Spanish   Robbie

minor participants: British   Spanish waiter

predicates:
Nouns verbs and adjectives used to describe/collocate with:

The Spanish:	*Robbie*:
factory for louts	sleepy
nurtured	quiet
pour alcohol	soft
create	neat
	cricket
	verbs to be/have (*states*)

agency: Spanish as agents.
Agent of the Spanish waiter's death: excesses (rather than the expected human agent with the verb 'murdered').

Effect: Spanish as active.
Robbie as passive.

B. Interpersonal Meanings

mood: Largely affirmative.

modality: Little modality, apart from deontic use of 'should'.

person: No first person singular reference; inclusive use of we in 'we should be ashamed'; We v. they (the Spanish); greater frequency of 'they' to refer to the Spanish.

Effect: Authoritarian; opinion presented as fact; depersonalising distancing of the Spanish through continued use of the pronoun 'they'.

C. Textual Meanings

theme: Robbie introduced first. The text establishes itself as about him personally (rather than the Spanish waiter for instance).

voice: Mainly active, use of passive in second sentence removes agency from Robbie.

cohesion: Little cohesion. Short sentences in first paragraph to create impact. Juxtaposition creates effect rather than use of connectors.

Effect: Robbie is highlighted – we identify with him. The detail of the Spanish waiter becomes incidental. Robbie is presented not as an actor but as acted upon.

Conclusion

Critical reading in the EFL classroom will take different forms with different groups of students. This is first because students will come with different levels of language and literary awareness drawn from reading and learning experiences in their first language context; second, they will come with a range of different linguistic resources. The fuller, deeper analysis which I was able to attempt with the third group of students was dependent on their having some knowledge of Hallidayan grammar, albeit of a much simplified and adapted kind. Work on ways of systematising a simple linguistic description for critical literacy purposes remains to be done.

Nonetheless there was evidence that Class 6 had begun to think of the roles of texts and readers and the media generally in more critical reflective ways. Yatsuko commented that she thought the BBC news was becoming increasingly biased. And Cathy, a student from Hungary, observed a divide in the class in the response to one particular text, between those coming from Eastern and Western Europe which she attributed to our different sociopolitical experiences. There was, in short a developing awareness that even authoritative texts, such as the BBC news, are ideologically loaded, and a more clearly articulated awareness of social influences on the interpretation of texts.

These are only beginnings. I shall continue to try to find more effective ways to help EFL readers feel more confident in taking up assertive positions against the text, to encourage them to feel they have options in the way they choose to read texts, and to help them feel in a more equal relationship with the writer.

Acknowledgements

I should like to acknowledge the cooperation of the following in the writing of this chapter: The students of 6A and 6E, the students on the courses: Diploma in the teaching of English to Speakers of other languages and the M.A. in English Language Teaching, Manolo Fernandez-Gasalla and John O'Regan.

References

Alderson C, Urquhart S 1984 *Reading in a foreign language.* Longman

Andersen R 1988 Overwriting and other techniques for success with academic articles. In *Academic writing: process and product,* ELT Documents 129. Modern English Publications in association with the British Council

Auerbach E 1990 *Making meaning, making change. A guide to participatory curriculum development for Adult ESL and family literacy.* University of Massachusetts English Family literacy project

Brice Heath S 1983 *Ways with words.* Cambridge University Press

Carter R, Walker R 1989 Literature and the learner. Introduction to *Literature and the Learner: Methodological approaches.* Modern English Publications, in association with the British Council

Eagleton T 1983 *Literary theory.* Blackwell

Fairclough N 1989 *Language and power.* Longman

Fish S 1980 *Is There a Text in this Class?* Harvard University Press, Cambridge, Mass.

Halliday M A K, Hasan R 1989 *Language, context and text: aspects of language in a social semiotic perspective.* Oxford University Press

Kress G 1989 *Linguistic processes in sociocultural practice.* Oxford University Press

Scholes R 1985 *Textual power.* Yale University Press

Smith F 1983 The promise and threat of microcomputers for language learners. *ON TESOL 83. The question of control.* Selected papers from the Seventeenth Annual Convention of Teachers of English to Speakers of other Languages. Toronto, Canada

Trew T 1979 Theory and ideology at work; What the papers say: linguistic variation and ideological difference. In Fowler, R et al. (eds) *Language and control.* Routledge & Kegan Paul

Wallace C 1988 *Learning to read in a multicultural society: the social context of second language literacy.* Prentice-Hall (originally Pergamon 1986)

Widdowson H 1984 Reading and communication. In *Explorations in Applied Linguistics 2.* Oxford University Press.

Appendix for chapter 3

Text A

Before the night was through they would reveal a lot more to each other than just their watches.

Copacabana danced below as he came face to face with her bewildering elegance.

Her movements held him spellbound as she slipped her immaculately manicured fingers inside her leather handbag to emerge with a cigarette pack.

It was the same American brand of Light 100's he always carried. Her pack was empty. "Have one of mine". Hesitating slightly, she took one and lit it herself.

That's when he noticed her watch. Like his, it was a modern Roman face with a stitched leather strap. "We obviously share the same excellent taste in watches, too. What's your favourite champagne?"

She laughed and spoke at last. "Same as yours?"

Text B

The brass rings, weighing about twenty pounds, hold the neck so stiffly that all movement is restricted. If the rings are removed, the head lolls forward, crushing the windpipe and causing suffocation. Why do the Padaung women of Burma submit to this age-old custom?

THE GIRAFFE-NECKED WOMEN OF BURMA

By Linda Grant

Every so often, women of the Padaung tribe in the wild mountainous regions of Burma, between Rangoon and Mandalay, slip across the border into Thailand under the armed guard of the Red Karen rebels. Muffled by scarves, they journey by boat to visit a hospital, chosen for its discretion, which will remove the encircling rings of brass from their necks. They are the giraffe women of Burma, whose heads are held stiffly by the coiled neck brace that restricts their movements.

Burma (renamed Myanmar earlier this year) is a socialist state with an ancient tradition of Buddhism. But it has been unable to suppress the traditional way of life of the tribal hill peoples, some of whom still practise animism, and who have been fighting for their independence since the British left the country in 1948. The Burmese Government has tried to bring the Padaung people into the twentieth century by forbidding what they see as an act of mutilation against women. But it has no effective control over the region where the Padaung live, which has been in the hands of the Karen rebels for many years. Indeed a third of the country is controlled by rebel tribes.

Why do the women wear the rings around their necks? According to Andrew Turton, a senior lecturer in South East Asian Anthropology at the School of Oriental and African Studies, 'There is no known anthropological study of the Padaung women, and very little is known about them.' Missionaries and officers of the British colonial service frequently visited the Padaung in the name of the King and the Lord and pronounced, in horror, against what they regarded as a savage and hideous practice. Content with description, they rarely thought to ask about its origin. When they did, they were fobbed off with evasion or smiling agreement to leading questions. One visitor, observing that the rings weighed up to twenty pounds, enquired whether the practice was inflicted by men to tether the women and prevent them from running away. The men laughed, which he took to indicate assent.

Burma is a secretive country. Until this year, tourists were allowed to enter for only one week. It has now been extended to two, but the territories controlled by the Karens and other rebel tribes like the Kachins are off-limits to foreigners. Because the villages are hidden in the forests, evading Government census, there are no estimates of the numbers who wear the coils. Certainly, the practice is diminishing as many young women ☞

Text B continued

☞ refuse to accept the burden.

Journalists and photographers who have entered the area have been offered three theories for the custom. The first relates the practice back to the time of the Shan princes, before the period when Burma was a colony of Britain. The Shan were the feudal rulers who, it was said, were in the habit of abducting young Padaung girls. The potential victims decided to make themselves as ugly as possible to avoid this fate and considered that encasing their necks in metal rings would be sufficient to deter any would-be abducter. They say that the rings were originally made of gold obtained by bartering with the Shan princes. Supplies of gold were exhausted generations ago and the Padaung were obliged to accept brass.

In another, wilder flight of fancy, the Padaung explain that they are descended from the Nagas, dragons of a past age. By extending the necks of the women, they are made to look more like these fabulous beasts, and the tufted head-dress is supposed to be modelled on the form of a dragon's crest. More practical, but perhaps equally fanciful, is the notion that the metal rings protect women against tiger bites.

Either the Padaung - whose name is derived from the Karen words *pa*, meaning to have round, and *daung*, meaning brass - do not want outsiders to know the reason, or they have forgotten. When the young women are asked why they submit themselves to having the rings put on, they argue that in doing so they become symbols of their tribe and that they mark themselves out from the alien Burmese with whom they do not wish to be assimilated.

The Padaung are not the only tribal peoples to affect elaborate dress. The Red Karens are so named because of their scarlet clothing. Another Karen tribe binds the legs of the women with decorative swathes which ensure that they waddle rather than walk. Still others are adorned with little more than an intricate set of tattoos.

For a Padaung girl, the brass ring procedure begins at the age of ten when the first ring is coiled around the neck by her mother, who recites magic charms which are believed to take away the rigidity of the metal. New rings are added every three years until 21 to 26, or even 28, brass rings encircle the neck. At the same time, the first of the leg spirals is placed between the knees and ankles.

The result is considerably restricted movement. Unable to bend their heads, women have to drink with the aid of a straw and sit with their legs held straight out in front of them. The deformity of the larynx caused by the elongation of the neck affects the women's voices, variously described as sounding 'as if they were speaking up the shaft of a well' by one Victorian observer, or as 'a high-pitched croak' by a German photographer who visited them in the early 1970s.

Despite these restrictions, the women labour in the fields as hard or harder than any other Burmese women, retreating further and further into the jungle to avoid discovery by Government troops, who would force them to abandon their way of life.

The Burmese state has been fighting a dozen insurgent forces for years with no lasting success: the revolt of the Karens goes back to colonial times when the tribe allied itself with the British, and many of them converted to Christianity against their traditional enemy, the Buddhist Burmese.   ☞

Text B continued

☞ The Padaung are a sub-tribe of the Karen and the men have been conscripted into the war against the Government. Last year the Karen National Liberation Army began to recruit women into the front line as soldiers, but women from the remotest tribes like the Padaung are allowed to carry on their way of life under Karen protection.

With their men away fighting, the women must do most of the work of the village. As well as transporting heavy baskets to markets many miles away and performing the traditional chores of women - pounding rice and carrying water - they have to till the fields, cultivate crops and hew wood.

Much time is spent in caring for the rings. In the heat and humidity the metals tends to oxidise and attack the skin, so the rings are kept clean by washing them in the river and polishing them with tufts of grass. Because of the stiffness of their necks the women wearing rings have to enlist the aid of other Padaung women to help them wash their bodies properly.

For decades, scientists have been fascinated by possible medical effects of the elongation of the neck. It is said that the punishment in the tribe for adultery is the enforced removal of the neck rings and banishment from the village. Because the neck muscles have atrophied, the spine is unable to support the weight of the head, which rolls forward and crushes the wind-pipe, resulting in suffocation. In the past few years those women who have made the illegal journey into Thailand to have the rings removed have needed many months of care, lying with the neck bandaged and braced to allow the muscles to strengthen. Some go there to volunteer for medical examination. X-rays reveal that the giraffe-like appearance is due not to the neck being stretched but to the shoulders being pressed down, compressing the chest.

For the Padaung, the traditional way of life embraces more than the wearing of neck rings. Certain inviolable taboos must be observed: a pregnant woman is not allowed to look at an ape, catch crabs or weave baskets for fear that the child will be born resembling one of these things. During pregnancy, she must cook her own food separately, over a fire used only by her. More progressively, men are allowed to attend and assist at the birth of the baby. After the birth, the home is thoroughly cleaned, symbolising the beginning of a new human being.

Although the Padaung follow courtship rituals involving moonlight visits accompanied by songs, these are a delightful pastime rather than a social necessity, for marriages are arranged by the parents using a woman known as a marriage agent. The price of the bride is paid to her parents in old silver coins dating back to the time of colonial rule. They are subsequently used as ornaments on festive occasions, festooned from the neck coils.

The giraffe-necked women have vexed many Western commentators. Some, mainly men, find them ravishingly lovely; others see the rings as a form of mutilation, like Chinese foot-binding, the lip-plates of the Amazon and the looped ear-lobes of the Iban. ❏

First appeared in Marie Claire Great Britain December 1989

Text C1

'THERE is nothing new about a married woman with children going out to work to help to supplement the family income. It has been done for generations in the poorer families where the wife has gone out to do domestic work, and in the cotton towns of the North where a great deal of female labour is used in the factories.

But the needs of modern society have widened the type of work available, and the changing status of women over the past 50 years has meant that many of them now choose to carry on some form of paid work outside the home.

Every girl now has to earn her own living between leaving school and getting married. Some of them take a long training and become so absorbed in the subject that they want to continue with it after marriage. For many of these girls the kind of work involved in running a house is not sufficient to use all their abilities and they feel they are not working to full capacity.

Text C2

No slackness

I DO not mean that the housewife has a slack time! For a short while after our twins were born I was without help and had to do everything myself including three-hourly feeds day and night, so I know how exhausting children and housework can be! As well as being exhausted, however, I felt nothing more than a drudge.

I had little to talk about when my husband came home in the evening and all the time I was consciously looking forward to what I called "getting back to work" - namely, to using some of the mental resources which I had been expressly trained to use for years. I was indeed "on the go" literally for 24 hours a day but I wasn't doing the kind of work that made full use of my own faculties.

When I returned to studies I was constantly asked, "How do you find the time?" The answer seems to be a perpetual mystery to the woman who doesn't go out to work and quite simple to those of us who do.

There are 24 hours in every day: the people who ask this question seem to be amazed at how much can be packed into them; I am astonished at how little some people seem to do.

The answer is this - you can achieve as much in a day as you set out to achieve if you think ahead and get everything well organised.

The days when I have only our home to think about are just as busy as when I have other things to cope with as well.

I am running about most of the time cooking, shopping and doing the housework and seem to have no spare moments. But all of this is done equally well when I have other things to do in addition, because I then make sure that everything is done with maximum efficiency in minimum time.

I see that the weekly order to the grocer really does include the needs for the week.

Shopping which can be done by 'phone is done that way after having a word with the butcher or other merchant about the quality and service that I like. All cookery operations are carried out in the best order so that not a minute is wasted. I quickly found that as well as being a housewife it is possible to put in eight hours' work a day besides.

Text C3

Husband must approve

THERE are certain factors which are essential if this dual role is to be successful. For a woman with a family there is, firstly, having trusted and competent help with the children. Without this it would be impossible to go out with an easy mind.

Some husbands can fortunately provide for this while in other cases the wife has to do so out of her earnings.

Secondly, having a husband who readily approves his wife pursuing another occupation.

Some men I know are far too ready with the phrase, "Women's place is in the home" - forgetting that their own daughters will almost certainly have to earn their living outside the home, at any rate for a time; and, further, while condemning women in careers in round general terms, they would be thrilled if their daughters were to achieve new and rare heights.

In many cases it would be impossible for a woman to comment constructively on her husband's problems without having some outside experience on which to base an intelligent and appreciative viewpoint.

There remains the important question of what is the effect on the family when the mother goes out to work each day.

The answer depends entirely on the woman concerned. If she has a powerful and dominant personality her personal influence is there the whole time and the children's upbringing follows the lines which she directs.

Of course she still sees a great deal of the children. The time she spends away from them is a time which the average housewife spends in doing the housework and shopping, not in being with the children assiduously. From my own experience I feel there is much to be said for being away from the family for part of the day. When looking after them without a break, it is sometimes difficult not to get a little impatient and very easy only to give part of one's attention to their incessant demands.

Whereas, having been out, every moment spent with them is a pleasure to anticipate, and a definite time each day set aside to give completely to them and their problems. Later on there will not be that awful gap which many women find in their lives when their children go away to school.

The general conclusion can best be summarised by saying it all depends on the woman. If she has no particular outside interest and finds her work in the home satisfying and absorbing then she must develop her interest from that as centre.

But if she has a pronounced bent in some other direction in which she has already achieved some measure of success then I am sure that it is essential both for her own satisfaction and for the happiness of her family that she should use all her talents to the full. With a little forethought she will find that most things are possible.'

• *Thanks to Harriet Jones, lecturer in the department of International History at the London School of Economics, for supplying this feature from the April 1954 issue of Onward, a Conservative Party publication.*

Text C4

'As well as being exhausted, I felt nothing more than a drudge.' Thus wrote Margaret Thatcher, one year after the birth of her twins, about her time as a stay-at-home mother. Luckily for her, her husband could afford a live-in nanny. The 1954 article, by the woman who has done little to support other working mothers, makes fascinating reading. It is reprinted below

Mother knows best

ONE of the new women barristers who were recently called to the Bar, Mrs Margaret Thatcher, sat for her final examinations only three months after her twins were born. She is 28, and at the last General Election was the youngest Conservative candidate. Margaret Thatcher believes in keeping busy and has definite views on careers for women. Her ideas and experiences show why.

Text D

Daily Maily, Thursday, August 3, 1989

EXPLOITATION THAT TURNED THE LAGER LOUT PROBLEM INTO A CRISIS

The blame that Spain must share

ROBBIE is not really a lager lout. He has been turned into one. He lives at home with his parents in a rather sleepy market town in Somerset. He's neat, quiet. He's got a job.

He's an enthusiastic supporter of his cricket club and his idea of a night out is a dance with his girlfriend, who was a bit upset he'd gone on holiday without her.

All of which makes the sight of him crumpled in a drunken heap among the cigarette ends on the floor of the Casa Padri Bar at 2.30am so depressing.

from
RICHARD KAY
IN SAN ANTONIO, IBIZA

How many people back home in Frome would have recognised that livid face, reddened by the sun and an excess of alcohol? That slurred, thick voice hurling out mindless, four-letter insults: his soft West Country accent twisted into ugliness? The yellow singlet his mother had ironed before packing for him, torn and stained with beer?

'Why is it you English behave like this?' asked the bar's proprietor Paco Munoz as we dragged Robbie out on to the pavement, spewing curses at everyone, before he recovered enough to lurch into the nearest disco.

A hypocritical question for a Spaniard to ask. The Spanish wring their hands and rightfully complain about the shameless excesses of British youth: excesses which have not gone away, despite their disappearance from the news, excesses that this week in San Antonio, Ibiza, caused the murder of young waiter Jesus Moreno.

We should be ashamed. But so, too, should the Spanish. For it is their ruthless and cynical exploitation of young tourists, pouring alcohol down their albeit willingly open throats, that has turned a potential problem into disaster.

The Spanish have, whether they like it or not, created a factory for lager louts. Right across the Balearics and along the Costas they have nurtured a climate where drunken, outrageous behaviour is almost inevitable. Drink is so available, so ridiculously cheap. ☞

Text D continued

☞
Taxes

Liquor stores sell vodka for around £3.50 a bottle. You can get Johnnie Walker scotch at £6.50, while cheap brandy can be bought for less than £3. The reason? Spain has one of the lowest taxes on alcohol in Europe.

There is a nationwide 30 per cent on drink - compared to the British average of almost 70 per cent - plus a local VAT, currently at 12 per cent.

'Clearly the price and availability of alcohol is a problem' said San Antonio's worried Mayor Antonio Tur. 'For many visitors our prices are just too cheap - it's too easy to get drunk.'

These few words of guilt are about the most you can expect from any Spaniard. Yet they, and their economy, share the responsibility for a young waiter's death.

They too must take part of the blame for the explosion of violence and crime that has blackened the name of British tourists abroad.

It is too easy for the Spanish to point the finger at young Britons - though they deserve it - while they continue to supply the very fuel of their appalling behaviour. The blame must lie squarely between us, as I now know from first hand experience of 'a night on the town' with a band of young Englishmen.

We all met in the Fisherman's Bar, around ten. It's hardly the place to loiter: a virtually impenetrable crowd, four deep at the bar, plastic tables and bar stools, and the purplish flickering of endless pop videos emanating from the gloom of one corner. These places are functional drinking factories.

We decided on one quick round of beers - pints at 60p - but the waiter brought another tray to our table without us even asking.

Two beers downed, we ventured outside and had only wandered 100 yards when a girl invited us into the Ozono Nightclub with the promise of free entrance if we went now. Normally, the boys explained, the discos were last on the itinerary. But a free trip, saving £2, was worth exploring.

Ambition

Inside, we started buying rounds at £4 a time. I think we had three rounds, and the drink was beginning to tell.

The talk was of home, their new friends, but mainly their triple ambition of finding a girl, getting her blind drunk (not difficult) and topping up their own consumption to ensure oblivion.

Only two hours into the evening, they were well on their way to the last desire. The other objectives looked easy to fulfil too.

Though it was not yet midnight, Cinderella had changed dramatically, I noticed. Girls, who had ambled through the streets in well-dressed, giggling but reasonably-behaved groups, were now sprawling over anyone who cared to chat them up, their make-up smudged, their clothes dishevelled. However, our boys didn't think much of the Ozono talent, so we agreed to move on. Eleven measures downed.

We staggered on to the Tropicana. Robbie was chasing his San Miguel lager with shots of fiery Jagermeister, a schnapps-like liqueur. It was after 2am. A half-hour stop at the Casa Padri, where Robbie had been 'helped out' and then the discos beckoned.

Around us, as we lurched from one noisy disco to another, groups of drunken men and women shouted and staggered in criss-cross paths. Finally we stopped at Rick's OK Corral. Rick, who's English, refused to serve   ☞

Text D continued

☞ Tequila Slammers. It was the first time all evening we'd been refused a drink. I thought it was going to cause some confrontation.

'Why?' snapped Robbie aggressively. 'They can be fatal,' said Rick simply, turning to other, less drunk customers.

Drug

Thankfully, Robbie and his friends lurched off to the cavernous Star Club, more than 20 rounds downed. There the cheap drink is only rivalled by the brazenly open sale of the drug Ecstasy.

Peddlers were asking 3,000 pesetas, about £15, for a tab that could keep you on your feet for another ten hours.

I saw Robbie and the boys on the beach just before writing this report. Barely recovered from the production line of drinks, a horrible cocktail no sane person would contemplate drinking, they were preparing for another onslaught. 'You get a taste for it after a while,' snorted Robbie.

It's a taste we could do without importing, a taste the Spanish should never have let them develop.   ❏

4 Making It Work – Communications Skills Training at a Black Housing Association

Pete Sayers

In the summer of 1986 I was asked whether I knew of any college courses suitable for two recently appointed staff to the newly established Manningham Housing Association in Bradford. They wanted a course on communication skills in order to improve the quality of the written English they produced in connection with their work. What they had to write included letters, reports and minutes of committee meetings. They also had to read a variety of incoming correspondence and be able to respond to it.

I knew of no courses that would exactly meet their needs. I had also, over the years, grown suspicious of the diagnosis that suggested there was a easy external solution to such communications issues.

The two people concerned are both Asian, one of Pakistani and one of Bangladeshi origin. One had a complete British education. The other had completed a full secondary education in this country. Both were young (early twenties) and had relatively little, if any, experience of housing associations before being appointed.

Housing associations are voluntary organisations that use public and private money to build and maintain low-cost rented housing. They specialise in either the type of housing they provide and/or the part of the community they serve. They are owned by their members and run by a management committee. In a small association like the one this chapter concerns the number of staff is small (four at the time of writing, and only two at the time of the events described above).

Housing associations receive their public funds through a government agency, the Housing Corporation. In the early 1980s housing associations and the Housing Corporation became aware that black people in Britain (by black I mean people of Asian as well as Afro-Carribean origin) were not being housed in proportion to their numbers in the community at large. Very few black people were employed by housing associations. Equal opportunities policies and their implementation became one of the topics for monitoring by the Housing Corporation. Additionally, pressure grew for new associations to be formed to meet the specific needs of the black communities in inner city areas. Manningham Housing Association is just such an association.

At that time I was employed in Bradford's Industrial Language Training Unit. Industrial Language Training units were funded through the Department of Employment's Training Agency (then the Manpower Services Commission) but based in the Further Education departments of local education authorities. Our job was to provide training in the workplace on topics relating to equal opportunities and communication skills. Employers contributed to the costs by paying fees for work done with their staff. In the late 1970s most of the work in Bradford was teaching English as a Second Language to Asian workers in foundries and textile mills. By the mid-1980s the demand for Industrial Language Training had shifted. Most of the work done concentrated on implementing equal opportunities and most of the participants were white professionals and office workers. There was some communications skills training for young Asians on Youth Training Schemes, but no in-company work. Manningham Housing Association (MHA) presented a unique opportunity – to return to teaching communication skills to Asian people and to revise our objectives and methodology from our experience of race awareness training.

The training agreed took the following format: weekly sessions of two hours – one trainer, two trainees. A training course tailor-made for the two members of staff at MHA was inefficient (in terms of bums-on-seats) but proved to be very effective training. Both participants and the others they worked with valued both the process and the results of the training. The agenda for each training session was negotiated between us at the beginning of each session. The initial course lasted six months.

In my first meeting with the two members of staff I outlined a number of themes which developed as the training progressed. One theme related specifically to spelling. (Both members of staff said that they had problems with spelling.) The other theme could best be labelled by the question 'Whose problem is it?' Both of these themes are affective: they are issues where people's feelings are important as determinants of learning. My idea in planning this training was that feelings about writing, spelling and reading would need as much, if not more, attention in developing learning than more traditional explanations or knowledge of the language.

My task here is to describe the training that took place and develop themes that interested me and which relate to critical language awareness (CLA).

Whose Problem?

English as a Second Language teaching for people who have come to Britain from the Indian sub-continent is well established. Funding has been available from a variety of sources, including the Home Office and the Training Agency, and is targeted at both school-children and adults. ESL teaching is politically safe. It rests on the assumption that Asian people in Britain have a 'language problem'. This assumption is widely believed to be a fact both in the white and black communities. It is related to, if not part of, the other key assumption underlying government policy on race, namely that black people in Britain are a problem – the assumption that underpins successive governments' immigration policy.

The two workers at Manningham Housing Association both diagnosed themselves as having a language problem, as do a large number of young people of Asian origin who have been through school in England. Even when their English is as good as a white person in the same social position (e.g. even when their English on an audio-tape would be indistinguishable from that of a white school-leaver) it is still likely that any deviations from standard English will be seen as an Asian person's language problem, rather than as a social class or quality of schooling issue.

The 'language problem' assumption is very powerful and has wide currency. ESL teachers have begun to challenge it by calling it the 'deficit' model of language teaching. Another facet of the deficit model is that it sees bilingualism as a disadvantage. Britain is a predominantly monolingual community. Foreign languages are rarely used and communities that speak other languages whether they be old established ones like Welsh and Gaelic, or more recently established ones like Punjabi, Bengali, Greek, Turkish, are politically and socially disadvantaged.

This is in itself not surprising but illustrates what the training I provided had to overcome in order to be able to look neutrally at the communication skills required by the two people employed at MHA.

There are alternatives to this set of assumptions about the position of Asian people in Britain. One alternative is to say that white British culture has a problem – one that stems from the underlying racism in British society, and that communication between racial groups is inevitably affected by it. This is the sort of assumption that has led to race awareness training for white people becoming a key component in implementing equal opportunities policies. Another alternative view that has developed within education is to see that bilingualism is an advantage, to be valued and encouraged within society, and that those Britons who are monolingual are the ones who are disadvantaged. My training looked for alternative ways of viewing business communication.

Dealing with in-coming correspondence

The two workers at Manningham Housing Association had to deal with a variety of official correspondence. Before the training got underway the deficit model determined their response to any piece of incoming correspondence they failed to understand. If they couldn't understand it, it must be their fault – owing to their language problem!

My approach was to look at the incoming text and work out why I found it difficult to understand. It came as a surprise to them to realise that white Britons might also have the same difficulties as they did in understanding English texts, and more surprising still that I – a teacher of English – should also find the text difficult. What was it about the text that made it difficult to understand and what motives might be ascribed to the writer to explain it?

The objective was to persuade the two workers participating in the training that the responsibility for not understanding could be shared, that they did not have to blame themselves for not understanding the text. One effect of the deficit model is that Asian learners come to believe that they are solely responsible for any communication breakdown. When it is realised that the responsibility is shared, they are more likely to feel confident and interested to understand more about the teacher's (or trainer's) interpretation of the text, and to develop their own strategies for understanding similar texts.

I can illustrate my approach with some examples of in-coming correspondence MHA received at the time the training was taking place.

One of the first letters received was from the European Commission in Brussels.

Subject: Your application for 22,000 ECU revenue

Dear Sir,

While preparing the procedure for disbursement of funds, some particular points have been raised by the Commission's Directorate-General 'Financial Control' which have to be cleared before funds may be released.

As suggested in your letter of 29th September, a detailed application for capital funds should be presented only once final approval for the 22,000 ECU has been received.

Yours faithfully, [signed].

This was a particularly difficult letter, but not untypical of what they had to deal with. My strategy was to process the text in a series of stages, as follows:

First   Scan the text. What's it about? What do you know of the context? Is this a reply to something that you've dealt with previously?

Second Look at the text in detail. Attempt to understand the vocabulary and syntax.

Third   Attempt a view (or views) of why the writer has chosen to express him/herself in this way. Is the writer being indirect, bureaucratic, formal or informal, etc.?

Fourth   Express feelings about this style and language (e.g. say aloud with feeling 'Why can't they just say what they mean?' – or whatever else arises while processing the text).

Fifth   Work out what the letter requires or expects you to do, and

Sixth   Work out how to reply. What do you want to say? What would you like to say but realise it might be better not to say? What style of language do you want to use?

I used the same strategy for many other letters received. These were not discrete stages, they often got mixed up, and it was not necessary to do each stage every time but the net result was that after a few goes at letters similar to this one, the two workers felt a lot happier and more confident about dealing with the mail, if only because it became more fun. The expression of feeling was crucial to this. Mostly it took the form of light frustration (an exasperated 'Why not just say . . . it would be so much simpler to understand?'), or open laughter when the meaning was finally grasped.

What was there to say about the 'disbursement of funds' (my nickname for this particular text)? First, there was the vocabulary. 'Funds' needed to be explained as another term for money. 'Disbursement' was a word which, in my opinion, was not English at all, but French, and which someone had forgotten to translate before sending out this letter to England. I explained that lots of business English involved words borrowed from French and Latin, and gave a few examples. I was also able to draw comparisons with the way Persian and Arabic words are used in Urdu, or Urdu words are used in Bengali.

'Financial Control' was something they were also likely to meet in other organisations they applied to for money. One of the workers said (in a tone of frustrated resignation) that they knew all the words (i.e. they were familiar to them as words of English), with the exception of 'disbursement', but they couldn't understand what this letter meant.

There was some background information. They knew that

MHA's management committee had sent off an application for EEC funding. This was presumed to be the reply. That still didn't resolve the difficulty that as a reply it was still difficult to work out exactly what it meant.

I tried reducing the text to a sequence of simple sentences using active verbs, wherever possible, to describe processes and relationships between ideas. It went something like this.

- *You (MHA) want to employ a director.*
- *You need £15,000 to pay the director's salary.*
- *You are asking us (the European Commission) to give you the money.*
- You filled in an application form.
- You sent us the form.
- You applied for £15,000.
- £15,000 is 22,000 ECU.
- We only talk about ECU.
- We don't talk about £s.
- We call money for salaries 'revenue'.

The statements in italics relate to ideas only retrievable from the background knowledge. The rest are deductions or assumptions I made in my attempts to process the text.

That much unscrambled the first line. We hadn't even got as far as 'Dear Sir'. It wasn't, in fact, necessary to provide that much detail for the two workers to understand the meaning. They already understood the processes implicit in the word 'application'. (It had not been long since they had successfully applied for the jobs they now had.) Because they understood the process of 'application' and could see how my simple sentence approach related to it, they were able to grasp how a similar process could unscramble the next line, which they did not understand. Because this letter arrived on the morning of the second session I had with the two people at MHA they were highly motivated to use it. That counter-balanced its inherent difficulties.

To explain the letter's first sentence properly I proposed the following ideas:

- We call giving you the money 'the disbursement of funds'.
- We decide whether to give you the money or not.

- This decision is often difficult.
- We sometimes take a long time to decide.
- We have a procedure for taking decisions like this.
- We are now starting this procedure.
- We call this 'preparing' the procedure.
- There is a department here called 'Financial Control'.
- People who work in Financial Control look at your application form.
- Those people are not happy about some things in your application.
- 'Some particular points' = some things.
- *We are not telling you in this letter what those things are.*
- The people in Financial Control want to clear those things.
- 'Clear' = sort out = feel happy about them.
- *We are not telling you in this letter who needs to sort those things out.*
- *It could be you, or it could be us.*
- We can't decide to give you the money before someone sorts these things out.
- We call deciding to give you the money 'releasing the funds'.

It is possible to come up with a different set of sentences to the one above and, indeed, to interpret the letter's underlying meaning and intent quite differently from the way I have. The italics, in this instance, are not interpretations of the text, but statements that recognise significant absences in the text. When reading the letter you need to be able to see not only what has been included in the text but also what has been consciously or unconsciously excluded. It is precisely because this kind of language is so open to interpretation that makes it difficult to understand. Using background knowledge of the context, or hypothesising likely contexts, is what makes it possible for the reader to construct some meaning from the letter. My list, above, is an attempt to make explicit just such a construction.

One of the most fascinating things for me about this letter was the wealth of interpretation it offered. How, for instance, was the second paragraph related to the first. Was there something in Manningham Housing Association's letter of 29th September that had caused those particular points which had to be cleared, or was the connection between the paragraphs much looser.

At this point I asked the people I was training to find a copy of the letter of 29th September. There was a brief interlude while the value of effective filing systems was experienced. (That was another part of their training, but not one I was involved in.)

The letter of the 29th was, in fact, the covering letter that went with the application for funding. It mentioned the possibility of later applications for capital funds. There had been no other correspondence. The most plausible hypothesis I could arrive at was that the second paragraph of the 'disbursement of funds' letter merely confirmed what MHA already knew and what MHA had stated it knew in its letter of the 29th.

The second paragraph appeared, as best I could gather from the evidence, to be quite disconnected from the first. I concluded that the letter was ill thought out and ill formed. It fitted my definition of gobbledygook. (I use the term the same way as the Plain English Campaign). Because the letter neither detailed the particular points that needed to be sorted out, nor who needed to do it, it made very little real sense and the best thing we (the readers) could do was have a laugh at its expense. So we did, and it proved to be very therapeutic. After analysing the text my message was simple – you cannot understand this letter because it does not make sense, because the writer was vague and indirect, and certainly not through any fault of yours. Your English is okay (I told the two workers at MHA). The European Commission, however, has a problem!

This reversal of the usual situation (someone else being judged as having the language problem) was quite liberating for them, even if presented jokingly.

There is a serious point here, too. Transactional analysis (Berne 1961, Harris 1973) is often used in interpersonal skills training and team development work. It advocates working towards an 'I'm okay – you're okay' position. This is a shorthand way of describing the most desirable outcome of any interaction as one where I feel okay about myself and also feel okay about the other party (or parties) to the interaction. All too often people find themselves in a situation where one party or the other does not feel okay about themselves as a result of an interaction. The situation I described earlier where Asian people are conditioned or educated into seeing themselves as having a language problem is a good example of an 'I'm not okay – you're okay' situation. The Asian people I was working with saw themselves as 'not okay' (they had a language problem) whereas white Britons and/or officialdom were 'okay'. As an interim step towards the 'I'm okay – you're okay' position, it is often necessary to move to the 'I'm okay – you're not okay'. The analysis of the 'disbursement of funds' letter enabled the two people I was working with to make that step. Having worked out an interpretation of the text of the letter, and concluded that any difficulties in it were due to failures of communication at the encoding (Brussels) end, the two workers at MHA were well motivated to work out the most suitable reply. They now felt much more confident about their own ability to do it. The letter sent (about a week later) read:

Re: Our application for 22,000 ECU revenue

Thank you for your letter of [date].

We note from your letter that there were some particular points which have been raised by the Commission's Directorate General 'Financial Control' which have to be cleared before we may receive the funds.

We should be grateful if you could let us know the points which have been raised, and if we could be of any help to you in answering them.

We look forward to hearing from you.

etc.

The reply, in itself, was not difficult to write. The time put into understanding the 'disbursement of funds' was repaid in the ease and speed with which it was possible to write the reply.

Another example of a letter that took some effort to understand arrived shortly after 'disbursement of funds'. It was from the agents representing the landlord of the MHA office. This is what it said.

Dear Sirs

Re: Rooms 9, 10 & 11, 6th Floor [named building]

I note from my file of the above accommodation that although your tenancy has only recently commenced, the expiry date is not far away.

You hold the premises on a one year lease from 6th July 1987 at a rent of £1,500.00 per annum and under current Landlord and Tenant legislation a minimum of six months notice to terminate this agreement by either party is required.

I have discussed this point with our clients and they agree with our view that it would be to neither the landlord's nor the tenant's advantage to terminate the existing agreement and then negotiate a further agreement for one year. We therefore propose to take no action at the present time but allow the tenancy to continue at the same rent etc. and we will review the situation next year.

We would point out that should you wish to vacate after one year's occupation (or at any date thereafter) please let us have the requisite six months notice at the appropriate time.

We hope that you will not vacate but that you will wish to continue your occupancy of these premises beyond the end of the first year and if this is the case, no action is required.

Should you require to discuss any of the above please do not hesitate to telephone me.

Yours sincerely,

The interesting thing about this letter was the emotional response it drew on first reading – and, more importantly, on reading the first paragraph. There were two underlying themes to this response. 'The last thing we want is a problem with our office premises' and 'Help, does this mean we're in danger of eviction?' The anxieties set up through this kind of interpretation of the first paragraph influenced the reading of the rest of the letter. In the second paragraph the key words on a first scan proved to be 'notice to terminate'. The anxiety increased. By the time they got to the second sentence of the third paragraph 'We therefore propose to take no action at the present time,' etc., they were confused, but not relieved. The anxiety set up by the initial scan of the first two paragraphs was very powerful. In presenting this letter to me at one of our training sessions the plea was 'What do we have to do?' The answer, from me, after twice reading the letter through, was simple – 'Nothing!' A look of incredulity crept over the faces of the two people I was training.

How could a letter with nearly a full page of text require nothing. One of them then started looking through the letter again, totally bemused.

We looked at the fifth paragraph in detail. The key message for them, as readers, was right at the end – 'no action is required'. The message would have been easier if the verb had been active rather than passive, e.g. 'You do not need to take any action', mainly because it would have more clearly linked the reader 'you' with the key message 'no action'. The most obvious problem, though, lay in the sequence the writer's ideas were presented in. The key message the reader needed ('no action required') came at the end, by which time the reader's anxiety level was such that confusion was the only outcome. This could be judged as sheer bad presentation, but there was more to it than that. The fifth paragraph was important not only because it contained the key message the MHA staff needed but also because it conveyed something of the writer's feelings. 'We hope you will not vacate.' In fact, if the sequence of the text reflects the priorities of the writer, then it would seem that the prime intention of that paragraph is to convey the writer's feelings – anxiety about continuing the tenancy.

The writer has the double task of both outlining the choices MHA has and expressing a preference about which option she/he would like MHA to take. The writer's feelings (her/his preference) is hidden in both the tentativeness of the presentation and the use of non-emotive, task-oriented words like 'advantage'. Paragraph four starts, 'We would point out that should you wish to vacate . . .' instead of a simpler 'If you want to vacate'. The two workers at MHA had not grasped that there was an 'if' clause in there at all, or that a choice was being presented. I summarised my understanding of the letter as 'You can now choose if you want to stay at these offices or not. We (the landlords) hope you will choose to stay. If you choose to stay, there is nothing you need to do for another year. The rent will stay the same'. When they realised that that was what the letter meant there was a huge sigh of relief and a puzzled 'Why couldn't they have said that in the first place?'

Attention to feelings is important in letters on sensitive topics and on topics where there is a substantial power imbalance between writer and reader. In this instance their landlords, through their solicitors, had substantial power over them, and any text sent on that topic would have a power imbalance built into it. The power imbalance would prevent a neutral interpretation of the text. Messages about what needed to be done would get mixed up with the feelings of the readers and possibly also the feelings of the writer.

More usually in their jobs the situation would be reversed. It would be MHA as landlords writing to tenants. The difficulties they had experienced with the content and the feelings engendered by this letter could give them valuable insights into the way their tenants might experience similar letters sent by them. So, what would they do differently, if they needed to get a similar message to their tenants? 'Well, I wouldn't write at all, I'd go and visit the tenant first', one of them said. That corresponded, in a way, with the last paragraph of the letter, which suggested telephoning – a less formal means of communication, and, in the opinion of the two people at MHA, a more appropriate place to start. 'They could've phoned or visited us, first. Their office is only downstairs!' 'If that's what you would do first,' I said, 'it's curious that the letter mentions that last!' I then started to wonder what this letter would be like if the ideas or items in it were expressed in reverse order, so that the content of paragraph six became the content of the first paragraph of a new letter, and so on. We discussed this for a while and came up with a new letter:

- This letter is to confirm our discussion/telephone call.
- You need take no action unless you plan to end the tenancy of your offices this year.
- We hope you will stay on in your present offices.
- If you do plan to move, please give us six months notice.
- We have discussed the tenancy with the landlords and decided that it is in both parties' interests to continue the existing agreement for a further year and to keep the rent at £1,500.00 per annum.
- We are mentioning this to you now because we note from our files that the expiry date for the existing agreement is not far away.

The text needed tidying up, but it was possible to see, I hoped, that writing the content of the letter in this reversed order produces a plausible presentation of the ideas. In the reversed order it is less likely to set up the anxieties experienced by the MHA staff when reading the actual letter. This happened right at the end of the training session in question, so it was never fully developed – one of the unpredictabilities of a training course that responded to immediate input, rather than a planned programme. This letter got nicknamed the 'no action' letter, and proved to be a powerful reminder to the two participants to be explicit about what they expected of tenants when writing their own letters.

One of the main points of having a black housing association is so that black people can receive a service from an organisation that better understands their situation and that knows how to explain its services in the language of the local community (or communities) – one that minimises the power gap. This entails both being able to use community languages such as Punjabi or Bengali, and also being able to use appropriate English. Appropriate, in this context, means English that is free from the kind of gobbledygook illustrated in the examples I am quoting here. Some, like the one below, presented the additional problem of interpreting and simplifying a text so that the information in them could be passed on to the client (the possible tenant) in simple and direct English.

This, my third and last example, is the text of a letter sent by another Housing Association that was collaborating with MHA over the transfer of properties from the county council. This happened shortly after the metropolitan county councils were abolished by the government. The letter below was sent to a tenant of the former county council. A copy of the letter was sent to MHA, who then had to decide what to do with it.

To the Occupier
13 [Street]
Manningham
Bradford 8

Dear Sir or Madam

We have been contacted by the West Yorkshire Residuary Body about the sale of property of which you are a tenant. As you know, the Residuary Body is closing its affairs and the properties which it owns are being disposed of. I believe that you have already been asked by a representative of the Body whether you would like to buy your property and that you have declined. Their next course is to see if Housing Associations are interested in purchasing these properties and if we are not interested then they are likely to transfer ownership to the local authority.

As you may know, Manningham Housing Association is a new charitable Housing Association working in the Manningham area. They have an allocation from the Housing Corporation to purchase properties either tenanted or vacant, for repair, modernisation and management. I believe that Manningham Housing Association might be interested in the purchase of your property from the Residuary Body and we would like to visit you, with them, in the very near future to discuss this matter further.

We can assure you that if we did decide to purchase your property there would be no pressure on you to move out or to have works done to it to which you did not agree. You would have the option of moving out to another property, either permanently or temporarily while your property had essential modernisation works done to it, or alternatively you could stay where you are and we would only carry out any necessary repairs as and when they arise.

We and Manningham Housing Association would like to visit you on Tuesday 2 February between 10.00 am and 11.30 am and I would be grateful if you would give me a ring if this time is not convenient.

Yours sincerely,

[Development Manager]

Apart from initial difficulties unscrambling the text to understand its vocabulary, context and intention, there were additional problems of audience. Could the occupier of the address above be reasonably expected to understand this letter which was (presumably) designed to communicate something especially to him/her?

The analysis we did on this letter was twofold:

(1) What don't you understand? (you = the two workers at MHA)
(2) What could you additionally expect the occupier of No. 13 might find difficult to understand?

At this point it should be said that in Bradford, like most cities in England, it is possible to deduce what sort of person is likely to live at any given house, if you know the street and postal district. Social class and ethnic origin determine where in the city people are most likely to live. Manningham is in the inner-city area of Bradford and where large numbers of people of Pakistani and Bangladeshi origin live. That's why Manningham Housing Association is there in the first place. The street in question is right in the middle of Manningham. The other housing association (which originated this letter) has its offices in the same area and can equally be expected to know that many of the local community find official English difficult to understand.

My judgement was that the style of this letter is inappropriate for its intended audience.

The key messages (the intentions of the writer) appeared to be:

(1) explain the choice of new landlord (given that the offer of purchasing has been declined)
(2) explain why this choice has to be made now (i.e. because 'the Residuary Body is closing its affairs')
(3) give some background information on housing associations and MHA in particular
(4) offer reassurance ('There would be no pressure on you to move out', etc.)
(5) inform the tenant of the planned visit (on Tuesday, 2nd February)
(6) ask the tenant to telephone if the planned visit is at an inconvenient time.

As in the previous letter, the order of items is such that the explanations come first and the specific information and request for action come at the end. The easiest parts to understand are key messages 5 and 6, and they come at the end. There is a danger (as with the 'No Action' letter) that by then the reader was so confused that she/he would be unable to spot them.

So what was it that made the first part of the letter potentially so confusing? Neither of the workers at MHA knew what the 'Residuary Body' was. They knew about the demise of the county council but the establishment of the Residuary Body to settle its outstanding affairs had not been publicised to anything like the same degree. The vocabulary used ('disposed of' instead of 'sold', 'declined' instead of 'said no') is likely to be difficult for the occupier of No. 13. The second paragraph of the letter reads like an internal memo, or an article in one of the professional housing journals. It was not difficult for the two workers at MHA to understand but they knew that it was only since starting their present jobs that they had learnt that 'an allocation from the Housing Corporation' was the technical term for all the money the government gives to housing associations or that 'management' as used in this paragraph is a technical term used in housing to describe the administration of rents and tenancies.

The specific point where confusion occurs is where the choice of landlord is presented, and the underlying complex set of relationships between the people named in the text. The way the letter is written it is not clear whether the person empowered to do the choosing is the tenant of No. 13 or the Residuary Body. The letter talks about 'their [the Residuary Body's] next course' and 'they [the Residuary Body] are likely to transfer ownership'. On the other hand, the tenant also appears to have some choices – whether to buy (already declined) and whether to have a housing association or the local authority as landlord. What power the tenant has to make this choice is not at all clear from the letter. By not making the choice clear, information is withheld, and the withholding of such information keeps power with the withholder. The information cannot be shared unless the information (particularly relating to choices) is clear and in language which the reader can understand.

One of the difficulties for the MHA workers in reading this letter was that another housing association was writing on their behalf and, more importantly, committing them to things that were contrary to MHA's stated policies. Quite why this other association was writing to the occupier of No. 13, instead of leaving the arrangements to MHA (as the potential buyer) I never did manage to work out, but it occurred to me later that the other association's way of collaborating with MHA felt paternalistic, and that paternalism is often found where white institutions attempt to share power with black organisations. In this instance I am convinced it is the hidden paternalism that causes the difficulty in understanding the letter. The letter has a surface presumption of equality expressed through phrases such as 'As you may know . . .' and 'We can assure you that . . .', but underneath the relationships are not equal and the power issues, the way choices are presented, are unclear.

After discussing what it was the letter was asking the occupier to do (receive a visit) and what we wanted the occupier to be clear about (the choices of landlord and tenant), the task I set the workers at MHA was to decide what from this letter they would choose to communicate to the occupier of No. 13, what else they would like to say, and in what order they wanted to present the items.

There were two additional factors. MHA does not give tenants the right to buy, whereas the Council does. The tenant's choice of landlord held within it a choice about whether or not to retain the right to buy the property. Their association's view was that they would modernise and they would move the occupier out to do it. They felt the letter as it was gave an impression of greater flexibility than was actually available. They would want to reword it.

As a training exercise, each of the two workers produced an individual draft version:

Draft One:

We have been contacted by your landlords (old County Council which is now called West Yorkshire Residuary Body) about the sale of the house you live in. You may know that the landlord are selling their house and you need to decide what to do in the future on the possibility are as follows:

1) You buy the house.

   Your landlords have told us that you do not want to buy the house from them.

2) Housing Association buy:

   If we decide to buy the house you live in, than you would pay the rent to us. What we should do to the house is to repair, modernis and manages. To carry out the repair and modernisation we would move you to another house

3) Local Authority (Bradford Council) could become your landlord if the option 1 & 2 above does not happen.

We would like to visit you to discuss the above possibilities on [date] between 10.00 a.m. and 11.30 a.m. If you can't make these times, than please ring in to arrange another time. One of us speak Bengali and other speak Punjabi

My first reaction to this draft was that it was much easier to understand, and much more likely to achieve the desired results. There were some parts where standard written English would need extra or different words, but those parts did not get in the way of understanding. The main point was that the information to be shared should be written clearly and simply, and that choices (if that is what the letter is about) are presented explicitly. The fine editorial work we could sort out later. There were some spelling mistakes too, which required special and sensitive attention. More on this below.

Draft Two:

Dear Sir, or Madam,

Manningham Housing Association is a Housing Association that buys houses in the Manningham area.

We were asked by your landlord (West Yorkshire Residuary Body) if we wanted to buy the house that you live in. We understand that you have told your landlord that you do not want to buy the house yourself from your landlord (WYAB).

The choices you have are:

1) To buy the house that you live in from your landlord.

2) If we buy the house that you live in from your landlord then you will become our tenant.

3) If we don't buy your house then you landlord will sell your house to the local council. You will then become the Council's tenant.

This Housing Association does not let its tenants buy houses from it even if you have lived in the house as a tenant for a long time.

The council does let tenants buy houses from it they want to.

We would like to visit you on [date] to talk to you about this. Please ring us at the office. My name is [name] and I speak Urdu/Punjabi, [name] also works here and he speaks Syletti [sic].[1]

Both these drafts were first attempts. Many of the grammatical and spelling errors would have been eradicated by the writers themselves upon re-reading. They were also only a training exercise on a sheet of lined A4, not a bona fide letter on the word processor. However, they gave the two workers at MHA an insight into the kind of letter that would have been more appropriate to the situation and some practice at devising a house style for letters to tenants or potential tenants that was suitable for both the tenant, and the philosophy behind the establishment of their housing association.

Spelling

It also emerged from this and similar exercises that although the two workers each made mistakes when drafting their own letters, they rarely made the same mistakes. There was potential for collaboration here. What stopped them was not the practicalities of error detection, but the feelings they had about mistakes, particularly spelling mistakes.

Spelling, in English-speaking communities, is a highly emotive issue. People are often judged and frequently damned for making spelling mistakes. MHA knows that its credibility as a housing association may be judged by the quality of English in its correspondence. Spelling mistakes catch the eye and distract readers' attention in a way that is quite out of proportion to the quality of the error. For most readers of English 'streat', e.g. in 'Oxford Streat is in London,' has an impact that is way beyond that of decoding what word is meant. The communicative effect of such spelling mistakes is largely affective. My contention in approaching this training was that if the problem is largely affective, then the solution lay in addressing the emotions and working with and through them.

The first step is to have an explanation of spelling mistakes that recognises different types of wrongness. We know 'streat' is wrong. We feel it is wrong. But it is very difficult to explain why it is wrong. When asked to explain why words like 'street' are spelt (or spelled) the way they are, teachers of English tend to get into lengthy explanations of the history of the language or just give up and say 'Because it is'. Neither help the student a great deal. In my experience 'Because the spelling system is daft!' works a lot better, not because it explains anything rationally at all, but because it shows empathy with the learner and allows some of the frustration out. Insulting the spelling system and distancing myself from it proved more effective, in the training I was providing, than defending or rationalising it.

My strategy was first to recognise and allow expression of feelings, and then to give an explanation that sought to get the spelling error in proportion. Examples of the kind of error I was having to deal with are found in the two draft replies to the 'Residuary Body' letter. The explanation went something like this: If someone spells the word 'street' (as in the name of a road) as 'zqrfh' that person does not know how to spell. They do not understand the system at all, and this rarely happens. If, on the other hand, someone spells 'street' as 'streat', they can, in my opinion, spell. They understand the English spelling system and can spell well, but they have not remembered the conventionally agreed spelling for the word.

Some spelling mistakes such as 'correspondance' for correspondence are often treated sympathetically. They tend to be those errors which many English writers make and which are accepted as difficult to learn. Even people in positions of power and influence (like me) make such mistakes. A second level of frustration is experienced with words like 'their' which often gets spelt 'there' or words like 'have' in 'should have' which often gets written 'should of'. This type of spelling mistake is usually judged to be more serious and therefore treated less sympathetically because, although lots of English writers make such mistakes, there is a grammatical component to the error. There is also a social class element to the judgement. 'Bad grammar' is similar to 'language problem' – a self-criticism that many of the British working class are led to believe about themselves. A third level of frustration is experienced when the written error, either spelling or grammar, is made by writers whose first language is not English. In addition to social class there is also a race component to the judgement. People with Punjabi or Bengali as their first language make other spelling mistakes, which are just as simple to make and occur just as frequently as the kind native speakers make, but because native speakers do not make them there is usually little or no sympathy from them, and the writer is likely to be ridiculed.

My message to the workers at MHA was that whereas they might escape being judged too harshly if they sent out an official letter with 'independant' instead of 'independent', they would not get away with 'than' instead of 'then' or leaving the 's' off 'speaks' (as in 'One of us speaks Punjabi'). Both were examples from 'Draft one' above. Such mistakes, on their own, were no worse or better than any other mistakes, but they would be judged differently by most people reading their letters.

I noticed in the training sessions that the two workers could spot about 90 per cent of each other's mistakes with relative ease. The question was then to look at how to make it easier for them to use this insight creatively. I explored the 'whose problem?' model one stage further. When I first met them, the two workers at MHA described themselves as having difficulty with English and with spelling. Their committee's feelings had been aroused by some correspondence that had recently been sent out, in which there were some inaccuracies of spelling and grammar. The two workers had a 'spelling problem' as well as, or as part of their 'language problem'. The difficulty, as I see it, with this judgement is that it unfairly locates the problem with the victim. Rather than people believing they have a spelling problem, it would be more helpful for them to believe the English language had a spelling problem, or looking at it another way, that the English had a spelling hang-up.

My aim was to make it possible within the culture of the MHA office to admit spelling errors, laugh at them, and seek help. There is then less of a face threat. Help might come from the dictionary or from colleagues, but would only come if people were not afraid to ask.

In Conclusion

My work at Manningham Housing Association was done as a piece of professional training not as a piece of action research for CLA, and in describing the work I did at MHA I have not sought to closely tie practice into theory.

In explaining what lay behind the discourse [as much as I could decipher] I had two intentions:

(1) to make easier the task of understanding and responding to correspondence, by offering information and techniques, and
(2) to make easier the process of understanding and responding by

addressing the emotional issues relating to the task, by giving people the opportunity to express and reassess those feelings of personal and group (e.g. ethnic group) inadequacy.

It is my contention that feelings of inadequacy underpin acceptance of dominant ideologies, and that awareness of those ideologies and their discourse conventions cannot be effectively counteracted without addressing that emotional underpinning. By addressing those feelings directly (but lightly) I was able to establish an awareness of the ideological issues behind using and understanding language that was relevant and important for the two people I was training.

As a new black housing association they were making a political claim to the middle ground between white housing associations and the black communities for whom discrimination in housing had long been a source of complaint. It was important that their language reflected their politics. MHA was seeking acceptability as a housing association and as such having to accept the dominant discourse of the housing bureaucracies. It was also, as a provider of housing, in a position to dominate. Black housing associations are in a double bind, as far as their choice of language is concerned. It is important for them to unscramble jargon from other agencies so that they and their clients can understand the nature of housing services available for their clients. This involves having a house style that is simple and direct. At the same time they have to convince those agencies (such as the Housing Corporation, local authorities, etc.) that they are to be respected as serious organisations by being able to correspond with them in conventional business English, correctly spelt. In short, they have, as organisations, to become bilingual – both in the usual sense of the word (e.g. English/Punjabi) but also in the sense of having two quite different house styles of English for official correspondence. This is not only a linguistic juggling act but also a political one.

Business correspondence is often unclear because it either withholds information (e.g. about choices, or about who is required to take what action) or holds back from explicit statements of feeling when preferences are described. By withholding information – either about facts or about feelings – individuals seek to make themselves more powerful. They are unlikely to talk about it in these terms themselves, but that is the nature of ideological stances.

By withholding they also distance themselves from others. This is not only true for bureaucratic relationships (of the sort I have described in this chapter) but also for personal relationships. The same social conventions and discourse patterns that support dominant ideologies also support the rationalisation of emotions in counselling interactions. There is not space in this chapter to explore this idea further. It is, however, likely to be a fruitful area for future research.

Note

1.   Sylheti is the dialect of Bengali spoken by nearly all the Bangladeshi community in Bradford.

References

Berne J 1961 *Transactional Analysis in psychotherapy*. Grove Press.
Harris J 1973 *I'm OK – you're OK*. Pan Books

5 Principles and Practice of CLA in the Classroom

Romy Clark

In this chapter I discuss my attempt[1] to introduce CLA into my Study Skills programme at a British University (Lancaster) and the dilemmas that both teachers and students can face when dealing with the dominant discourse conventions in the academic community: to conform or not to conform.

I focus in my discussions on the teaching of academic writing to university students and in particular on my work with students from the Department of Politics and International Relations. I begin by briefly examining the notion of academic discourse community and the difficulties students have in entering this community. I then refer to the principles of CLA I draw on in my own work, describe the so-called Study Skills programme I have developed and give a brief account of the workshop procedures I follow. In the final section of the chapter I discuss the tension that exists for student writers between rights and obligations and how I attempt to resolve the dilemma of providing access to, while also challenging, the dominant conventions in academic writing.

Academic discourse community

Chase, Director of the Western College Program Writing Center at Miami University, Ohio (1988: 13) registers a new emphasis in the teaching of writing and composition skills. In addition to the focus on the cognitive 'process' approach teachers and researchers are beginning to pay more attention to the social dimension of writing.

Approaches are developing which view academic writing as a social activity which takes place within a specific socio-political context. This specific context is the 'academic discourse community'.

The notion of an academic discourse community implies that there is a set of shared values and beliefs, of discoursal conventions. These conventions establish what is legitimate knowledge, what are the appropriate ways of learning and writing about that knowledge and what are the legitimate roles and behaviours of the members of that community. Not all forms of knowledge or ways of telling that knowledge are accepted.

As Chase says: 'discourse communities are organized around the production and legitimation of *particular* forms of knowledge and social practices at the expense of others, and are not ideologically innocent' (ibid: 13; my emphasis). Moreover, the academic discourse community, like all other communities, is not monolithic: power in the community is unequally distributed. Different members of the community do different things: lecturers teach to their agenda, set the assessment methods and criteria and evaluate the students' work. Students of course also 'assess' their lecturers, but their evaluations rarely carry the weight that lecturer assessments of students do.[2] It is the senior members of the community, the teaching staff, who establish the rules of behaviour for the community and it is easier for staff to flout those rules than students. Lecturers and published authors are allowed to act as authorities and present their opinions as legitimate knowledge. This is much more difficult for students to do (see p. 120 for an example).

An important part of the teaching of academic writing, then, in my view, is to critically explore with the students the notion of academic discourse community and how it is that certain forms of knowledge and ways of telling that knowledge have evolved in the way that they have. This is the first step, via CLA, towards *empowerment*, through the awareness of what the discourse conventions of the community are, where they come from and what their effects are so that students are no longer naively manipulated by them. By 'empowerment' I mean, then, the process by which students become aware of what the conventions are, where they come from what their likely effects are and how they feel about them. The second, important, step is to develop ways of challenging some of the discourse practices and of producing alternatives which allow the 'excluded' values and experiences to shape alternatives. This is a step towards *emancipation*, in other words using the power gained through awareness to act.

I shall return to these two concepts of empowerment and emancipation when I discuss classroom practice. From a pedagogic point of view, the challenge is to develop classroom practices which allow teacher and students to develop this critical awareness and which provide the students with opportunities to decide whether to conform to the perceived norms or whether to draw more creatively on their knowledge of them, by combining them with alternatives or by ignoring some or all of them.

Entering the academic discourse community as a student

In this section I describe some of the difficulties many students have in finding out about the conventions of the community they are moving into and in learning how to respond to what is expected of them. In the words of Bartholomae, a teacher in the Department of English at the University of Pittsburgh (1985: 134):

> every time a student sits down to write for us [university teachers] [she/he] has to invent the university for the occasion – invent the university, that is, or a branch of it . . . The student has to learn to speak our language, to speak as we do, to try on the peculiar ways of knowing, selecting, evaluating, reporting, concluding and arguing that define the discourse of our community.

Sometimes some of the conventions of the particular 'branch of the university' are made explicit, but mostly they are not. At my university the Engineering department explicitly tells its students to use passivisation in order to maintain objectivity. Some other departments give students very general written guidelines on assignment writing which are often mainly concerned with 'technical' aspects of assignments such as length, spacing, etc. Mostly the students have to try to pick up signals from their department lecturers and subject textbooks and journals.[3]

The following example is, in my experience, unusually explicit in terms of *who* the student is allowed to be. It is also a good example of resisting the explicit 'lesson' in conventions![4]

One of my students (a mature postgraduate from Africa) received the following comments on one of his essays for his department: 'Your arguments are undermined by the use of the personal pronoun. [Name of student] is not an established authority ... or not yet, anyway. Avoid the use of personal pronouns and expressions like "in my view" in all academic work.' The student in question was delighted to receive confirmation of one of the academic conventions we had been discussing in our Critical Language Awareness programme. His reaction was that it was his lecturer who was wrong and not him. He felt very strongly that he both had the right and the duty to use the personal pronoun 'I' and other personal expressions. This conviction grew out of discussions we had had in the classroom about such topics as 'writer identity', 'responsibility and commitment in writing' and about the dominant academic convention of so-called 'objectivity' in academic writing (for some more details see the section on the Study Skills course p. 125). The student was so confident in fact that he went to see his lecturer to discuss the point further and explain his own point of view.

In our discussion of this episode, the student told me that he would never have had either the sense of personal responsibility and commitment so clearly and consciously or the confidence to insist on expressing himself in the way he chose if we had not had the discussions on academic conventions. So this was a successful outcome for one student of critical analysis, awareness raising and challenge of dominant practices within one discourse community where he was 'constructed' as a non-authority.

In discussions with me another student, a mature British student of Afro-Caribbean origin, who was referred to me by her department because of 'problems with writing', told me how she feared being turned into a 'robot' in the university, which is why she resisted what she saw as some of the expected academic conventions. She also feels exasperated by comments on her essays telling her that what she says is 'interesting and relevant' but has 'no structure' or 'no organisation', while giving her no useful suggestions as to how she might restructure her material in an appropriate way for the lecturers.

These examples illustrate the conflict between the 'right' of the students to be themselves and to express themselves in a way that feels comfortable to them and the dominant expectations about 'good' academic writing in a University. I shall develop this point in the last section of this chapter.

In the following sections I describe the theoretical assumptions and pedagogic principles which I try to base my work on.

Theoretical assumptions

In this section I describe two main assumptions which underpin my work in CLA. The first assumption concerns the relationship between language and ideology. The second one has to do with the nature of discourse as a social practice.

The first assumption, the relationship between *language and ideology* is in part based on the seminal work of Roger Fowler and his colleagues at the University of East Anglia (1979). They argue that it is possible to pin down in linguistic terms the underlying attitudes and beliefs – or ideology[5] – which are encoded in text. Following Halliday, Fowler et al (1979) argue that natural language carries social meanings embodied in the lexical and syntactic structures. But much of social meaning is not explicit so critical interpretation involves a process of unveiling or demystifying. What is needed is an instrument of analysis for uncovering what is implicit – the underlying ideological content. In their essay, 'Critical Linguistics', they attempt to offer such an instrument in the form of a check-list of linguistic features which they have found significant. Their check-list has five headings:

(1) *the grammar of transitivity* (cf. Halliday's 'ideational function')
(2) *modality* (cf. Halliday's 'interpersonal function')
(3) *transformations* (e.g., passivisations, nominalisations)
(4) *linguistic ordering* (the grammar of classification)
(5) *coherence, order and unity of the discourse* (cf. Halliday's 'textual function')

However, their approach is, in my view, somewhat deterministic – it seems that if only readers have the linguistic tools at their disposal they can get at the 'true meaning' of the text. To counteract this danger I also draw on the work of the sociologist of culture Stuart Hall (1980, 1982).

Hall (1982) perceives meaning as a social production, and if meaning is not 'given' but socially produced this then implies that different meanings can be ascribed to the same events. This would further imply that there is no such thing as 'neutral reality', rather the encodings of reality will differ according to the social ideologies underlying the different perceptions of reality. Hence the 'struggle over meaning'. What we need to explain is how one meaning wins credibility or legitimacy over other available meanings. In order to explain how partial accounts of reality appear as 'the truth' Hall elaborates on the key concept of 'ideological presupposition' and argues that it is ideological presuppositions that make a text ideologically coherent. An ideological presupposition is a set of implicit ideological assumptions which are taken as true and which make an explicit proposition ideologically coherent. For example, when the President of the World Bank argued, in the context of starvation in the so-called Third World that 'It was "alarming" that many governments did not implement *family planning policies*' (*The Guardian*, 28.9.88, my emphasis), the link between lack of 'family planning' and starvation only makes sense if one accepts a number of linked implicit propositions. These are that 'people are a burden', 'People are not an asset', 'starvation is caused by overpopulation in the so-called Third World', 'starvation is *not* linked to issues of land access or dependency on the so-called First World', and so forth.

Hall (1980) develops a useful dynamic view of the reader–writer relationship which counters the somewhat one-sidedness of the Fowler view in which the writer is the more powerful of the two 'actors'. Hall's model is more concerned with what goes on during the readers' interaction with the text and the different decoding positions they read from (1980: 136–8).

The work of Fowler et al. and of Hall is particularly useful for the students in their reading, of course, but it is also very relevant to themselves as writers. By focusing on production of text (rather than on text interpretation as envisaged by Fowler and Hall), it is possible to use these concepts to help students see how their own language choices convey a picture of themselves and their attitudes towards their message and their readers to their audience and how they might try to take more control of the identity and attitudes they want to show through. For example, many students are unaware of the offence they may give by choosing to use the so-called generic pronoun 'he' and the image of sexism they project.

It also helps them in building their own arguments based on their reading if they can, for example, expose some of the presuppositions embedded in the texts which contain the knowledge they are supposed to draw on. An example of this is being able to unpack, in order to challenge it, the world-view contained in the assumption that family planning is the answer to hunger in the so-called Third World referred to above.

The second assumption is based on a view of discourse proposed by Fairclough (1989). I share the view expressed by Fairclough and others in this book that in order to account satisfactorily for both the production and interpretation of text (spoken and written) we need a model that integrates analysis of text (what), the socio-cognitive processes involved (how) and the socio-historical context in which the text occurs (why). Figure 5.1 shows the model developed by Fairclough (ibid.: 25).

This view of discourse, and my earlier comments on the nature of the academic discourse community, entail three fundamental pedagogic principles which I discuss in the following section.

Pedagogic principles

The first principle is that Critical Language Awareness (CLA)

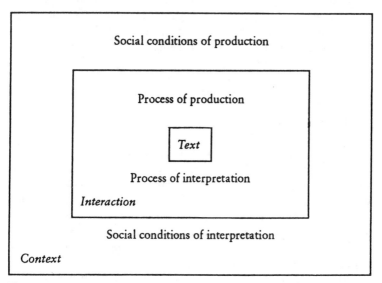

Figure 5.1

should focus on all of the three layers of discourse (see Figure 5.1) and on how they are interrelated. Language forms cannot be considered independently of the way in which they are used to communicate in a particular context. Individual acts of communication in context cannot be considered independently of the social forces which have set up the conventions of appropriacy for that context (see also Fairclough, this volume).

Second, students' awareness should emerge from the production and interpretation of *real* language – not from contrived examples brought in by the teacher. That is, students should be given the opportunity to develop their critical awareness while actually struggling with academic conventions in order to make their own meaning. This gives the students a real *purpose* for examining the conventions and deciding how to deal with them, with a *real* reader in mind and *real* consequences to their decisions.

Finally, CLA should *empower* language users in terms of developing their awareness (knowledge) but should also help them on the way to *emancipation* by giving them the chance to challenge existing conventions and the right to offer alternatives in order to help shape new conventions (action).

This last principle, of empowerment and emancipation, is the main focus of the rest of this chapter. Putting it into practice, in my view, in the context of teaching academic writing means raising the following broad issues which are at the centre of the dilemmas for both teacher and students:

WHAT you are allowed to say: content

HOW you are allowed to say it: form

WHO you are allowed to be: social subject

Discussing what you are allowed to say as a student, how you are allowed to say it and who you are allowed to be raises conciousness about the processes by which certain kinds of knowledge are legitimised and orthodoxies established (content), how formal conventions have been shaped (form) and how students are constructed as social subjects by the discourse practices within the academic community (social subject). The example given on p. 120 is a good illustration of the student being explicitly constructed by a lecturer as a non-authority who is not allowed to express personal opinions. Or rather, this was an *attempt* to construct the student in this way – which was resisted.

I shall now begin to describe my own practice in more detail.

My own practice

First I need to say a few words about the context in which I am operating. As I mentioned at the beginning of the chapter, I am responsible for organising the provision of Study Skills support for students already enrolled in departments of the university. For the purposes of this chapter I shall refer to just one part of my work, the teaching of writing, and I shall limit my discussion to two aspects of this work: subject-specific writing workshops for one department (Politics and International Relations) and 1:1 tutorials. I am convinced that, as Bartholomae says (1985: 139), it is hard to see how 'writers can have a purpose before they are located in a discourse since it is the discourse with its projects and agendas that determines what writers can and will do'. It is equally hard to see how writers can develop a sense of writing for a specific audience without having a real audience in mind.

I have, therefore, tried to make the teaching of writing more specific to actual departments. I have negotiated with a number of departments[6] to run workshops where students work on *real* assignments for their department. The staff I talked to were quick to see the benefits of such an approach when I presented my reasons for wanting to move away from general classes. They have been instrumental in the success of the courses both by their active support and their availability for consultations when I need help.

Study Skills (CLA) provision for students of Politics and International relations

The course caters for students following the postgraduate Diploma in International Relations and the three MA programmes offered by the department of Politics and International Relations. The course was originally set up for overseas students who did not have English as their first language, but increasingly 'native' speakers of English are attending the course.

As I suggested earlier, the 'materials' of the course are the written assignments that the students have to complete for their department. These form the basis for both workshop discussions and 1:1 tutorials. I keep a diary of our sessions in which I record student comments and my own evaluation of sessions and issues raised by students. This allows me to base the workshops around student-generated agenda.

The course marks a significant departure from the previous study skills programmes in the university – and indeed, to my knowledge, from the practice of other universities. Previously, study skills programmes had been organised on a mixed-discipline basis around the general academic skills: reading, writing, listening, etc. The tasks were obviously of a very general nature and were provided by the Study Skills tutor. In other words the classes provided 'practice' in academic skills *outside* the specific sections of the academic discourse community in which the student was actually having to operate. This meant that the writing had no real purpose. A further major disadvantage was that particularly those students who were having most difficulty in entering the community and therefore under the most pressure time-wise were having to spend extra time doing work which had no *direct* bearing on their own work. That is, they were doing *extra* work for the Study Skills' teacher. The most significant benefit of doing subject-specific work is that students have a vested interest in the discussions. This is because they are not only *directly* related to but also grow out of their own work and affect the outcome of their assignments and eventually their success in the course. The students are therefore quite willing to spend time and effort getting their writing as effective as possible.

The course procedures

Figure 5.2 shows how the course is articulated across two terms and integrates awareness of the writing process with collaborative writing workshops and explicit critical awareness of linguistic resources and conventions. In the figure arrow 1 represents the way in which the consciousness raising activity leads into the writing assignments. Arrow 2 shows how problems which arise in the students' own writing feed back into the ongoing discussions. Arrow 3 shows how generalising about what they are trying to do in writing leads to talking about the linguistic resources and

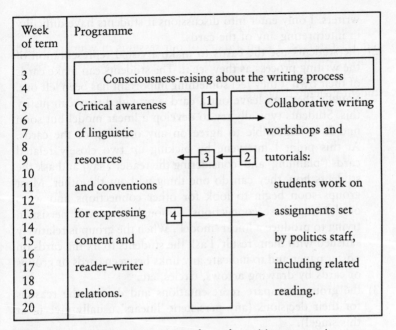

Week of term	Programme

Figure 5.2:   Consciousness-raising about the writing process in Study Skills course structure

conventions available for achieving these ends. Arrow 4 shows how students can feed the explicit discussions of linguistic resources back into their own writing.

I now focus on the consciousness-raising exercise on the writing process which takes up the first two sessions of the course. This exercise has been more fully discussed in Clark and Ivanič (forthcoming) so I will limit myself here to a short description of and a brief comment on the purposes and benefits of the exercise.

The exercise is based upon seventeen cards, each of which contains one component of the writing process. The components can be seen in the representation prepared by students, given in Figure 5.3.

The students work in small groups. Each group is given a set of seventeen cards and the exercise proceeds as follows:

(1) the students discuss each card in turn in terms of what they think the card means, drawing on their own experience as

writers. I only enter into discussions if students have difficulty in interpreting any of the cards.

(2) the students use the cards to make a visual representation of the writing process as they see it. The students can make cards of their own if they feel something important has been left out. Equally they can leave out a card – provided they can justify this. Students typically try to develop a linear model but soon find it is impossible to agree on any ordering of the cards. At this point I intervene by picking up two closely related cards ('planning' and 'considering the reader', say) and ask the students how they can do one thing without the other. Most groups soon begin to look for other connections and ways of showing these connections, although some will persist in trying to produce a linear 'model'. When the group is relatively satisfied with their 'result' I ask the students to fix the cards on poster paper and to indicate any links between cards or groups of cards by drawing arrows, circles, etc.

(3) the groups compare representations and discuss the reasons for their decisions (any persistent 'linears' usually give in at this stage!).

(4) the whole class compares their representations with one that the Teaching of Writing Group I belong to produced and discusses the similarities and differences.

(5) the whole class discusses what they have learnt from the activity and any implications they see for their own writing.

Figure 5.3 shows a representation produced by a group of students in the Politics and International Relations department.

The purposes of the above activity are several: to provide an opportunity to reflect collectively on their past experience as writers and their expectations about future writing; to provide a shared reference point and a minimal meta-language for future use in discussions; to provide an opportunity to air anxieties about writing; to place on the agenda a number of issues concerning the academic discourse community and its conventions and to begin a critical examination of them.

The main benefits of the exercise are the following. First, students become aware of the complex nature of the writing process, a process which they have usually never examined before. Most have been taught following a fairly rigid 'product' approach: plan,

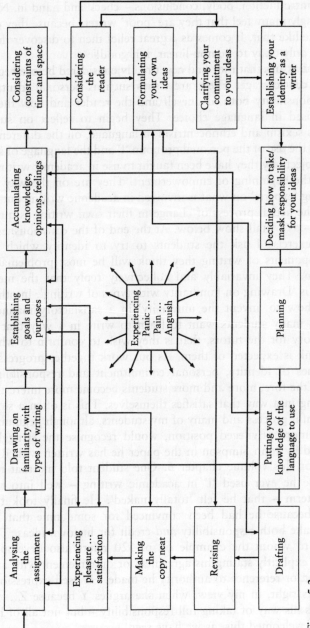

Figure 5.3

write – introduction, body, conclusions – check and hand in. Not surprisingly many feel that they are 'poor' writers because they do not write like that. It comes as a great relief then to discover that it is not only okay to be non-linear, but good!

Second, issues that they had never really considered before begin to take centre stage. These are issues such as personal identity and responsibility both to oneself and the reader and how these are realised in language choice. They begin to reflect on such issues as sexism and ethnocentrism in language, on the difference between the use of the personal pronoun 'I' and the language of so-called objectivity they have been taught to use in academic writing. This is the beginning of empowerment. They are on the way to becoming 'experts' on what is involved in academic writing but of course the actual process of change in their own writing is quite painful – as I shall show below. At the end of the consciousness-raising exercise I ask the students to try to identify which of the components of writing they think will be most problematic for them. They invariably and collectively reply that the most difficult is 'Drawing on familiarity with types of writing'. In other words, how to 'invent the university' in a satisfactory manner. Initially, many students want to learn to write in a way that is satisfactory for the tutors, that is they wish to conform to what they think is expected of them. As our work together progresses and issues of identity, personal commitment and responsibility come to the fore, more and more students become more interested in writing in a way that satisfies themselves. This is often a slow and painful process and many of my students, although beginning from a more privileged position, would recognise the struggles described by John Simpson in the paper he has written with Roz Ivanič for this volume chapter 6. One student told me that the first time he ever used 'I' in academic writing – well into the second term – that he felt 'totally naked'. He finally took the plunge because he had been convinced for some time that he had to take both responsibility *and* credit for his own ideas. The student to whom the example on p. 120 refers also developed ways of explicitly stating his agreement or disagreement with any quotation or reference to authority he made. He used expressions like 'X is right, in my view, when she argues Y because Z . . .'. This was his way of taking full responsibility – but not all of his lecturers welcomed this, as we have seen!

Yet another student moved further and further away from the impersonal language he had been taught to use and had used as an undergraduate. In his own words (in Clark et al.: forthcoming):

> in my first essay using language such as 'The analysis below will attempt . . .' was a way of attempting to imply academic objectivity and denied any personal commitment – the analysis was in fact mine and did not have an independent life of its own! Similarly, by using language such as 'examination of the historical development of strategic deterrence . . . suggests' and 'the history of the nuclear arms race suggests' I attempted to imply objectivity . . . I am now more likely to write 'In this essay I shall argue . . .'

Of course some students continue to play it safe, but at least they do so with open eyes – not out of ignorance. Others take more and more risks, both in content and style, because they come to see that ultimately they have a chance, through their essay writing, to explore ideas and make a positive contribution to the thinking in their discipline rather than simply reproducing the orthodoxies – usually western ethnocentric ones!

So in order to deal with this aspect of writing – i.e. drawing on familiarity with the conventions of academic writing – I introduce the following activity. The activity, as I hope will become clear, also provides an excellent opportunity for bringing into the open the dilemma of whether or not to conform to the perceived conventions and the possible consequences of any decisions the students make in this connection.

I take in copies of a past essay from which I have removed all comments by the assignment marker. I have chosen this essay for two reasons. First, because it is a reasonably good one but not one that is impossible to aspire to. Second, because it is very conservative in the way the writer draws on the rules of the game and so provides a useful lesson in typical academic conventions and their possible effects on the reader.

I ask the students to read the essay individually and then to discuss it in small groups which then report back in a plenary session. Only then do I give the students the lecturer's comments and the grade. I ask the students to focus in particular on three aspects they and I have discussed in the preceding consciousness-raising activity: 'considering the reader' (i.e. bearing in mind who you are writing for and using language in a socially responsible manner), 'argumentation strategies' (i.e. quoting, exemplifying, counter-arguing, drawing on your own experience, etc.) and 'writer identity' (i.e. what image of yourself you wish to portray to your readers in as far as you can control this). I choose these aspects to concentrate on for two reasons. First, because they are issues which generate the most discussion in the earlier consciousness raising activity. Second, because they focus on the key dilemma for the students, that is: now I know what the rules are and what a reasonable essay looks like, do I play by the rules or not? In the two years that I have used this particular essay, many of the students have been especially critical of two characteristics: the overuse of 'appeals to authority', particularly direct quotations, and the lack of explicit writer positioning. Others, however, and mainly students from overseas who are particularly anxious about meeting expectations, put their finger on the central dilemma and argue the following case. If this student got a goodish mark for this essay then should we not do the same kind of writing: with lots of long quotations, lots of appeals to authority, no polemics, no obvious writer position, lots of passivisations and impersonal expressions, no 'I', etc. This issue has led in the past to passionate discussion about personal commitment and integrity and responsibility to the reader and the whole question of the purpose of essay writing. It leads to further issues concerning membership of the community and the rights as well as obligations of students, something most of them had not considered themselves to have. In fact, at the beginning of the course many students ask 'Who am I to have opinions, to be critical or challenge the experts?'

In fact all of the students I have worked with – some more than others – feel that they both are, and are treated as junior members of the academic community. This despite the fact that many of them are experienced professionals in their own right. It is therefore helpful to remind them of this and to help them value their own experience as worthwhile knowledge to draw upon.[7]

The discussion resulting from the essay evaluation is a valuable starting point for future discussions, focusing as it does on the central dilemma of how far to conform or not to expected student behaviour. The first concrete outcome is a hand-out, 'Some characteristics of a good essay' (see The Appendix) which summarises and attempts to systematise the points the students themselves have made. The second outcome is a more focused discussion on personal integrity and responsibility based on another hand-out which builds on the earlier discussions, 'Responsibility and commitment in writing' from which I give a few examples below. For the specific CLA content of the course, this is another crucial session because we focus explicitly on the linguistic realisations of dominant conventions of academic discourse and potential alternatives to them.

We examine a number of issues including how to indicate or mask the difference between 'fact' and 'opinion' or 'interpretation' – compare

1. The author *says* . . .
2. The author *seems to be saying* that . . .

whether or how to indicate the strength of our commitment to ideas – compare:

3. This *will lead to* decreased stability . . .
4. This *may lead to* decreased stability . . .

how to avoid committing ourselves too strongly by hedging – compare:

5. In discussing whether aid works we have to consider *a number of variables, such as political stability.*
6. There are *three variables* that we have to consider and they are political stability, size of population and patterns of land ownership.

We examine the implications (e.g. for attributing responsibility) of transformations – passivisations and nominalisations:

7. *Poverty* on today's scale prevents a billion people from having even minimally acceptable standards.

After these initial sessions the students are encouraged to draft in the classroom so that other people are to hand to help them if they get stuck. They are encouraged to act as critical readers for each other and to comment on each other's writing. This gives them further opportunities to put into practice the insights gained from the earlier CLA sessions. When the students are ready to discuss a complete draft with me, they arrange a 1:1 tutorial. I read their text in advance, write down my responses to it as a reader and then discuss my responses with the students. I do not correct students' writing, for in my view three very good reasons (for an excellent discussion of responding to student writing see Zamel, 1985): first, there is no guarantee that my interpretation of what a student is trying to say is accurate; second, I believe that the students learn from having to try to solve problems themselves first, once the problems have been pointed out to them; third, and perhaps most importantly, I do not want to focus on grammatical accuracy but on the ideas the writer is expressing, and how they and the writer come across to me as a reader. Here are some typical comments on student writing:

student 1:	'Nuclear weapons and security a nation feels go hand in hand.'
my comment:	'In your view? Some people would disagree, I think.'
student 2:	'Conventional forces act as a deterrence as well as theatre nuclear forces.'
my comment:	'You present this as a "fact" – many people would disagree. Should you rephrase this, maybe?'
student 3:	'In the 1950s *theorists* argued . . .'
my comment:	'*All* of them?! No dissent?'
student 4:	'This paper will discuss . . . reasons for Truman's actions will be examined . . . finally this paper will try to evaluate . . .'
my comment:	'Is this impersonal style a deliberate choice on your part? Why? Let's discuss this.'

Where the grammatical accuracy is a serious obstacle to the ideas coming across to the reader I usually indicate that I do not understand and then ask the student to tell me what she or he means. Where necessary we try to reformulate the text together – or the student works on it by her/himself if she/he feels able to. The student then hands in the work to the department lecturer for assessment.

The tension between rights and obligations

In this final section I try to present the dilemmas that in my experience both teacher and students face when deciding how to deal with the dominant discourse conventions of academic writing.

For me, the teacher, there are two problems. There is a tension between the need to provide access to the kinds of linguistic practice which are required in order to succeed in education and the need on the other hand to develop a critical awareness of dominant conventions and alternatives to them. I also worry that by encouraging students to flout some of the conventions – when they themselves want to, of course – they will somehow be penalised for it in their marks or in the attitude lecturers may adopt. There is also a risk of moving from one kind of prescriptivism to another, namely the imposition of another set of teacher-preferred conventions. It is therefore always important to make clear to the students that ultimately it is *their* decision as to which conventions to adopt.[8]

But above all the issue is to help students 'unpack' the university and find out what is expected, what their obligations and rights are. So, throughout the discussions that take place, both in the classroom and in the tutorials, I am very conscious of the tension between the need on the one hand to develop the students' knowledge of the academic conventions and on the other hand their right to express their own identity as they see fit. The tension between recognising the right of the Afro-Caribbean student to refuse to conform to what she sees as straitjacketing practices and the fact that her lecturers find her writing unacceptable. The conviction of another student that what she is writing is good dramatic prose and my and her lecturer's sense that her style is more appropriate to popular journalism. The tension between the ethnocentricity of demanding western-style structuring of an argument and the right of the student to include moral lessons in his writing on nuclear weapons, which he feels very strongly about.

This tension has forced me to try to formulate some sort of basic distinction between conventions. By this I mean placing recognised writing conventions into two categories, of acceptability and/or floutability: those you should not flout and those you can and/or should. Although this grouping is entirely personal it is based upon the range of reactions from subject tutors to my students' work, on discussions with colleagues in the Teaching of Writing Group (mentioned in note 1) and partly on the nature and consequences of non-conformity. So the conventions which I would recommend that students do *not* flout are:

(1) *you must substantiate your arguments*: this encourages students to think through their arguments carefully.
(2) *your arguments must be relevant to your stated aims*: this helps the students focus more persuasively on the specific arguments they want to develop. If the writer gets lost so does the reader.
(3) *you must not plagiarise*: this is dishonest by any standards and can lead to severe punishment.
(4) *you should follow a recognised referencing convention and be consistent*: this makes it easier for readers from many different parts of the world to understand and follow up any interesting references.

The other conventions, particularly those to do with so-called objectivity and 'academic style', are in my view open to legitimate challenge. For example students should be encouraged – but not obliged – to take responsibility for their ideas by using 'I' and other personal expressions instead of masking their position behind the pretence of objectivity with impersonal language. They should be encouraged to avoid unnecessarily 'big' words, long sentences and name-dropping through excessive referencing because they are elitist and excluding practices. The word 'should' of course leads to the other dimension of the problem: am I simply replacing one prescriptivism with another? My answer to this is that the teacher should not attempt to impose her/his own view of what should be challenged, with the exception of racist and sexist or ethnocentric discourse. As Graddol and Swann argue (1989: 193) this is a very different kind of prescriptivism from that which rules that certain syntactic varieties of English, for example, are incorrect. In my view, encouraging students to avoid sexist or racist language is a question of valuing the rights of others and therefore an important ethical issue. With respect to the other issues, of course I make my own views and the reasons for them very clear. However, I see my job as facilitating the students' examination of the conventions of the academic discourse community they are operating within, of helping them to find alternatives where they wish, but above all providing them with as much knowledge as possible so that they can make their own informed decisions.

To sum up, I return to the two key concepts mentioned earlier, empowerment and emancipation. Empowerment is the key to the resolution of the problem for the teacher. By providing information and knowledge, by helping the students to reflect on their own views and practices, by giving a systematic explanation of the way language works the students are empowered. They learn what the rules of the game are and why. Theirs is the decision whether to accommodate to all or some of them or whether to challenge them by using alternatives. The teacher cannot emancipate the students, they can only be helped to emancipate themselves.

Conclusion

In this chapter I have described my attempts to introduce CLA into my work in Study Skills at a British University and the tension that exists between the need to provide access to conventional discourse practices and the need to develop alternative practices. I have argued that it is essential to make CLA and the teaching of writing purposeful activities. This means working with students within the academic community they are located in on real assignments for their subject tutors. I have further argued that a crucial aspect of CLA is to empower students by providing them with the opportunities to discover and critically examine the conventions of the academic discourse community and to enable them to emancipate themselves by developing alternatives to the dominant conventions.

Notes

1. Many of the ideas that I base my work on have been developed in the Teaching Of Writing Reasearch Group, an interdisciplinary group that meets regularly at Lancaster University, particularly by Roz Ivanič, Joan Allwright, Rachel Rimmershaw and Anne Marshall-Lee. The CLA aspects of my work have similarly been, at least in part, the result of collective thinking in the Language Ideology and Power Group, also based in Lancaster.
2. A colleague from the Lancaster Language Ideology and Power group recently reported on work she had done on student evaluation questionnaires. She showed that lecturers on the whole used the information they got from students, whatever the statistical distribution of responses, to back up their own views on the course being evaluated.
3. One student (undergraduate from Hong Kong) told me that she 'copied the language from psychology journals to [her] level'. The

result was a mixture of psychology jargon and entangled grammar! Another student (MA from USA) deliberately toned down her own position in one assignment because her perception from lectures was that the lecturer would not accept 'liberal' points of view.

4.   This example was first used in a paper jointly produced with three students from the Politics and International Relations class, one native speaker and two non-native speakers (Clark et al.: 1990).

5.   The term 'ideology' is used here to mean 'a systematic body of ideas, organised from a particular point of view' (Kress & Hodge: 1979).

6.   One of the issues that was discussed in these negotiations was a view of education as collaboration rather than competition: the emphasis on the collective rather than the individual. One department refused to allow me to work on real assignments (economics) because it would have been 'difficult to assess on an individual basis'. The other courses at the moment are for the Departments of Linguistics, Accounting and Finance, and Business Analysis.

7.   At a recent discussion of the Teaching of Writing and Research Group, two students (mature women undergraduates) Denise Roach and Angela Karach, talked about how the academic community undervalues the role of experience, women's experiences in particular, and does not consider it to be 'legitimate knowledge'.

8.   One student in particular (an MA student from Singapore) consciously decided that he would stick with the accepted conventions because on the whole he felt more comfortable conforming. He writes about this decision in the paper mentioned in note 4.

References

Bartholomae D 1985 Inventing the university. In Rose M (ed) *When a writer can't write*. Guilford Press

Chase G 1988 Accommodation, resistance and the politics of student Writing. *College Composition and Communication* 39(1): 13–22

Clark R, Constantinou C, Cottey A, Yeoh O C 1990 Rights and obligations in student writing. In Fairclough N L (ed) *Language and power, proceedings of the BAAL annual meeting, Lancaster 15–17 September 1989*. CILT

Clark R, Ivanič R forthcoming Consciousness-raising about the writing process. In Garrett P, James C (eds) *Language awareness*. Longman

Fairclough N L 1989 *Language and power*. Longman

Fowler R, Hodge B, Kress G, Trew T 1979 *Language and control*. Routledge

Graddol D, Swann J 1989 *Gender voices*. Basil Blackwell

Hall S 1980 Encoding and decoding. In Hall S, Hobson D, Lowe A, Willis P (eds) *Culture, media, language*. Hutchinson

Hall S 1982 The rediscovery of ideology: return of the repressed in media studies. In Gurevitch M, Bennet T, Curran J, Woollacott J (eds) *Culture society and the media.* Macmillan

Kress G, Hodge R 1979 *Language as ideology.* Routledge

Zamel V 1985 Responding to student writing. *TESOL Quarterly* **19**(1): 79–101

Appendix for chapter 5

Some Characteristics of a Good Essay:

1. Reader-friendliness:

- well-typed and double-spaced (or neatly handwritten and double-spaced)

- the spelling and punctuation are not too erratic and are consistent

- the language and the examples that the writer uses are neither racist/ethnocentric nor sexist

- the text is divided into easily-digested chunks – paragraphs (one main idea in each) and sections

- the sections have headings which summarise the content for the reader and do not mislead him/her

- there are no over-long sentences and the language is not unnecessarily complicated

- the introduction informs the reader of what is to come: a brief statement of the main theme/argument and a short outline of the paper

- there is a conclusion which restates the main argument, briefly rehearses the steps in the argument examined in the body of the paper and indicates any consequences, further developments, etc.

- the writer's intentions and progress through his/her ideas are clearly signposted to the reader by the use of 'semantic markers'

- any technical terms are explained and where possible examples are given

- there are illustrations (diagrams, charts, tables, etc.) where appropriate
- referencing is clear and consistent

2. Argumentation:

arguments are well-substantiated by a *variety* of means:

- appeals to authority: quoting, paraphrasing and/or summarising
- reference to empirical evidence
- use of examples
- reference to own experience where relevant
- pointing out the flaws in existing arguments or positions
- there is a balanced and judicious use of reference material – primary and secondary (overquoting is as bad as underquoting)
- opinion is not 'dressed up' as fact
- the writer's position is made clear
- arguments are presented coherently
- arguments are relevant to the task in hand
- there are no contradictions: between writer's stated aims and the aims achieved; in the line of reasoning followed

6 Who's Who in Academic Writing?

Roz Ivanič and John Simpson

1 Introduction

We belong to a small group of students and researchers in Lancaster who are jointly learning and researching academic writing. We are the two longest-standing members of the group, having worked together sporadically since 1983. As co-researchers we have each played a different role. John is a student who has recently entered higher education. He is in a particularly good position to make observations about academic writing: because of his long, bumpy journey through the education system he is more critical and more demanding than most students. Academic writing and all its trappings have failed to 'suck him in' as the Progressive Literacy Group (1986) puts it. Roz is a teacher and a linguist. Her role has been to read relevant theory and see what's in it, to recognise conventional and unconventional writing and to question where it is coming from.

Our way of working has been to identify parts of an academic assignment which John was pleased with and parts he was unhappy with. In earlier years he was pleased with parts which conformed to conventions of academic writing, using conventions which he had been taught at various stages in his education or acquired from reading in his subject areas. Critical discussion of these conventions has led us to recognise that they often distracted from, distorted or buried what John actually wanted to say, and they created an image of him as a person with which he did not want to identify. We tried to 'clear away the debris' and unearth what he really wanted to say, and what sort of identity he wanted to create by the way he writes. This joint critical language study has increased our critical language awareness with two spin-offs: research findings which we are reporting here and language development for us both as writers.

Finding your own language is more difficult in writing than in speaking. Whereas we all have the option to 'be ourselves' and 'speak with our own voice' when talking, we are under pressure to submerge our individual identities when writing. Written language is 'standardised': that is, it is designed to conceal differences. It has been shaped by cultures which are distant from most people, so becoming literate in itself involves an acculturation process. So there is no ready-made alternative variety of written English for someone wanting to 'write with my own voice'. Rather, it is a question of making choices from a range of alternatives within academic writing, trying to find ones which are most in harmony with our sense of ourselves.

Each individual's language is a hotch-potch of elements they have picked up from their different experiences of language throughout their lives. It's difficult to say precisely: 'This is my language' and 'This is someone else's language', because on the one hand it all originated from other sources, and on the other the present mix is unique to the writer. So creating your own identity as a writer means taking responsibility for choosing the bits that make up your own unique mix.

For us the question: 'Who's who in academic writing?' is one of the keys to being able to write. Through experience of reading and writing academic texts we have begun to realise that the identification of 'I' is critical to meaning and credibility. Students need to identify the people behind the texts they read, establish an identity for themselves as readers and writers, and recognise the relationship between themselves and the tutors who will read their work.

We have three purposes in writing this chapter. The first is to outline what we have found out through our own critical consciousness-raising about the people behind academic writing. The general idea that texts are inseparable from their producers and interpreters is not new, but we think that the particular application of the idea to academic writing is worth spelling out in detail.

Our second purpose is to propose that the more visible all these people are, the easier it is to read and write academic texts. The third purpose is to explain why we think this sort of critical language awareness is useful. Just as awareness of these language issues has helped John enter and survive higher education without losing his own sense of identity, so we believe it would be of value to other adults returning to study, and indeed to everyone.

We will be referring to ourselves in an unusual way. 'We' refers to things we have done together, including thinking and writing this article. 'John' and 'he' refer to things John did alone, for example writing the assignments we were studying together, and making his own observations on them. In places where we generalise about what 'a student' does, we will use 'he', 'him', 'his' to emphasise the fact that any tentative generalisations we make are founded in John's experience. To use non-sexist generics would obscure this. 'Roz' and 'she' appear less often. They refer to things Roz did alone, for example making a linguistic commentary on particular examples we are discussing.

We will use 'I' in two ways. In some places John will write about his own experience: in these places 'I' refers to him. We will use the expression 'the "I"', always with 'I' in inverted commas, to refer to the presence of the writer's identity in a text.

We are taking a critical position towards the language of books in the way we are writing this chapter for a book. We are trying to be as clear as we possibly can about 'who's who' in what we are writing ourselves. We are also trying to write in such a way that any student like John could understand what we have written.

In section 2 we will explain what we mean by recognising the 'I' in the reading and writing process. In section 3 we will set out the cast of characters who in some way enter into academic writing, describing their roles from the point of view of a student faced with an assignment. In section 4 we will present examples of the way in which John interacted with other characters in some of the assignments he did during his first year as an undergraduate. In section 5 we will explain how we see our collaborative research as a way of developing critical language awareness, and suggest why and how others might benefit from working in the same way. We will discuss these issues from the perspective of the writer, and only mention reading where it is directly connected to writing. We believe, however, that critical awareness of your own identity applies just as much to the reading process as to the writing process.

2   The 'I'

In this section we will first explain what we mean by 'the "I"', and then explain why we think it is important. By the 'I' we mean recognising that writers not only construct their texts but are also constructed by them. That is, they are both creating the writing and participating in it at the same time. Taking account of the 'I' sometimes means actually putting the word 'I' into the writing, but it is not only that. More generally it means realising that everything you write says something about you, and making sure as far as possible that you are showing yourself as the sort of person you want to be.

Choices in language affect not only the meaning which is conveyed but also the impression of the writer which is conveyed, including the sort of relationship the writer wants to set up with the reader. We reject the idea that academic writing is objective and impersonal. If writers do choose an objective style, depersonalising ideas, this is when the writing can run into trouble both for the readers and for the writers themselves. For readers an impersonal style makes it difficult to work out what the writers really mean, and where they stand. Writers trying to use an impersonal style often lose track of what they really mean, winding up in long, contorted sentences. They are not cutting themselves out of their writing; instead, they are creating an image of themselves as people who have an objective view of knowledge.

We believe that the 'I' is the most important part of any kind of writing, because all writing should start with the one essential question: 'What do I want to say?' This question helps writers to fulfil two interrelated requirements: one is a responsibility to themselves and their ideas; the other is a responsibility to their readers.

Taking responsibility for your ideas commits you to truthfulness. The 'I' makes you write your ideas, thoughts and convictions. Good academic writing is about progression; it is not static. Academic writing is not for saying 'Look at me: I am an expert in this field and agree with the rest of the academic world.' It's for saying 'Hold on, I think we got it wrong and this is what I think.' This is where truthfulness is so essential, because the real person is showing through, not hiding behind a screen of impersonal objectivity. Academic writing should be done to inform, question, disagree and substantiate. It should not be like a bland game of pat-a-cake[1] where a point is thrown backwards and forwards like a plaything.

Finding an 'I' in writing also helps you to find clarity. In our work, for example, using the 'I' meant we could unwrap long sentences to find out what John was trying to say. The 'I' is a very simple tool for doing this because it lets you stand away from the writing and look at what you are trying to say. This allows you to go back to the writing with a freedom because you have asked yourself about your writing and ideas.

Writers who achieve clarity and truthfulness in academic texts get the readers on their side. The readers get what they want and expect from writers: a full conviction in putting their ideas forward. They will be able to read what writers actually think about the subject they've been writing on. They may not agree with the ideas but it will certainly make them think and question. Purely by being a writer you run the risk of being criticised and disagreed with. If you do receive criticism and disagreement it means the writing is alive and is provocative and you have succeeded in communicating your ideas.

Everything we have said in this section applies to all writers: recognised experts whose writing students have to read, and student writers trying to write assignments. In the next section we will focus our attention on student writers in relation to the other people who affect their writing.

3 The cast in order of appearance

To some extent all texts have the same characters: writers, writers of prior texts which they draw on for content or style[2], and readers[3]. However, the specific characters who appear in specific texts are very different from one text to another. In the academic community something written for publication by an established scholar has a very different population from an assignment written by a student for assessment purposes. For this reason we will not treat academic writers and readers in general, but rather we will trace more or less chronologically the people a student encounters in the process of reading for and writing an academic assignment.

In each sub-section we will contrast an objective, impersonal view of academic writing with our own view that texts are populated and these populations should be acknowledged and as visible as possible.

3.1   Who is the person who sets the assignment?

This person is usually the same as the reader of the assignment, and we'll say more about her/him in that role in section 3.5. below. However, there are some important things to say about the role of 'assignment setter', which we'll say here. This person is posing a challenge and a threat to the student, and positioning him as a writer, and exercising control over him. However stimulating the assignment may be as an intellectual exercise, it is also face-threatening because it will be judged. She/he positions him, not as a writer with a responsibility to inform his reader, but as a student who has to perform a certain writing task in order to be assessed. She/he exercises power by defining the content and form of the essay.

To some extent individual tutors can choose how much power they exercise over student writers in assignment setting. For example, by encouraging students to choose their own assignment topics they may reduce their control. However, most of what we have described is not in the hands of the individual tutor, but is constructed by the way she/he in turn is positioned by the institution of higher education, with its brief to maintain standards (whatever those are) and discriminate among candidates for degrees.

3.2   Who are the writers of the books that students read?

John's answer is:

> Remarkably the answer is quite simply ex-students. It may be hard for a student to realise that the 'great academic' authority they are sat reading at one time was a student. In essence this one question and answer outline the whole problem of academic writing and reading. These writers are often sucked in, trapped into reproducing what they are sucked in by.
>
> Why do academic writers write? Before actually moving into higher education I believed they wrote because they had something to say about the subject they were writing on. I now see it more in terms of: 'Through this subject I can say more about myself.' This 'I' ('ego-I') says 'look at me first: look at how intellectual I am. Look: I'm doing the right thing and may gain recognition for

myself and my place of work.' These incitements to write usually result in academic writing which says very little about the subject, does not stimulate new ideas in the writer or the reader, and is unwilling to take risks and question existing ideas.

As a reader I want authors to make me stop and rethink my position. I want them to make me read what they are saying; whether it is agreement or disagreement, reaction is essential. Most of all I want to see that the author is writing the book because she/he has true convictions and feelings about what she/he is saying. In any of my previous writing whether it has been academic or creative, Roz and I have always worked out writing problems from the standpoint of what I'm trying to say. Always underneath we search for the 'committed-I' and what was the idea that coexisted with the 'I'. (We will describe this process in more detail in section 3.3.2 below.)

However, with the bad academic I read this cannot be done because the 'ego-I' gets in the way. As a student I want academic writers to promote their ideas but not themselves. By promoting their ideas they are guaranteeing themselves to be remembered and talked about for years to come because they make the reader think, agree or disagree. The 'ego-I' writers on the other hand make themselves a solid notch in oblivion. Readers complain that they have not found out anything more and wasted time, so then these writers are not recommended as a source. Even if they are on a reading list they provoke the familiar cries of: 'Don't bother, it takes too long to say so little,' 's/he managed to make a really interesting subject boring,' and 'they hardly say anything about the subject, but more about themselves.'

The 'ego-I' is withdrawn, impersonal, disengaged. The 'committed-I' is more like a writer getting into a conversation with the reader about something s/he cares about: more like informal speech. Table 6.1 shows some of the things we have noticed which are signs of the 'ego-I' compared with the 'committed-I' in writing.

The characteristics of the 'ego-I' are common in the books John reads. Although they may be essential for expressing some ideas, we believe writers fall into this style far more often than necessary. It frequently has no function other than to exclude many readers from access to information and intellectual development.

The 'ego-I' appears to be more common in some fields than others. In the last thirty years some writers in some fields have been trying to break away from the conventions we listed under 'ego-I',

Table 6.1:   Characteristics of the 'ego-I' and the 'committed–I' in academic writing

The 'ego-I'	The 'committed-I'
• impersonal language • using few pronouns other than 'it' or 'this' • long, nouny sentences • densely packed abstractions • generalisations	• more use of the pronoun 'I' (or 'we' for joint authors) • more verbs of thinking and saying • more words for people • more examples

and write more in the 'committed-I' style. For example, here is an extract from Wells (1987) which illustrates how academic writing is becoming less segregated from informal speech:

> Before going on to discuss the differences we observed in greater detail, however, I want to emphasize the very great achievement of *all* the children we studied. Indeed, in the population as a whole, all but the tiny minority of seriously handicapped children do succeed in acquiring functional competence in their native language. In the Bristol sample of 128 children, there was not a single child who had not mastered what might be called 'basic English' by the age of five. Rosie was the least advanced child in the follow-up study . . .

It would take a lot of space to discuss his language choices in detail. Briefly, though, notice his use of '*I*' and '*we*'; the verbs of saying: '*discuss*' and '*emphasize*'; his use of examples: '*In the Bristol sample of 128 children*', '*Rosie . . .*'; not too many abstractions: '*differences*', '*achievement*', '*population*', '*minority*', '*competence*', but no more; sentences not exceptionally long.

We, too, are trying to push back the barriers of academic language and write in a way which is as committed, informal, and accessible to readers as possible. This chapter is an example of our efforts.

John finds it easier to read the 'committed-I' type of source material, and prefers to absorb that style for himself. We will not exemplify these here, as our focus is on the student's writing. There are examples of John's attempts to bring the 'committed-I' into his writing in section 4 below.

3.3 Who is the student?

3.3.1 – as reader

This is John's account of the interaction between himself as a reader and the writers we described in section 3.2.

> Students have to read certain texts to gain insights into certain areas. As a student reader I go to a textbook as a means of expansion and authority. However, I usually find that I have to battle through a book to gain a small amount of either. The question then arises: 'What happens that makes understanding such a chore?' The simple answer is that a contract between the reader and the author has been broken. There is a contract between the writer and the reader that the writer will give information, spark ideas, increase understanding. If the writing doesn't do this the contract is broken.

Students tend to think the content and the style[2] must be right because books are printed, and written by academics. But any reader has a right to take a position as a reader, including a student reader. Taking a position entails asking four critical questions:

(1) *Do I understand it?*
   A student has a right to criticise what he reads on the grounds that it isn't clear for him. One reason for criticising may be that the writing contains many abstractions and generalisations, disconnected from people and experience. If a student has to ask of a book 'What are you trying to say?' then something's wrong. You've got to trust yourself: you have the right to say it's wrong because it's not working for you. We expect this principle to be controversial: many people would argue that it's the student's fault if he doesn't understand.

(2) *Do I agree with it?*
   A student has a right to question and disagree with the content of what he reads (or hears or sees). A student may disagree with the ideas and/or the choice of words. John's experience is that few students or tutors operate with this principle.

(3) *Do I like the way it's written?*
   A student has a right to decide which style[2] in what he reads he wants to identify with, and which not. In our experience few

students or tutors outside linguistics departments have given any thought to this principle.

(4) *Do I want to be the sort of person this text is written for?*
A student has a right to resist being constructed as the sort of person who thinks in the way a text imposes on him. For example, here is a sentence John had to read for one of his courses:

> The desire to minimize negative, and maximize positive emotion can affect both specific thought contents and more general information processing strategies (see Bruner, 1947, for the influence of conditioning on perception). (Weston 1985: 36)

In order to read this John has to become the sort of person who defines emotion and thinking in this way. He also has to accept the command 'see Bruner . . .' as the way to understanding these issues further. Most students respond to this by feeling inadequate to their role as student. We suggest that it is legitimate to respond by resisting the role which is set up for them.

All four questions focus on the 'I' – making the reader himself an active participant in the reading rather than a passive receiver of transmitted knowledge. Current views of the reading process emphasise this active role of the reader, but it is not often applied to study skills courses.

3.3.2 – as writer

In this sub-section we will first contrast a traditional with a critical view of the relationship between reading and writing for a student. We will then present John's experience of being a student writer.

In a non-critical view of academic writing, published books and articles have two roles for the student writer. First, they contain the source material the student is supposed to draw on for most assignments. Their writers are supposed to be authorities on their subjects. Second, they are supposed to provide models of the language students should be using in their own writing. Table 6.2 represents this conventional relationship between student and

Table 6.2: A non-critical view of the relationship between
reading and academic writing

	Content	Style[2]
Reading	1. Work out what the published writers mean.	3. Simultaneously absorb the language they use.
Writing	2. Decide what you want to write.	4. Decide how to write it.

source material, which doesn't take account of the identity of the
writer.

In Table 6.2 there is a direct relationship between the content
and style of what the student reads and what he writes, represented
by the unbroken arrows. The danger in this is that a student writer
can get trapped by what he is reading. He can be trapped into
attempting to reproduce the content; he can be trapped into trying
to imitate the language and through that the sort of people who
write like that[3]. This imposes another person's construction of
knowledge and language on him, not allowing the 'I' through. In
our analysis of John's work before he entered college we found
that this resulted in

- repetition
- long sentences
- not saying what he really meant.

However, a critical approach to academic reading and writing
makes the relationship less straightforward. In Table 6.3 critical
language awareness (CLA) intercepts the arrows.

3.4   Who are the people who are written about in academic writing?

This may seem like an odd sub-section. Academic writing is thought
of as being about ideas and facts rather than people. Readers expect
to find characters in novels, not in essays. However this is not as
clear-cut as it may seem, as some of the examples we give in
section 4 will show. In the social sciences there are people behind
the generalisations and statistics, whether they surface in the text

Table 6.3:   A critical view of the relationship between reading
and academic writing

	Content	Style[2]
Reading	1. Work out what the published writers mean.	3. Simultaneously absorb the language they use.
CLA	Recognise writers and readers behind ideas.	Select features you want to identify with.
Writing	2. Decide what you want to write.	4. Decide how to write it.

or not. This is a whole topic for investigation in itself, which we
are not pursuing in this chapter. There are also people behind the
opinions: these could be other students, tutors, or published writers
(see 3.2).

3.5   Who are the readers of students' essays?

Readers are generally in a less powerful position than writers. But
the readers of students' essays always have power over the writers,
which makes writing an entirely different process. Student writers
are constantly in a position of being told what to write, and then
judged on it by their tutors, according to criteria which are often
shrouded in mystery.

In the next section we will illustrate how these 'characters'
populate academic writing, using John's own writing for examples.

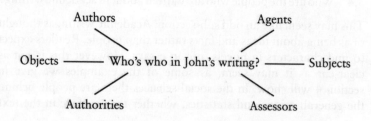

4 Who's who in John's writing?

In this section we will describe specific examples of John's writing on the degree course he is currently taking. The examples are taken from three assignments on different courses in the first year of the degree. Each represents a different relationship between the people present in the text. This approach makes student readers less dependent on the content and style of their sources. They still need to work out what the published writers are saying (box 1 in Table 6.3), but they will recognise it as the view of an author, rather than a truth. They still need to decide what they want to write (box 2 in Table 6.3), but they will be more in control of this by being aware of their own identity as writers. They will not so much absorb the language in which the sources are written as critically assess it, consciously adopting only the features they would like to identify with, and using these in their own writing (boxes 3 and 4 in Table 6.3).

John finds that concentrating on the 'I' helps him to resist being mystified and positioned as a reader and to be in control as a student writer.

I believe that to embark on an essay you not only have to know what the question means but you must also know the complexities of the essay itself. An essay is not a flat piece of writing on a flat piece of paper: if it was, essay writing would be a very much simpler process for writer and reader.

When I read an essay title ideas begin to spark but in no orderly sequence. Along with ideas come memories of articles and books I have read, lectures I have listened to and information from the TV. The information I have is in a semi-chaotic state. Because the thoughts are all sparked from the one central essay question they are all somehow interlinked with each other. How do I sort this out?

I think that the answer is to ask yourself our title question: 'Who's who in academic writing?' First look and see where the 'I' comes in to writing. In fact discovering where the 'I' is is one of the most selfish, indulgent and rewarding academic tasks there is. This sorting out of the 'I' gives me the chance to clear away all the academic waffle and pretentiousness that we read in course books. I consider this part to be the student's revenge and indeed can be very enjoyable.

The next question that arises is how do I go about finding this

'I'?. There are a number of ways. One is to translate your ideas from academic essay language to your own everyday language. Obviously the form your own argument takes may need to be softened slightly but in actual working circumstances there have been very few occasions when 'the language of the "I"' has been too severe. There is one sure way you can find your own language and that is by actually speaking what you think. When you get really annoyed with writing you have the chance to find yourself: to clear away the anger and the heat and what you're left with is the core. Then you need confidence and trust in yourself. This is a gut reaction and it's rich because the books, the learning is all there ready to find expression.

Even though this may seem to be going away from the academic forms it lets you know where you are. Later on when you come to find quotations to back up your points, they back up your own writing not just by expressing the same point but by complementing your ideas. For the actual practicalities it is better to have someone to listen to you then they can note or remember what you say because once you find the 'I' it tends to be like opening the floodgates.

We want to emphasise that putting the 'I' into writing is not a matter of choice. The student writer, like any writer, is a participant in his own writing whether he wants to be or not. Our experience has shown that student writers often get stuck precisely because their identity is at stake and they don't realise it. We believe that conscious awareness of the 'I' in writing helps writers to be in control of the self they are creating. Here are brief details of the three assignments and why we have chosen them as examples.

A   The 'Infanticide' essay

If infanticide is morally permissible in certain circumstances, then should it be legally permissible in those circumstances? (In answering this question you should take into account the active/passive distinction.)

This assignment is an example of what is often called a 'discursive essay', an 'expository essay' or an 'argumentative essay', in which the student is expected to put forward his point of view, and justify it. He was expected to use evidence from his reading to support his position. John got a good mark for the assignment – 2.i. class.

Most of our examples come from this typical assignment, but

we will illustrate some additional points by briefer reference to two others.

B   The 'Adult Literacy' essay

PLACEMENT ESSAY: Provision for adult education should be totally client-centred (Munion 1982). Discuss this statement with particular reference to adult literacy programmes.

This assignment is very different from the Infanticide essay. It was based to a large extent on the work John did for his placement in the Adult Basic Education Department of the local College of Adult Education. It therefore includes a narrative section, describing what happened on the placement. Another difference is in the sort of evidence John used to support his position in answer to the question. In addition to the views of other published writers, he was expected to draw on his own experience in the placement. However, in John's case there was a further source of evidence: as a student who had come to higher education through adult basic education, he has experience of the topic himself, and insights to offer based on this experience.

John got an excellent mark for this assignment – 1st class.

C   The 'Welfare State' essay (CYS)

Discuss the view that the welfare state has done little more than reinforce traditional gender relationships.

This assignment differs from the other two because of the tutor who would be marking it. In this course John knows that the tutors have particularly strong views on this topic and he has to take this into account in the way he argues his position. In spite of the obstacles we describe below he got a 2. i class mark.

We discussed each of these assignments after John had finished it, using them as the basis for critical language study, with the aim of raising our own critical language awareness. What we write about them here is drawn from tape recordings of these discussions.

We will use the same sub-headings as in section 2 to introduce the people who surround and enter into these pieces of writings:

the tutors who set and read the assignments, the people who wrote what John read, John himself, and the people he wrote about. The headings are not so neat and discrete as we made them appear in section 3: the populations of texts in reality crowd together and interact with each other in complicated ways. Nevertheless we hope the headings will be a useful way of thinking about who's who in academic writing. We have sub-divided some of the sections into 'content' and 'style' [2] where both seem to have been influenced.

4.1   The tutors who set the assignments

4.1.1   Content

In the 'Infanticide' essay the tutor prescribes not just the content but also part of the argument students should use in their answers: 'In answering this question you should take into account the active/passive distinction.' She defines what type of writing is required: the question: 'should it be legally permissible?' calls for the expression and justification of a value judgement.

In the 'Adult Literacy' essay it is not so much the official wording of the assignment as the tutors' spoken instructions which guided – or failed to guide the – students. The same topic had been assigned to another group of students earlier in the term and they had been criticised for failing to make sufficient reference to the placement they had undertaken. For the previous group of students a set of expectations was operating of which they were not aware. The tutors told John's group about this, and knew they should integrate some reference to their placement, but they didn't know how they were expected to do this. John felt angry that the tutors hadn't explained the conventions for the task: 'If they want me to do these things at least let me know what they are.' He also felt pressure from the tutors to treat this as a regular academic essay, with the usual conventions such as 'include about eight references'. John recognised this expectation coded in the wording 'Discuss this statement . . .'

In the 'Welfare State' essay John felt pressure not from the written rubric nor the spoken instructions, but from what he knew about the tutors' views. He knew that the view mentioned in the rubric 'that the welfare state has done little more than reinforce traditional gender relationships' was the view of the tutors, and it is also the view presented in the key reading they were recommended: *Social Policy – A feminist analysis* (Pascal 1986). All the time he was writing, particularly in one place where he wanted to criticise Pascal, he felt a conflict between expressing his own view and writing what his tutors would agree with.

The Appendix contains the section of the essay in which John criticises Pascal for misrepresenting Beveridge. We will discuss this extract in detail here: this discussion bridges all our sub-sections and we will be referring back to it later. We want to show how various participants in the text interact: the tutors who will read it, the writers whose books John read, and John himself. John as writer has to referee this encounter: a delicate task.

The encounter began when John read the book by Pascal. He felt that she was being unfair to Beveridge, criticising him without taking account of the historical conditions in which he wrote his report. As a man reading a feminist critique he felt something of a personal slight: 'Hold on! Men do do some good as well.' When he checked the original report by Beveridge he found that Pascal had misrepresented him by quoting one sentence of his report without the paragraph which precedes it and qualifies it. John felt that this was absolutely appalling, dishonest: one step away from plagiarism in the catalogue of dirty deeds.

So John wanted to criticise the recommended book for the assignment. This in itself is an act of identity, but more so when we take into consideration the fact that he knew the tutors who would be assessing the work approved of Pascal. When we discussed what, if anything, John had done to cope with the fact that he expected his criticism would be badly received, he pointed to the choice of:

In Beveridge's defence it is only fair to point out . . .

He started by defending Beveridge, not criticising Pascal. Even in his strongest statement, he does not attack Pascal directly:

the criticism levelled at him by Pascal is distorted. She quotes him too selectively.

By making '*the criticism . . . is distorted*' his main clause, he avoids stating directly that Pascal is responsible for the distortion. In fact all Pascal is responsible for is levelling criticism. At this point John is obviously finding fault with her, but he phrases it in an indirect way. From here on he continues to defend Beveridge, making him the main topic of the last paragraph in the extract.

This is an example of how a writer needs to be acutely aware of his own position in relation to other participants in academic writing, and tread a delicate path in order to present his own view in the face of potential opposition.

4.1.2   Style[2]

It is strange to think of the tutors who set assignments influencing John's choice of language. However in our discussions of these assignments we have identified two places where John was constrained by the way in which the task was worded. First, in the 'Welfare State' essay, sentence 1:

> In this paper I am going to show that the welfare state has and still does reinforce the 'traditional gender relationships'.

In this sentence Roz commented on the structure of '*the welfare state* has and still does reinforce the "traditional gender relationships"'. Here John has not written out the whole verb 'has reinforced', but has left out 'reinforced' because it is being repeated in the verb 'does reinforce' immediately after. This sort of omission[5] seems to be characteristic of written language, and very far from spoken language (according to Perera 1984). John says that he is led into constructions of this sort by attempting to link back to the title of an essay, something he has been told to do in his introductions. The way in which the title has been formulated by the tutor imposes a form of words on him, and he has to turn his ideas into words which will more or less link in with the tutor's. So here the style of the tutor's rubric is 'sucking him in' to a particular grammar. Here is exactly the same thing happening in the third sentence of the 'Adult Literacy' essay:

> I will use the experience and insight I gained from my placement to back up this statement and show that for adult basic education to be effective it must be totally client centred.

Here John had to use 'that for' to get back into the title. He had to wrestle with the words and grammar to sort out what he really meant, and he ended up with a long, complex sentence.

4.2 The people who wrote what John read

It would take up too much space to include here all the writers John encountered in his reading for the assignments: each has a bibliography of ten to fifteen books and articles. We will focus on the ones he drew into his own writing, either explicitly as part of the 'content', or generally as influences on his 'style'.

4.2.1 Content

Under this heading we include not just official 'course texts', but also other sources of ideas – for example, television programmes. We are focusing here on the way in which these authorities populate John's writing with their ideas. In this respect they become 'people he wrote about' and belong simultaneously to sub-heading 4.4. Sources can be paraphrased, summarised, or quoted.

John does not use paraphrase or summary. After reading and notemaking he puts notes aside, makes a 'flimsy plan', and writes from his head. He takes full responsibility for decisions he makes such as what to include in the argument, and what position to take. He recognises that these will have been influenced by the reading he did before writing, but he feels he is 'making them his own' by writing without direct reference to the sources. For example, in the 'Infanticide' essay John wrote:

> Pain is obviously just one of the criteria that makes the discussion of infanticide possible.

He may have learnt from the tutor, seminars or reading that the argument needs to go beyond the single issue of pain. However, John sees no need to credit this insight, as it is coming from his own head at the time of writing.

John does use quotations. While he is writing, and/or after he has finished he checks his notes and uses a quotation where it helps him to support or develop his argument. He believes that a quotation should always have a use: serve his needs as a writer. If a quotation does not work in this way then he believes this would make him merely a reporter of other people's ideas rather than responsible for creating his own argument.

In the 'Infanticide' essay John uses quotations to support his own argument, never to contrast with it. However, exactly who is brought into the essay by the quotation is different in each case.

(a) The opinion of the writer of the passage quoted:

> Since young children 'belong' to their parents, it is the parents who are the proper decision makers with regard to the treatment or non-treatment of severely defective newborns.

This is the view of H. Tristram and J. Englehart. They become important contributors to the essay by supporting John's own argument in favour of this view.

(b) The opinion of a published authority other than the writer of the passage quoted:

> McCormick insists, however, that the decision to allow an infant to die 'must be made in terms of the child's good and this alone'. That is he would exclude utilitarian considerations such as the emotional and financial burden of caring.

John quoted this from a book by A. Mappes and J. Zembaty, but it is not their view he was interested in. They distance themselves slightly from McCormick's view by introducing it with the speech representation verb 'insists that' but they are incidental to John's purposes. It is McCormick who counts as an authority in favour of the view John is presenting.

(c) The opinion of a judge involved in one of the legal cases which have been through the courts:

> Court Judge David G. Roberts ordered the surgery to be performed. He ruled 'At the moment of live birth there does exist a human being entitled to the fullest protection of the law. The most basic right enjoyed by every human being is the right to life.'

Again this is a quote within a quote, this time specific to essays which concern legal cases. John is appealing to authority to support his position, but this time the authority is not a published academic in the field, but a judge in a court. The writers of the passage quoted, A. Mappes and J. Zembaty again, are mere reporters.

(d) The opinion of parents involved in a case:

> Her parents refused their consent for the operation, because she had a mental handicap and no one could tell what her future life would be like; they believed that 'God or Nature had given the child a way out'.

Here A. Shearer, the writer of the book in which this passage appears, is scarcely present. Certainly John is not interested in his view. He is merely a reporter of information about the case, and useful in that he also reports, apparently verbatim, the view of the child's parents. Of course, he is not totally invisible: his language constructs the child's parents, presents as fact their refusal and their reason for it. Nevertheless, A. Shearer's identity is fairly peripheral to John's writing.

In the 'Adult Literacy' essay John uses five quotations. Two of these are short case studies of other students, quoted from Pugh, Volkman and Butterfield 1986, to contrast with the studies he had presented from his own placement. John's intention was to bring these other adult learners into his essay as 'characters' – people who are part of the content of the essay. However, he could not avoid importing Pugh, Volkman and Butterfield too. They invade John's essay with their choice of language – language John would never have used himself to describe adult learners: 'was an inadequate writer', 'presented a sad story', 'was totally illiterate'.

The other three quotations in the 'Adult Literacy' essay contain the findings of small-scale surveys and/or the opinions of the writers. In this particular essay John faced a dilemma as to whether or not to include quotations of the opinions of others. On the one hand, he is working within an institution and has to play their game. The unstated rules say that a student writer has to back up what he says with quotations from sources, to show that 'it's not just an opinion'. On the other hand, John is a far greater authority on what it feels like to be an adult basic education student than anyone who has published books or articles on the subject. 'Who feels it knows it', as the title of a book points out. John's solution was to play the game, but reluctantly. Here is how he brings an acknowledged authority on adult learning, Jennifer Rogers, into his essay:

> If any other provision is used, for example group provision or group centred learning, then problems arise in confidence and anxiety as Jennifer Rogers points out:
>
> > 'This was my first encounter with one of the most striking features of adult students, their anxiety that they might be making themselves look foolish, or that they might be exposing themselves to failure.'

In place of 'as Jennifer Rogers points out' John could have written 'as I know from my own experience'. Who has more authority? By the rules of the academic writing game Jennifer Rogers does, but we challenge the value system which produces such a nonsense.

In the 'Welfare State' essay John quotes mainly from Pascal and Beveridge, as we mentioned above. These writers enter much more robustly into the essay than anyone John quoted in the other two essays. Instead of appearing to back up John's views, they appear as combatants in a battle John has staged. They are the people John is writing about, also belonging to section 4.4 below, more than any of the writers quoted in the other assignments.

4.2.2   Style[2]

As we said in the introduction, John has consciously rejected the language of some of the sources he reads, consciously incorporated some of it in his own way of writing, and is no doubt unconsciously incorporating some now which he will eventually choose to reject. He is well aware that the way he writes now has been fashioned by his diverse language experiences throughout his life. Although there is no sharp dividing line between 'his language' and 'academic language', he senses a pressure to identify himself with the 'ego-I' conventions of academic writing: a pressure he wants to resist. Here we will take one sentence from each of our three sample essays to illustrate how John is making choices from a range of alternatives within academic writing, trying to find ones which are most in harmony with the identity he wants to convey.

An example of a convention John has encountered in his reading and adopted is the formulaic introduction. Here are sentences from the first paragraph of each of the three essays:

a) 'Infanticide' essay, sentence 3, following a definition of infanticide (see appendix A)

> In this paper I will show that infanticide is 'morally permissible' in some cases and indeed in other cases it is immoral not to practise it.

b) 'Adult literacy' essay, sentence 1

> In this paper I will show that adult literacy programmes can only really function in a beneficial way if they are totally client-centred.

c) 'Welfare State' essay, sentence 1

> In this paper I am going to show that the welfare state has and still does reinforce the 'traditional gender relationships'.

John thinks of the expression 'In this paper' as a very secure opening: a useful piece of terminology to get you going. You don't have to think about it: you can just step off. However, it is important to recognise an act of critical awareness in the choice of this particular phrase. Of the various options available, John has chosen to represent 'the paper' as the location, rather than the agent of the verb 'show'. This is because he is strongly committed to using the word 'I' in this opening sentence – saying to the reader: 'Remember it's ME.' (We'll write more about this in section 4.3.1.) An equally common opening to academic papers which John has chosen not to use is:

d) 'This paper will show that . . .'

This formulation suggests that the writing exists independent of the writer: a view of writing which John doesn't share.

In sentence (b) Roz drew attention to the expression 'function in a beneficial way' as a paraphrase for 'work well'. John finds that 'in a beneficial way' is a useful expression he'd like to identify with, meaning something more specific than 'well', whereas 'function' is an unnecessarily academic word he's absorbed; he'd prefer to use 'work'. This illustrates how easy it is to be 'sucked in' to ways with words which have social meaning but do not add anything to cognitive meaning. His choice of the phrase 'in a beneficial way' sets him up to use another Graeco-Roman word 'function' against his will.

4.3   John himself

John is committed to showing himself as an active participant in his writing, and does so in several ways. We have selected five, because we are able to exemplify them from the essays we discussed. However these are only illustrations, and not a comprehensive list of ways in which writers are participants in their own writing.

4.3.1   Using 'I'

John uses 'I' frequently, and for several distinct purposes. We will illustrate this from the 'Infanticide' essay. In 774 words of writing in the 'Infanticide' essay John used 'I' eleven times, for five different purposes.

a) He takes responsibility for his own beliefs

> If a child is born with a severe ailment, that needs surgery to extend its life, but by extending its life the child will have to continually suffer then I believe infanticide to be morally correct.

> I can see very little reason in such a case to make a child suffer for even two years.

This is certainly the most frequent use of 'I' in this extract. However, 'giving your opinion' is not the only place for being explicit about the existence of the writer. Here are four other uses of 'I' exemplified in the extract.

b) He tells the reader his own uncertainties:

> I am not able to give an instant answer to the second part of the question.

c) He states what he thinks the issues ought to be:

> I think the real question with Baby Jane Doe that should be asked is why was active infanticide not considered?

Of this John said that he doesn't know whether the tutor agrees with him: this is the result of his own reflection on the topic, not a regurgitation of an analysis he has gathered from elsewhere.

d) He takes responsibility for the definitions he's working with:

> Purely for the purpose of this paper I will class infanticide as the killing of a child that has been born.

e) He tells how he's going to structure the essay:

> In this paper I will show that infanticide is 'morally permissible' in some cases and indeed in other cases it is immoral not to practise it.

The use of 'I' is one way for the writer to have a presence in his writing. Another is that any statement of opinion or value judgement is understood to be the writer's opinion. John believes 'I' should be attached to as many of these as stylistically possible.

However, he doesn't always follow this principle. An example of a more impersonal wording is

> The central ethical concern in relation to infanticide, be it active or passive, would seem to return to: if 'medical expertise' is available, should it or should it not be applied?

4.3.2 Saying what he thinks

John resists the temptation and pressure to reproduce other people's ideas, unless he has made them his own, as we mentioned in section 4.2.1. He wants to present his own view, even if he knows it is controversial, or will be unpopular with his tutors, as our discussion of the extract from the 'Welfare State' essay in section 4.1 illustrates.

4.3.3 Drawing on his own experience

Like other mature students in our research group, John has life experience which is a relevant and valid source of wisdom and knowledge. Yet he knows that this is often dismissed as anecdotal and irrelevant: theory produced by recognised members of academic institutions, based – at best – on recognised research procedures, carries weight where life experience doesn't. In the Adult Literacy essay he did include insights and examples drawn from his own experience. John said:

> You can't get a better authority than me and I felt a lot needed to be

said about A.B.E. [adult basic education]. It was a deliberate policy to say what I wanted to say, but I was scared of handing it in.

For example, he wrote:

A client must be able to choose what they want to do and at what rate they want to do it. The only type of assessment that should take place is from the client and their tutor.

When student writers make value judgements of this sort, with 'must' and 'should' in them, tutors often demand evidence and justification. John felt that he had the authority to state such views on the grounds of experience. Possibly they were accepted because the tutors recognised this authority; possibly because they happened to concur with the tutors' views anyway.

He also mentioned sensitive issues:

Basic Education is exactly what it says it is, teaching people the basics.

problems arise in confidence and anxiety

These two extracts represent John's own painful experience, although he didn't make this explicit by writing 'and this is how it was for me'. When we discussed this we realised that writers might often write something that has burning personal significance which is not apparent to the reader. Academic writing usually discourages people from identifying and exploring personal experiences which they feel strongly about – as if it's better if it doesn't matter.

4.3.4   Choosing what to refer to

In choosing which sources to mention John saw it as an act of identity to mention Christian Scientists in the 'Infanticide' assignment. The information comes from a television programme, not from any of the sources recommended by the course tutor. However, John doesn't credit the makers of the television programme as his source, so they are invisible contributors to his writing.

In the 'Welfare State' essay the tutors had recommended one source, the book by Pascal mentioned above. However, at one stage Pascal criticises the Beveridge Report on Social Insurance and Allied Services (1942) which was the policy document leading to the founding of the welfare state. John made his own decision to find out exactly what Beveridge wrote, and bring Beveridge himself into his essay to stand up against Pascal's criticism. (We discussed this in detail in section 4.1.1.)

4.3.5 Using his own style[2]

John never wants anyone to say anything for him: that would be cheating. It is very difficult to identify his own style and separate it from other influences. As we said in the introduction, the way everyone writes is both unique and borrowed: a personal selection from the words and structures they have encountered throughout their lives. Here is a short extract from the Adult Literacy essay which illustrates how John is evolving his own academic writing style, bringing together features he has adopted from different sources.

> It occurred to me ~~their and then~~ that what Brian needed was for the interest and motivation he showed about motorbikes to be transferred into the lesson involving spelling. Brian did not know what he wanted to do. He was on ET "just for something to do". I believe it is only by keying into a persons' needs and interests that adult education can work at all and Brian seems to exemplify this point.

One feature of style John has consciously adopted is using 'I', as we described in section 4.3.1. 'keying in' is a metaphor which he feels vividly expresses what he wants to say. 'exemplify' is a word a friend used recently which John finds serves his purpose. He crossed out 'there and then' because it didn't seem to fit – perhaps because it belongs to a different style[2]: fiction or autobiography. When asked about the phrase 'can work at all' John said 'That's me': it comes from language he has chosen to identify with, not an academic style which has been forced upon him. Some of the clauses are short; some have human subjects: these are characteristics of spoken language. He rounds off an example from his case study with a generalisation (I believe . . .): this is a technique he has noticed in academic writing.

We would like to be writing about particular characteristics of speech which John is consciously preserving in his writing, but he doesn't feel in control enough to do that yet[6]. John feels that he is still a long way away from writing as he would like to write, but using the word 'I' is a step in the right direction:

> In academic writing I can never express myself with the power that I can verbally. But because I find it such a struggle to write then it obviously means that some of the force, the rawness and the gut feelings can't come through because I have to concentrate on presenting it in a certain way. The rules do stop me: there are accepted ways. I've got to phrase things as required, and quote. I can say that I had to play by their rules but that 'I' is always there. Provided the 'I' is there I don't feel I'm sucked in.

4.4   The people John writes about

John writes about people who hold particular beliefs. In most cases these are the writers of books and articles he read: we have written about them in section 4.2.

Social sciences are special among academic disciplines in that they are about not only what people think, but also about people's lives. Although we are not exploring this issue here, it is an important one to keep on the agenda.

4.5   The people who read what John writes

The readers of these three essays were the tutors who had set them. We have already written about some of the ways that they influenced John's writing in section 4.1. Here we will focus on how John reacted to the fact that they were going to read and assess what he wrote. When he handed in all three essays he was nervous about how they would be received. In the 'Welfare State' essay the tutors as assessors were uppermost in John's mind while he was writing about the Pascal/Beveridge issue.

In the 'Adult Literacy' essay John felt uncertain about what was expected of him, as we mentioned in section 4.1. He also had a deliberate policy of drawing on his own experience and saying what he believed as a result of it. He said: 'I wanted people to be assaulted by it and pushed that little bit'. However, he was scared about handing it in because he thought he might have gone too far and jeopardised his chances of a good assessment. John expected the response, 'That's OK but it's not what we want.' It greatly reassured him and restored his faith in the academic endeavour when he received such a good mark.

In the 'Infanticide' essay he felt that he was writing the essay as part of the academic game, and that the tutors would be assessing how well he could display what he had learnt from reading. The comment on the end of the paper was:

> Some interesting ideas here – a difficult subject tackled well. You might however want to check whether or not you really are *developing* ideas as opposed to simply presenting them.

What motivation is there to a student writer to develop ideas when he's positioned as someone displaying knowledge rather than someone making a contribution to it?

5 Critical awareness of who's who in academic writing

We've written about things we have become acutely critically aware of: the way in which people populate what John reads and writes, and especially the fact that he himself is a part of the cast. In this section we will first explain why we consider our work to be an example of critical language awareness. Then we will describe the benefits of this work to each of us, and how we think other student writers and researchers can reap the same benefits.

The discussions we have about John's writing, including the ones which led to the writing of this article, are critical language study: they raise our critical language awareness. Our way of studying language is 'critical' in the sense that we are not studying just the 'proper', 'correct' or 'appropriate' way of writing. We are looking at ways in which the standardised conventions of academic writing often leave people out. A lot of academic writing is impersonal: it doesn't appear to be about people, and it excludes readers and writers who aren't familiar with it. We are interested in challenging this by making the writer's responsibilities and rights more explicit, and by recognising that the type of language a person is using is a part of them.

Our critical language awareness-raising discussions have two valuable outcomes. First, they are providing us both with insights about language and language learning, some of which are contained in this article. Second, they are simultaneously contributing to our development as writers: more directly for John, since we are discussing his writing, but indirectly for Roz too.

We believe that critical language study of the sort we have done together could and should be part of all language learners' development. We had the advantage of working as a pair in our own time, but the same issues could be raised in class discussion. We think this is particularly valuable for adults returning to study, but it could be relevant to language learners of any age. Here are two suggestions as to how work like ours could be done in larger groups.

Any group of learners could list the people in their writing. If they don't think of mentioning themselves as writers and their teachers as readers, the teacher could add them. Class discussion could then focus on different ways of representing yourself as writer – something which is rarely mentioned in traditional approaches to learning to write.

Learner-writers can read each others' writing or published writing, and build up their own picture of the writer on the evidence they have in the text. They can list the evidence they have used for building this picture, thereby developing a critical awareness of the way in which language positions its writers as well as its readers. They can discuss how they respond to that sort of person: whether that is the sort of identity they would like to present for themselves as writers.

6.   Conclusion

Throughout this chapter we have examined the roles people play in academic writing, focusing on the writer's responsibilities and rights. Ideas are the responsibility of the writer. They are important because they are precious things that need to be shared. Through our work together we have found that using the 'I' in academic writing brings ideas out. This makes the writing clearer for the reader. Readers of academic writing have the right to understand and enjoy what they read. Writers of academic writing have the right to do more than just using the recommended sources to regurgitate standard ideas in the standard patter. Writers have the right to express what they think and feel.

We hope the illustrations of how we use the 'I' in essays will be able to guide you as a writer into a type of writing that has part of yourself in it. We can't guarantee that 'I-essays' will get good marks, because marks are an issue in themselves. The only thing we can say is that if you put the 'I' into your writing, it will definitely have you in there and no matter what anyone else thinks, that YOU is important.

Dedication

for Hannah

Acknowledgements

The ideas in this chapter are part of continuing discussions in our group and belong also to Chris Benson, Romy Clark, Angela Karach and Denise Roach, among others. We are grateful also to Norman Fairclough and Mary Talbot for their helpful comments.

Notes

1. 'pat-a-cake' is a playground game in which children throw a ball backwards and forwards as they sing a rhyme.
2. We are using the word 'style' because we hope it is easy to understand for all readers. As a linguist Roz would prefer to use the term 'register' or 'discourse conventions'.
3. This idea has been developed by Mary Talbot (1990). She uses the term 'text populations' to talk about the characters in discourse. The same idea is often called the 'subject positioning' of writers and readers, as in some other chapters of this book.
4. Brooke (1988) discusses imitation as a process of identifying with a writer rather than copying a style. We agree with the way Brookes defines imitation, but take a critical view of it.
5. 'ellipsis' in linguistic terms.
6. These issues are discussed in more detail in Ivanič and Roach (1990).

References

Brooke R 1988 Modelling a writer's identity: reading and imitation in the writing classroom. *College Composition and Communication* 39 (1).

Ivanič R and Roach D 1990 Academic writing, power and disguise. In Fairclough N et al. (eds) *Language and power: proceedings of the BAAL conference*. CILT

Perera K 1984 *Children's writing and reading: analysing classroom language*. Blackwell

Progressive Literacy Group 1986 *Writing on our side* Progressive Literacy Group, Vancouver, BC

Talbot M 1990 Intertextuality and text population. Unpublished ms.

Wells G 1987 *The meaning makers*. Hodder & Stoughton

Works quoted in relation to John's studies

Beveridge W 1942 *Report on social insurance and allied services*. HMSO

Mappes A and Zembaty J 1981 *Biomedical ethics*. Random House

Pascal, G 1986 *Social policy – A feminist analysis*. Tavistock

Pugh A K Volkman C and Butterfield C 1986 *Aspects of adult literacy*. The Goethe Institute

Rogers J 1973 *Adults learning*. Penguin

Shearer A 1984 *Everybody's ethics*. The Campaign for Mentally Handicapped People

Tristram H and Englehart J 1981 Law and morality in cases of infanticide. In Mappes and Zembaty (eds)

Weston D 1985 *Self and society: narcissism, collectivism, and the development of morals*. Cambridge University Press

Appendix

The section of the 'Welfare State' essay in which John criticises Pascal for misrepresenting Beveridge.

In Beveridge's defence it is only fair to point out that he could not have possibly been foresighted enough to have conceived such developments as the pill, abortion and the strength of the women's movement. He did look at women's issues but within a traditional framework. Beveridge did see how important they were and he also allowed for some change as this excerpt illustrates:

> Taken as a whole the plan for social security puts a premium on marriage, in place of penalising it. The position of housewife is

recognised in form and in substance. It is recognised by treating them not as dependants of their husband, but as partners sharing benefit and pension when there are no earnings to share.

(Beveridge 1942)

Beveridge may have seen women in the typical gender role within the family but the criticism levelled at him by Gillian Pascal is distorted. She quotes him too selectively. For example:

In the next thirty years housewives as mothers have vital work to do in ensuring the adequate continuance of the British race and of British ideas.

(Beveridge 1942)

She has used the last sentence from the paragraph I have just quoted. Even though I have not quoted the paragraph in full my quotation illustrates Beveridge's wider considerations while Pascal's quote shows him to be narrow. Beveridge did try to look forward and he did try to implement financial support for women. It may seem that he did nothing 'more that reinforce the traditional gender relationships' of man and wife, but how could he have seen the changes of the last 50 years?

One way of looking at social policy would be to describe it as a set of structures created by men to shape the lives of women.

(Pascal 1986)

Beveridge could not have got the social policy of the welfare state right in one go. We now have had 50 years to make the welfare state understanding and flexible in its attitude towards gender.

7 · The construction of gender in a teenage magazine

Mary Talbot

Looking at language critically is a way of 'denaturalising' it – questioning and 'making strange' conventions which usually seem perfectly natural to people who use them. It can help make people more sensitive to language, more aware of the sociolinguistic worlds they inhabit, and more critical of them. This can help to 'empower' people, in the sense of giving them greater conscious control over aspects of their lives. One thing people can become more aware of in this process is how language shapes or 'constructs' them as particular sorts of social subjects, affecting various aspects of their social identities, including their gender identities – their identities as women or men. In this chapter I focus in particular on the construction of femininity through language – on how language helps construct women as 'feminine'.

What I am going to do is propose and demonstrate a way of examining mass media texts that cater for teenagers' interests. My specific purpose is to show how femininity is constructed for them. Taking one sample text from *Jackie*, a magazine for teenage girls, I examine it as a 'population' of real and imaginary characters into which the reader is drawn. On the basis of this analysis, I suggest a set of questions that can be used to stimulate critical awareness of how mass media texts construct social identity. But before launching into this, I must first of all spell out how it is that written mass media texts construct social identities for readers. I must also explain the notion of 'text population', which is what I use to examine who we 'associate with' through the mass media.

I will then suggest a range of features to focus on for drawing out this population and explain my choice of data.

The construction of readers

In reading a written text, we engage in interaction. Written discourse is a relatively passive and one-way process, in comparison with, say, interaction face-to-face or over the telephone. It is nevertheless an interactive process, establishing addressers and addressees. Unlike face-to-face interaction, it may be far from clear who these participants are. In producing discourse, an addresser always speaks from a social position; she necessarily establishes a social identity for herself and at the same time some relationship with her addressee. In mass media discourse, the positions available for interactants are not interchangeable: the reader cannot become the copywriter (any say she has in what goes into the magazine, through the post bag, is mediated on the publishers' terms). Interaction in mass media discourse is one-sided and there is a great distance between producer and interpreter. The *Jackie* writer is an entertainer who provides information and advice of which the reader is beneficiary. The writer doesn't know the actual social identities of her readers and since she cannot observe them, she cannot monitor their individual responses. She has to construct an imaginary addressee. A reader is synthesised.

There is an increasingly common feature of types of discourse used to address mass audiences which Fairclough (1989) has called 'synthetic personalisation'. He describes it as 'a compensatory tendency to give the impression of treating each of the people 'handled' en masse as an individual' (p. 62). This synthetic personalisation is extremely common in the mass media: in magazine articles and advertisements, in junk mail, etc. It involves the construction of an imaginary subject as if she were an actual individual and also the construction of a persona for the producers. Consider for example, how advertising addresses millions of identical *you*s. The construction of an identity for one of these imaginary *you*s is not just a shot in the dark. Advertisers have market research behind them to help them construct an imaginary addressee with a specific set of interests, attitudes, likes and dislikes. Moreover, modern advertising offers potential consumers membership of imaginary communities based on consumption, as much as offering actual commodities for consumption: i.e. buy this and you will become a certain kind of person, buy this and be one of us. All we have to do to belong to these communities is buy and consume.[1]

In taking up places in interaction through the mass media, readers are constructed by producers. Writers make informed guesses about the targeted audience of a particular publication. As actual readers, we have to negotiate with the position of the reader synthesised. Whether we accept this position depends very much on who we are. It is far easier for someone outside a targeted readership to contest the kinds of attitudes and preoccupations that the reader synthesised is given. A male adult reading *Jackie*, for instance, is unlikely to fit comfortably into the position of the reader constructed. He would have no difficulty in contesting the writer's notions of who he is and what interests him. For example, presupposed ideas attributed to the reader, such as the one carried in a text opening with the words: 'When you're trying your hardest to impress that hunk in the sixth form . . .', would fall on stony ground indeed. A 13 year-old girl on the brink of adulthood, on the other hand, might have the impression that trying to impress hunks in the sixth form is one of the things she *should* be doing! I won't go into this further here, but refer the reader to Chapter 13 which examines the effect of addressee's subject position on interpretation in some detail.

Test population

What I intend to do is look at some of the 'population' of a two-page feature. But I will not be looking at the text in a traditional way as the product of a single author containing a clearly defined cast of characters or *dramatis personae*. Instead I will examine it as a 'tissue of voices', a mesh of intersecting voices of characters inhabiting a text. The writer and reader interacting through the text are part of the population I investigate. As readers we can ask, 'Who is speaking to me? What identity does she set up for herself in different segments of the text?' and 'What sort of identity does she set up for me, i.e. who does she think I am?'

With this view of a text, we can examine a text's population by looking for traces of people addressing one another, traces of characters' words or thoughts and traces of different kinds of conventional 'voice' used by a character. For convenience in presenting the features to focus on below, I have found it helpful to divide the 'population of characters' into three categories: interactants, characters, and subject positions. This will enable us to distinguish between three elements of a text population:

(1) *Interactants* are people addressing one another. In the case of a written text, the reader participates passively, but the writer may simulate direct face-to-face interaction with the reader. Writer and reader are not the only interactants possible in written discourse, however. The writer may simulate interaction between characters in her text. These are interactants too.

(2) *Characters* are people, whether real or imaginary, whose words or thoughts are represented in a text. These words or thoughts may be embedded in a text by being quoted, reported or simply presupposed.

(3) *Subject positions* provide people with conventional kinds of 'voice' with which to address one another. A writer may address a reader from a range of subject positions. Her identity is not the same at every point in a text; she may even contradict herself. Corresponding subject positions are set up for the reader.

We must bear in mind, however, that members of a text population do not obligingly slot into just one of these boxes: after all, one character given lines to say inside a text may be established as an interactant with another. The reader may be established as a character in a text, as well as a passive interactant with the writer. She may, for example, be given actual lines in a dialogue, as in the opening sentence of the column in the sample pages: 'Ask any clever advertiser how to suggest femininity with a product, and he'll probably tell you "a kissprint".'

Some features to focus on

The way of examining the text that I propose involves focusing on features contributing to setting up a text population. I present a range of suggested features to attend to under the headings of *interactants*, *characters* and *subject* positions.

Interactants

Features we can attend to in order to determine what kinds of exchange are taking place between interactants are speech functions and adjacency pairs. Basic speech functions are statements, offers, commands and questions; these establish addressers in the roles of giver of information, questioner, etc. Adjacency pairs are kinds of utterance that occur in pairs and contribute to the orderly organisation of talk; e.g. an addresser's question 'expects' an addressee's answer, offers 'expect' acceptances (or refusals) etc. A mass media writer's use of response-demanding utterances addressed to the reader contributes to the simulation of a reciprocal, two-way discourse between producer and audience. The writer may also use adjacency pairs – response-demanding utterances and responses – in her representations of interaction between characters in her text.

Characters

Perhaps the most explicit cues to characters are visual ones: the photographs. Other than this, we may be able to spot the words of characters because they are marked off by speech marks, and/or cued by a verbal or mental process verb (e.g. *saying, asking; thinking, wishing*). In other words, they may be quoted or reported. As well as cuing a character's words, reporting verbs may tell us something about the reporter's implied viewpoint (e.g. in using the reporting verb *claim*, she is dissociating herself from what she reports). The attitude taken up by the reporter is part of her identity.

Reportage can be said to conjure up characters from thin air. The characters, whether real or imaginary, are created by the writer. They are usually people of course, but they can also be inanimate objects. When an inanimate object is the grammatical subject of a verbal or mental process verb it is created as a character through a process of 'grammatical metaphor' (possible examples are: 'My watch *says* it's half past ten' and 'This pickle doesn't *want* to come out of the jar').[2]

Sometimes the writer may state a character's likes and dislikes quite straightforwardly; particular mental process verbs to look out for are *like, prefer* and similar terms indicating choice or preference. There may be other less explicit traces of people's thoughts in sentences containing 'fact' nouns (e.g. the *fact* that . . ., the *superstition* that . . ., the *way* that . . .).[3] Other potential clues to the presence of characters' thoughts may be where one clause appears to contain some kind of reason or motivation (e.g. *because . . ., (in order) to . . .*). These 'giving of reasons' postulate a source (in other words, they must come from somewhere) but in a rather less explicit way than quotation or other reportage.

Presuppositions may be set up as taken-for-granted ideas in characters' heads. These presupposed ideas may be cued by a wide range of presupposition 'triggers'. For example, '*when* did you *stop* biting your nails?' which presupposes that 'you used to bite your nails'; 'do you want *your* coffee *before* you wash up?' which presupposes 'you have some coffee' and 'you are going to wash up'; '*the* trouble with girls is they're soft', which presupposes 'there is something wrong with girls'. I suggest that careful selection of examples relating to girls' experience can bring to their attention what presupposed ideas are being placed in their heads.

Subject positions

The subject positions I attend to below are set up specifically by magazines. We also need to bear in mind that social identities are bestowed on writers and readers at a more general level: they are children or adults, female or male, working-class or middle-class, schoolchildren, employees, daughters, sisters, etc. People take up constellations of subject positions.

Magazines contain a repertoire of activities and topics for entertaining and instructing readers. They involve participants in recognisable activities with expected purposes and topics. Conventional kinds of topic and activity, such as narrating a history of lipstick or giving instructions on how to use it, assign subject positions to the people involved. In a narrative the writer, obviously, has the 'voice' of a narrator. In giving instructions she has the 'voice' of a facilitator. In each case the reader takes up the corresponding position of the recipient.

Certain kinds of feature proliferate in the mass media which contribute to synthetic personalisation and establishing an informal friendly relationship between the producers of mass media texts and their audience. We have seen some of these already; the response-demanding utterances introduced under Interactants above contribute to the simulation of friendly face-to-face encounters in one-way discourse in the mass media. Here I outline other elements which contribute to the synthesis of friendly personae for the writer and like-minded reader.

There are various strategies a writer can use to establish a friendly relationship with a mass audience. She can do this by claiming common ground (e.g. in reports or presupposed ideas attributable to both writer and reader), by 'speaking the same language' and by showing that she knows what the reader is like, what she thinks (e.g. in presupposed ideas attributable to the reader). The use of informal words contributes to setting up a friendly 'chatty' relationship with the reader (examples of these in *Jackie* are 'choccy', 'dosh', 'vids'). At the other extreme is the formality of the small print (in the sample pages – see the Appendix – 'kind courtesy' in the 'facts and figures' section is a clear example of this). We can look at vocabulary to help us to decide whether the editorial is 'speaking the same language' as her targeted readership or in some other persona.

In examining the relationship established between writer and reader in mass media texts, something else to look at is the writer's use of the pronouns *we* and *you*. In the mass media, the pronoun *you* is often used in direct address to the reader. I referred to its common occurrence in advertising in my preliminary discussion of the construction of readers above. The pronoun *we* may be used 'exclusively' (the 'editorial we'), or 'inclusively' to refer to producer and interpreter together. In using the 'exclusive' *we* mass media producers identify themselves as an editorial team. In using the 'inclusive' *we*, the editorial includes the audience in this group and makes an implicit claim to the right to speak on its behalf.

Choice of data

The magazine *Jackie* is part of teenage girls' initiation into feminine womanhood: it teaches young people all kinds of things about how to be appropriately feminine adult women in modern consumerist society. *Jackie* has been critically examined by a few people in the academic world. These have chiefly been researchers and students in cultural studies, who have tended to focus on the romance fiction element it regularly contains. An exception to this is the first work done on *Jackie*. This is McRobbie's '*Jackie*: an ideology of adolescent femininity' (McRobbie 1978). One observation she makes is that the publication presents its teenage readers with 'a *false* sisterhood'. I will look for evidence of this sisterliness in the sample of data in the Appendix for this chapter (pp. 197–9). The sample I have chosen is a consumer feature: a combination of editorial material and advertising which has been around in women's magazines since the late 1930s.

There are advantages in using such data with CLA programmes. Learners' own light reading is tailored for them, already familiar ground for them and relevant to their own experience. They are the targeted readership, proficient in the language variety or varieties used. This has two consequences. On the one hand, this makes them the experts, on their own ground. On the other hand, the social identities and relationships bestowed upon them are likely to appear obvious or 'natural'. In the case of advertising-related texts, the kinds of gendered identity constructed for us centre on patterns of consumption. This is so ordinary, so much a part of everyday life, that most of the time we are scarcely aware of it.

The consumer feature I have chosen is a 'beauty feature'. It tells readers about lipstick, including how to put it on, and even provides a symbol for femininity: the 'kissprint'. The two-page feature contains various elements; a column of text covering an assortment of topics relating to lipstick (reproduced on p. 197 and the first paragraph of p. 198, and referred to below as 'the column'), testimonials from ordinary lipstick wearers, 'lip tricks', a do-it-yourself (DIY) element on how to apply lipstick, a 'facts and figures' section giving a selection of marketing details and a history of lipstick illustrated with pictures of media 'personalities'. This feature offers readers entertainment in the form of information and advice about a single commodity. As McRobbie says, the editorial is bestowing 'useful feminine knowledge' as an older sister might do, as part of their 'feminine education'. The article is reproduced in the appendix at the end of this chapter without the photographs and the proliferation of 'kissprints' which adorned the segments of written text when they appeared in *Jackie* magazine.

Sample analysis: the population of a consumer feature

The purpose of examining the population of a mass media text is to see who the audience is 'associating with' in reading it. I divide the analysis of the 'beauty feature' into two general areas, using the range of features introduced above to pick out the interactants, characters and subject positions forming the text population of each area. I focus first on the community of lipstick-wearers. In doing this, I will also refer to various personae taken on by the editorial: interviewer, historian, etc. Then I consider what kind of producer and interpreter are set up in the consumer feature and what kind of relationship is constructed between them. This begins with an assessment of the writer's social identity, with particular attention to her subject position of editorial-as-friend. This subject position is of particular significance because the writer's identity as a friend is tied up in her construction of the reader.

A community of lipstick wearers

The testimonials section provides the most explicit cues to characters in the beauty feature; namely, four snapshots captioned with names and ages and four texts marked off with speech marks. Four individuals are quoted by the editorial-as-interviewer. In her interaction with the reader, the editorial indicates that she is quoting prior discourse by other people. Presumably actual interviews took place at some time, and constitute the historical context of this section of the beauty feature. Whether or not actual interviews did take place, the interviewees have been constructed both as interactants (with an interviewer) and as characters – they are set up textually for the reader.

The speech functions are mostly statements, but there is one command ('wait!', in Clara's testimonial) and one question ('My first lipstick?' in Rhona's). Rhona's question can be seen as an element of two adjacency pairs. It is identifiable as the first part of a question–answer pair. The next sentence is the answer and completes the exchange:

Question: My first lipstick?
Answer: I stole it from my sister's drawer.

In other words she answers her own question. Her question can also be interpreted as a rhetorical strategy for responding to a question from the interviewer, an utterance which has not appeared on the page:

Question: [When did you get your first lipstick?]

Answer: My first lipstick? I stole it from my sister's drawer – I
was about 12.

I take the statements to be the interviewees' responses to
questions which would, on the basis of the first interviewee's
answers, have been something like: 'How often do you wear
lipstick?' 'What's your favourite shade?' 'When did you get your
first one?' The interviewees' supposed 'own words' are structured
by the interests of the editorial-as-interviewer, who has set the
agenda.

The girls are strongly foregrounded. As an interactant, the
interviewer is present only as a shadow cast by questions. The
quoted texts contain self-reports by the interviewees, constructed
of course by the writer. Mental process verbs proliferate: e.g. 'I
like pinks and deep reds' (Rhona); 'I *don't know* if I can *remember*
my first lipstick!' (Clara)). (The italics used in quoting from the
sample are mine.) The writer establishes these people as characters
with feelings and attitudes towards things. So what are the social
identities of these people, Margaret, Emily, Clara and Rhona, and
what kind of relationship are they involved in with their addressee?

Most of the presupposed ideas presented as givens are biographical details. The presupposed idea 'I had a first lipstick' is
in three of the four interviewees' texts (Margaret, Clara, Rhona).
They are all responding to the same questions in interaction with
the interviewer. Here we need to suppose that the presupposed
'first lipstick' they attribute to themselves in each testimonial
was preceded by a presupposed 'first lipstick' the interviewer has
already attributed to them in her question. Another 'attributive'
presupposition is in Margaret's text. In saying 'My favourite shade's
a sort of brown-and-red mixture', Margaret is presupposing 'I
have a favourite shade'. Other presupposed ideas are cued by
when-clauses. Clara's 'when I was wearing it ["Choosy Cherry"]'
presupposes 'I used to wear it'. These presupposed ideas concerning
the possession and use of a commodity are given the same
commonsensical status as other kinds of biographical detail also
established in presuppositions, which really are shared by everyone.
Or one of them at least; namely, Emily's 'my mum gave me a bright
red lipstick to play with', which presupposes that she had a mother.
Another is Margaret's 'when I was ten', which presupposes that
she was once ten. Another biographical detail is presupposed in

12 year-old Emily's opening words: that she habitually goes out.

The self-reports and presupposed ideas of these individuals establish the normality of lipstick use, of being a habitual consumer and having developed preferences, of being an early starter, of first lipsticks being memorable, and of having decided upon a favourite shade. The testimonials construct a bunch of people with shared 'newsworthy' experiences about their lipstick use. The reports and presuppositions establish common ground. The writer constructs characters who share biographical details in terms of consumption with the editorial-as-interviewer and the reader. The testimonials from consumers contribute to the establishment of a lipstick-using community; a community in which having a mother and having a lipstick are set up as the same kind of thing, in which a first lipstick is something universal and memorable in women's lives and to be shared with other women. This is not an actual community but an advertising construction; the consumption of a commodity is all that is needed to become a member of it.

There are other characters inhabiting the interviewees' lipstick-centred world. Some of these are reported: the 'everyone' in Clara's section, for example, who responded to the first lipstick she wore (cued by the reporting verb *ask*):

It was called 'Choosy Cherry' by Mary Quant – everyone used to *ask* me if I was ill when I was wearing it!

Two other people (who do not get a word in) are Emily's mum as the provider of lipstick and Margaret's anonymous lipstick donor.

The lipstick wearers in the testimonials are the only characters quoted by the writer, but the feature contains other characters, some of whom are also lipstick wearers (lipstick producers and advertisers are other people in the text I turn to later). There are six professional studio photographs of media 'personalities' in the illustrated history on the right, which introduce six more lipstick wearers. These studio photographs are uncaptioned but the film stars' names appear in the text. Although these women are visually prominent, they are not quoted. Their actions, thoughts and motivations are represented, but as part of the writer's own knowledge: information which she is imparting for the reader's enjoyment. The thoughts and motives attributed to them relate to the wearing of lipstick.

According to the second paragraph, female film stars of the 1940s wore lipstick for purely personal reasons:

> By the 1940s, female film stars wore their lippy *to reflect their own characters*.

In the same paragraph, the editorial-as-historian reports the thought processes of two characters best known for screen roles in the 1940s, Bette Davis and Joan Crawford: 'Bette Davis and Joan Crawford *preferred* the wide-mouthed "stiff upper lip" look'. Another possible candidate in the same paragraph is Jean Harlow, who '*went for* absolute kissability' (whatever that may be). However, the photographs of these characters are the work of a studio. They are not snapshots, as the photographs of the interviewees are in the testimonials. The styles of appearance or 'looks' displayed in the illustrated history are products of huge amounts of professional activity. These 'looks' are not personal preference but big business.

Similarly, in the column of text below, changes and variations in lipstick 'looks' are accounted for in terms of personal preferences in 'self-expression' through appearance:

> dark colours and the style of 'drawing' on little pursed lips meant that women looked cutesy and doll-like. Later on, in the forties, film stars *wanting* to look 'little-girl'ish continued this, while the newer breed of dominant women *opted* for a bolder look, colouring right over the natural 'bow' in the lips.

Other lipstick wearers are 'most girls in the 60's', at the end of the same paragraph, who '*concentrated* on over-the-top-eye-make-up and face painting'.

A lipstick-wearing character who is not so easy to spot in the column is 'a woman' in sentence two who is set up in some kind of clichéd scenario about marital infidelities (leaving traces of lipstick on men's collars, etc.):

> Lipstick on a collar, a glass, his cheek – they all suggest a woman was there.

This sentence contains a grammatical metaphor. It is the smudges of lipstick that are presented as the 'speaking' characters, not the woman herself, whose presence they 'speak' about: the grammatical subject of the verbal process verb suggest is 'Lipstick on a collar, a glass, his cheek – they all'. These eloquent smudges signify (presumably to everybody) not just the presence of a woman, but some amorous relationship with a man. The connection between lipstick and kissing is made in other parts of the feature; notably in the 'kissprint' itself. This connection is made again in the last sentence of the column, in the copywriter's description of the pleasurable role of consumer:

> And with some companies churning out batches of lipstick at a rate of 9,000 an hour, that's an awful lot of kisses to get through!

The connection is also made in the 'facts and figures' section, at the end of the first segment, in the alternative wording of lipstick as 'coloured kisses'.

I will look at one more group of 'users', some early lipstick-wearing 'ladies' in paragraphs two and three of the column, and then turn to the people I need to say most about: writer and reader. In the writer's capacity as lipstick historian, she does not quote the early users' supposed own words, but reports their motivations:

> Before the days of lipstick as we know it, ladies used vegetable or animal dyes like cochineal – beetle's blood – *to colour their lips.*
>   The reason behind it wasn't simply *to make themselves more beautiful* – superstition lingered that the devil could enter the body through the mouth, and *since red was meant to ward off evil spirits* 'lipstick' was put around the mouth *to ward off his evil intentions!*

In this extract, the writer presents us with the motivations behind ladies' use of dyes in antiquity. They used them in order '*to* colour their lips', but not simply in order '*to* make themselves more beautiful'; '*since* red was meant to ward off evil spirits', they used them in order '*to* ward off his [the devil's] evil intentions!' The word *superstition* is a 'fact' noun; it cues a reported belief that the reporter does not go along with, that 'the devil could enter the body through the mouth'. There are other characters in this extract whose beliefs and motivations are not reported, namely evil spirits and the devil; these are hostile entities, and apparently male ('*his* evil intentions!').

Writer and Reader

Other members of the text population are writer and reader. So what kind of producer and interpreter are set up in the beauty feature and what kind of relationship is constructed between them? Starting with the writer, there are many ways in which a social identity is set up for her. She is constructed as a person with feelings and with attitudes towards things. Starting with a straightforward example of her choice of vocabulary, we know that she is no feminist, because she uses the pejorative abbreviation 'Women's lib' for the Women's Liberation Movement. Other examples require rather more elaboration. For instance, a writer's non-alignment with what a reportee says (the way she distances herself from the reported statement of another) presents her as someone with an implied viewpoint. This can be seen in the column, paragraphs four and five, where the producer distances herself from the projected statements of the experts, both 'Experts in human behaviour' and 'Other "experts"' who we can call folk-psychologists:

> These days there are more complicated (and ruder!) theories. Experts in human behaviour *say* that it's all to do with sex (what else?!).
> Other 'experts' *claim* that the shape of your lipstick can reveal a lot about your character – i.e. if you wear the end flat you're stubborn, if it's round and blunt you're fun-loving, etc., etc. – but don't seem to take into consideration the fact that each brand of lipstick is a different shape to start with and it's easiest just to use it accordingly. So much for the experts!

Notice how the writer responds to the words of the characters she has created. Her response to the statement of the 'Experts in human behaviour' is ambiguous; is she endorsing it or ridiculing it? With the 'Other "experts"' she expands on their words ('i.e. . . .') and comments unfavourably ('but . . .'), then dismisses both kinds of 'expert' in psychology on the basis of this comment. Exclamation marks very often attribute to the writer some kind of friendly, enthusiastic emotional state; here, I think they also contribute to establishing her distance from scientific, and even pseudo-scientific, statements.

She begins the next paragraph by presupposing that what preceded it was not interesting. This presupposition is cued by an emphatic assertion: 'What *is* interesting is . . .'. The new topic,

changes in lipstick use in terms of fashion, is introduced as part
of the shared common sense of *Jackie* by means of the 'fact' noun
way:

> What *is* interesting is the *way* that fashions have changed over the
> years. (*is* has italics in the original)

All in all, the ancient history and psychology why and how type
of consideration comes over as pretty silly.

What is worth knowing relates to consumer fashion. Contrast
the challenge to intellectualism in the column with the respect
for companies in the 'facts and figures' section (in the formulaic
expression: 'by kind courtesy') and the respect for advertisers in
the first sentence of the column. In the opening sentence of the
column, we can see the reader being set up as a character and
interactant in hypothetical interaction with an advertiser and
some anonymous interpreter of symbols. We can pinpoint this
hypothetical interaction by picking out the verbal process verbs:

> *Ask* any clever advertiser how to *suggest* femininity with a product,
> and he'll probably *tell* you 'a kissprint'.

Notice that the hypothetical response '"a kissprint"' is attributed
to 'any *clever* advertiser'. The writer is implicitly classifying
advertisers: 'clever' ones are those whose response to the reader's
question would be the one the writer proposes. Of course, the whole
imaginary dialogue into which the reader is drawn is constructed
by the writer in the first place. In constructing this dialogue, the
writer is asserting knowledge of advertisers' likely approach to
marketing products for female consumers. (Advertisers themselves
are assumed to be male.) So the writer is someone who associates
with, and has great respect for, admen. In the following sentence,
she explains the advertiser's choice of symbol for representing
femininity (the scene with the lipstick smudges we looked at
earlier). She also appears to be in a position to speak for men in
general, judging from the third and last sentence of this opening
paragraph, where she reports their thoughts: 'When men think of
make-up, they think of lipstick.'

The producer appears in the text twice as a pronoun, in the
caption under the title and in the testimonials, as an editorial

we and *us* respectively. *We* appears in the self-report in The Header: '*We* kiss and tell the whole story behind lipstick!'. This establishes the anonymous editorial team as a group of friendly gossips. The editorial '*us*' also sets up a relation between the editorial-as-interviewer and Clara, who 'wouldn't tell *us* her age!', one of the interviewees we met earlier. There is an inclusive *we*, referring to both writer and reader, in the second paragraph of the column: 'Before the days of lipstick as *we* know it . . .'. Personal reference to the reader as *you* is a common feature of the synthetic personalisation practiced in the mass media. Instances of the reader being placed in the text as if she were an individual addressee can be found in the instructions and in the opening sentence of the column.

The writer addresses the reader as a friend, using various means to set herself up as a member of the same social group as her teenage readers. She minimises the social distance between herself and readership, claiming common ground and a social relation of closeness. This common ground claimed by the writer is set up in various ways; in presuppositions, for example, which place ideas – assumed beliefs or experiences – in the reader's head, and in fact-projections. By presenting facts, projections attributable to common sense or everybody, the writer is setting herself up as the kind of person who takes the projected facts for granted, but she is also setting up the reader as a like-minded person. (I give examples of each of these below.) The writer's establishment of a friendly, 'sisterly' identity, then, is wrapped up in her construction of an addressee and we can say little about the constructed writer without also considering this reader. A significant contribution to the writer's establishment of an identity for herself and a friendly, 'close' relationship with the reader is achieved through her claims to common ground, to her assumption of shared knowledge and experiences; to her knowledge, in short, of who the reader is. In the establishment of this common ground, the reader is also constructed. To 'be the same kind of person', the writer needs to construct who she's being the same as!

How does the writer show she is the same kind of person as the reader? One way the *Jackie* editorial does this is by 'speaking the same language'. Some of the vocabulary selected ('cutesy', 'lovable', 'awful' and perhaps 'churning' in the column, and 'lippy' in the illustrated history) contributes a little to the construction of a youthful, female identity for their writer, matching the targeted audience by approximating the readers' (supposed) fashion of speaking. Consider also the rewording in the second paragraph of the column: 'cochineal – beetle's blood'. This seems to be eliciting a response of disgust about 'nasty' creatures/substances (in other words, the writer wants the reader to go 'eugh!'). She is also asserting a dislike of 'nasty things' as something she shares in common with them.

Another way in which the writer claims common ground with the reader is by producing a report attributed to an inclusive *we* in the column: 'lipstick as *we know* it'). More frequently, common ground is claimed in reports for which it's hard to find any source, so that they are attributable only to some vague common sense or everybody, as in fact projections and presuppositions. So, for example, it is taken as an agreed fact in paragraph 6 of the column that 'fashions in lipstick have changed over the years', as we have already seen. In paragraph 5 there is another fact-projection presenting agreed knowledge (in this case, that 'each brand of lipstick is a different shape to start with'): 'the *fact* that each brand of lipstick is a different shape to start with'.

Similarly vague in attribution are presuppositions, such as the 'existential' presupposition that 'there is a right shade of lipstick' in the DIY section, 'Lip tricks!': 'Choosing *the* right shade of lipstick is easy'. Presuppositions of this kind, which simply take the existence of something for granted, are triggered by the definite article *the*. Other examples of 'existential' presuppositions can be found in the first paragraph of the illustrated history:

> Clara Bow, the 'It' girl of *the* 1920's who first set *the* fashion for wearing make-up

which presupposes that 'there was someone called an 'It' girl in the 20s' and that 'there is a fashion for wearing make-up'. Three more presuppositions, this time in the 'facts and figures' section, establish fashion change as common knowledge:

> Women wear more lipstick now than ever before, though *the* trend is towards subtler shades, rather than *the* brilliant reds favoured by previous generations, to reflect *the* 'natural' look of the 80s.

The presupposed ideas that 'there are such things as trends', that 'brilliant reds were favoured by previous generations' and that 'the

80s look is "natural"' are presented in a commonsensical way. Furthermore, the last of these presuppositions is contained within a clause giving the motive for a mode of action, which is difficult to attribute to anyone in particular. The mode of action is the use of 'subtler shades'; the motive is in order '*to* reflect the "natural" look of the 80s'. It appears to be reporting what everyone knows to be the case, and requires the reader to form a bridging assumption: namely, that the 'natural' look is achieved by using subtler shades than brilliant red.[6] This short passage is full of taken-for-granted ideas about fashions in cosmetics.

In showing that she is the same kind of person as the reader, the writer has to set up a postulated reader with whom to align herself. But she can claim to know 'who the reader is' in other ways as well. For instance, in the DIY section the emphatic assertion ('you *can* achieve a long-lasting look!') cues a contrasting negative assumption in the reader's mind that 'I think I can't achieve a long-lasting look'. (Note that this bit of advertising discourse can only reassure the reader by first setting her up as a failure, or perhaps just a faint-hearted pessimist.) Scare quotes too can contribute to the construction of the reader, giving the impression that the writer knows what the reader thinks. Marking words with scare quotes can cue distancing of different kinds from the terms marked. The writer may be using them to signal what is assumed to be an unfamiliar term or divergence from (what is assumed to be) 'normal' usage, thus setting up the familiar and the normal for the reader. Examples of this use of scare quotes I suggest are used for 'bow' and 'drawing' in the column, and 'bleeding' in the DIY section. Thus by placing 'bleeding', for example, in scare quotes the writer constructs a reader who does not normally use, and is possibly unfamiliar with, this term in its painting and craftwork sense of 'seeping over a line'.

So an identity constructed in the text for the producers of the beauty feature is the editorial-as-friend. The editorial speaks in different voices, however; she is not the same persona throughout the two pages but has multiple identities. I have mentioned already the editorial-as-interviewer and the editorial-as-historian when I was talking about lipstick-wearers earlier. We can also say she takes on the social identity of editorial-as-advertiser in numerous places, editorial-as-market-researcher in 'facts and figures' and editorial-as-facilitator in the DIY section. I don't mean by this that she takes on different roles, as an actor might do, but that as she shifts from one activity to another her language use shifts accordingly. We can see this shift by looking again at the point in the column where the editorial-as-friend tries to make her reader think: 'eugh!'. Contrast the writer's view here with the editorial-as-market-researcher's presentation of information about lipstick ingredients. These personae harbour contradictory attitudes towards lipstick ingredients. In the column they are 'nasty': 'cochineal – beetle's blood'. In 'facts and figures' they are presented in relatively technical terminology and apparently not 'nasty' at all:

> Lipstick is basically made up of oils and animal fats, particles of raw colours and pigments held together with waxes, and added perfume.

Consider how easily the writer could have changed the wording of this section so that it would make readers go 'eugh!' An alternative wording, sounding unpleasant rather than technical, could have been 'whale blubber and bits of gunk stuck together'.

These subject positions or personae are not clear-cut. For example, the editorial-as-facilitator in the DIY section is fulfilling the important function of teaching the skills needed to use products. She makes conventional use of commands in providing numbered instructions for the (extravagant!) application of lipstick: '1. Outline . . . 2. Fill in . . . 3. Blot . . .' etc. In the same section she is still promoting a product:

> 1. Outline the lips with a toning lip-pencil – this will help stop your lipstick from 'bleeding' around your mouth (a touch of Elizabeth Arden's Lip-Fix Creme, £4.95, provides a good base to prevent this, too).

The editorial-as-advertiser in the last two paragraphs of the column produces what sounds just like advertising copy, attending to commodity availability and range: 'more colours available than ever before . . .' etc.. In the last sentence, she slips from promotional language back into friendly and informal 'girls' language' in giving the bizarre representation of the production and consumption of lipstick we saw earlier:

> with some companies *churning out* batches of lipstick at a rate of 9,000 an hour, that's an *awful* lot of kisses to *get through*!

I find this concluding sentence interesting because it contains the only reference to the mass-production process and the distinct activities of production and consumption: they produce, we consume. Consumption is pleasurable, however, since it involves 'getting through' kisses!

The writer guides the reader's attitudes towards texts, postulating the reader's sympathies towards the various characters who are supposed to have produced them. The reader is constructed as a person with certain kinds of attitudes: mistrust of 'experts' giving scientific statements, respect for manufacturers, a host of presupposed notions about spontaneous fashion changes, 'budget brands' and so on. The reader is positioned as someone who assumes real lipstick is a 'modern invention' in paragraph two of the column: 'It's hardly a modern invention' (negation presupposes a corresponding positive assertion, otherwise why bother to make negative statements at all?). This person is presented with contradictory attitudes towards lipstick ingredients. But their unpleasant aspect is safely placed in the vague and distant past associated with some primitive Ur-lipstick used by superstitious people, all of which is subsequently presupposed to be uninteresting in any case. As we have seen, modern lipstick ingredients are apparently not 'nasty'.

Writer and reader, then, are synthesised in a friendly relationship. As an older sister might do, the editorial demonstrates the application of lipstick and gossips about it. Ironically, the actual producers of the 'beauty feature' may well of course have been men. The two pages synthesise a friendly 'all girls together' relationship, based on becoming feminine consumers: on a form of sisterhood in consumption. The beauty feature presents a feminine consumption community consisting of free individuals whose identities are established in pleasurable consumption. Lipstick is presented as a natural part of female experience, set in a historical framework of fashion and the whims of individual celebrities.

Conclusion

In this chapter I have looked in some detail at the text population of one sample text. The following set of questions summarises the approach, for application to other mass media texts:

1. Who are the *interactants*, i.e. who's talking to whom?

2. What *characters* are in the text and what are they doing there?
3. Does the writer engage with them, either in criticism or agreement? Is the reader one of them?
4. What *subject* positions are there, ie. what kind of identity does the writer set up for herself?
5. Is she being friendly?
6. And what kind of identity does she set up for us, the readers, i.e. who does she think we are?

The range of features to focus on that I gave above is intended to help us to answer these questions. Applied to an advertising-related text, this set of questions can be used to examine the consumption community constructed in it and the synthetic personalisation through which the reader is offered membership of this community. Consumer features which are based entirely around testimonials are frequent in *Jackie*, and lipstick is a common topic. They always contain an imaginary consumption community, and the writer always has the composite identity of interviewer, advertiser and friend. We can use them to stimulate learners' critical awareness of the extent to which our identities as gendered consumers are constructed for us in magazines, under the guise of 'sisterly' friendship. We can also examine the populations of other kinds of article, shifting attention from gendered identity in consumption to other aspects of gender.[7]

Acknowledgements

With thanks to DC Thomson for their kind permission to reproduce the pages of *Jackie* magazine. Thanks also to Leo Baxendale and Norman Fairclough for their invaluable comments on drafts of this chapter.

Notes

1. I have taken this notion of a consumption community from Leiss et al. (1986). Leiss et al. explain that in the transition from industrial to consumer culture,

   'consumption communities' . . ., formed by popular styles and expenditure patterns among consumers, became a principal force for social cohesion in the twentieth century, replacing the ethnic bonds that people had brought with them to the industrial city. (p.53)

2. This term comes from Halliday (1985).
3. The words/thoughts of characters may in addition be cued by verbal/mental process nouns (e.g. the *assertion* that ..., her *decision* to ..., the *feeling* that ...). All these different features share the common grammatical property of being able to 'project' texts. According to Halliday, projection is a kind of grammatical relationship in which a clause functions as a 'representation of a representation' rather than 'as a direct representation of (non-linguistic) experience' (1985: 227–8). Fact projection is on the boundary between representing 'a representation' and representing 'the world'.
4. This is according to White (1970).
5. There is some confusion between 'character', in the sense of 'personality-type' here, and 'look', a look being a specific style of appearance. The two terms seem to be almost interchangeable, which is perhaps not surprising when we consider the extent to which women are made visible in modern society and the importance placed on women's appearance.
6. The term 'bridging assumption' is used by Brown & Yule (1983), drawing upon work on comprehension (Haviland & Clark (1974). It refers to an implicit piece of background knowledge which has to be inferred to make a coherent connection between two utterances. For example the two utterances:

   Mary got some picnic supplies out the car. The beer was warm.

   require the following bridging assumption:

   The picnic supplies mentioned include some beer.

   We make bridging assumptions that fit in with our knowledge of the world automatically. They are even more difficult to spot than presuppositions and fact-projections, which at least have some tell-tale formal properties (a *when-* clause, for example). I couldn't see the bridging assumption in the sample text until Norman Fairclough pointed it out. For me it was a matter of common sense!
7. For instance, there are regular features offering help in dealing with social relationships, particularly boyfriends. The following short extract, for example, is from an advisory feature called 'Hanging on the telephone':

So you've turned down a party because he promised he'd ring you. . . . Last night, he really wanted to see you again but now, in the cold light of day, he's had a change of heart. Boys often ask for phone numbers without thinking (the fact that you'll hover over the phone for many an hour won't even occur to him).

In this passage the writer is a friendly counsellor who claims to know exactly what boyfriends are like, and the mass audience is constructed as a single character with particular preoccupations, which are presented as a matter of common sense.

References

Brown G, Yule G. 1983 *Discourse analysis*. Cambridge University Press
Fairclough N L 1989 *Language and power*. Longman
Halliday M A K 1985 *Introduction to functional grammar*. Edward Arnold
Haviland S, Clark, H 1974 What's new? Acquiring new knowledge as a process in comprehension. *Journal of Verbal Learning and Verbal Behavior* 13: 512–21
Jackie 20 September 1986. D.C. Thomson
Leiss W, Kline S, Jhally S 1986 *Social Communication in Advertising*. Methuen
McRobbie A 1978 *Jackie*: an ideology of adolescent femininity. University of Birmingham: Centre for Contemporary Cultural Studies (CCCS) Occasional paper
White C 1970 *Women's magazines: 1693–1968*. Michael Joseph

Appendix for chapter 7

LIPS INC.

We kiss and tell the whole story behind lipstick!

Ask any clever advertiser how to suggest femininity with a product, and he'll probably tell you 'a kissprint'. Lipstick on a collar, a glass, his cheek — they all suggest that a woman was there. When men think of make-up, they think of lipstick.

It's hardly a modern invention — women have been adding artificial colour to their lips for centuries now. Before the days of lipstick as we know it, ladies used vegetable or animal dyes like cochineal — beetle's blood — to colour their lips.

The reason behind it wasn't simply to make themselves more beautiful - superstition lingered that the devil could enter the body through the mouth, and since red was meant to ward off evil spirits 'lipstick' was put around the mouth to repel his evil intentions!

These days there are more complicated (and ruder!) theories. Experts in human behaviour say that it's all to do with sex (what else?!).

Other 'experts' claim that the shape of your lipstick can reveal a lot about your character — i.e. if

you wear the end flat you're stubborn, if it's round and blunt you're fun-loving etc etc — but don't seem to take into consideration the fact that each brand of lipstick is a different shape to start with and it's easiest just to use it accordingly. So much for the experts!

What *is* interesting is the way that fashions in lipsticks have changed over the years. When lipcolour first came into fashion at the beginning of this century, dark colours and the style of 'drawing' on little pursed lips meant that women looked cutesy and doll-like. Later on, in the forties, film stars wanting to look lovable and 'little-girl'ish continued this, while the newer breed of dominant, business-like women opted for a bolder look, colouring right over the natural 'bow' in the lips. By the sixties 'women's lib' was in style and most girls abandoned lipstick altogether, or used beige colours to blank out the natural pink of their lips, and concentrated on over-the-top eye make-up and face painting instead.

Now, in the eighties, there are

more colours available than ever before - right down to blue, green and black! 'Glossy' lips, popular for a while in the seventies, are out again, and the overall trend is for natural pink tints, with oranges and golds in summer, on big, full lips.

Large cosmetic manufacturers will have upwards of 70 shades available at a time, introducing a further three or four shades each season to complement the fashion colours of that time. And with some companies churning out batches of lipstick at a rate of 9,000 an hour, that's an awful lot of kisses to get through . . .!

LIP TRICKS!
Choosing the right shade of lipstick is easy — making it stay on is a bit more tricky. By applying lipcolour correctly, you *can* achieve a long-lasting look!

1. Outline the lips with a toning lip-pencil — this will help stop your lipstick from 'bleeding' around your mouth.

2. Fill in using a lip brush loaded with lipstick — a lip brush gives you more control over what you're doing, and fills in tiny cracks more easily.

3. Blot lips with a tissue, dust over lightly with face powder, apply a second layer and blot again.

MARGARET (15)
"I wear it all the time, because I always wear make-up. My favourite shade's a sort of brown-and-red mixture — I usually buy Boots 17 or Max Factor lipstick. I got my first one when I was 10, for Xmas — it was a sort of pink colour, I think it was just for me to play with."

EMILY (12)
"Usually I just wear lipstick when I'm going out, but sometimes for school, I like pinks, oranges and plain glosses. I was about 7 when my mum gave me a bright red lipstick to experiment with — I think I've worn it ever since!"

CLARA (wouldn't tell us her age!)
"I always wear red - dark red - and usually from Mary Quant or Estee Lauder. I don't know if I can remember my first lipstick — wait! yes I can! It was called "Choosy Cherry" by Mary Quant - everyone used to ask me if I was ill when I was wearing it!"

RHONA (18)
"I like pinks and deep reds. I don't wear it all that often. My first lipstick? I stole it from my sister's drawer — I was about 12 — dying to look grown-up even then!"

Clara Bow, the "It" girl of the 1920's who first set the fashion for wearing make-up — she wore her lipstick in a perfect Cupid's Bow.

By the 1940's, female film stars wore their lippy to reflect their own characters. Jean Harlow, the platinum blonde pin-up girl, went for absolute kissability with a lip-line as unnatural as her eyebrows — while no-nonsense dramatic actresses like Bette Davis and Joan Crawford preferred the wide-mouthed 'stiff upper lip' look.
By the 60's, innocence was IN - models like Twiggy abandoned lip colour altogether, and all the emphasis was on the eyes instead.

Into the 80's, and Madonna brings back bright lip colour with the most famous pout since Marilyn Monroe.

LIPSTICK FACTS AND FIGURES

Rimmel, the largest-selling 'budget' brand of cosmetics, sell over 5 million lipsticks every year, at an average price of 94p each — that's a staggering £4,700,000 plus spent on coloured kisses from Rimmel alone!

Out of all the lipsticks sold 47% are 'pink' shades — Rimmel's top seller is 'Pink Shimmer'.

Lipstick is basically made up of oils and animal fats, particles of raw colours and pigments held together with waxes, and added perfume.

The average price of a lipstick is £1.39.

Women wear more lipstick now than ever before, though the trend is towards subtler shades, rather than the brilliant reds favoured by previous generations, to reflect the 'natural' look of the 80's.

The biggest business in make-up is with young women. On average, every woman in Britain under 24 buys 20 make-up items each year, including four lipsticks and one lip pencil or crayon. For over 35's however, the figures plummet to just 6 items per year, of which only one will be a lipstick.

(Statistics by kind courtesy of SDC and Rimmel.)
Reproduced from 'Jackie'
20th September 1986

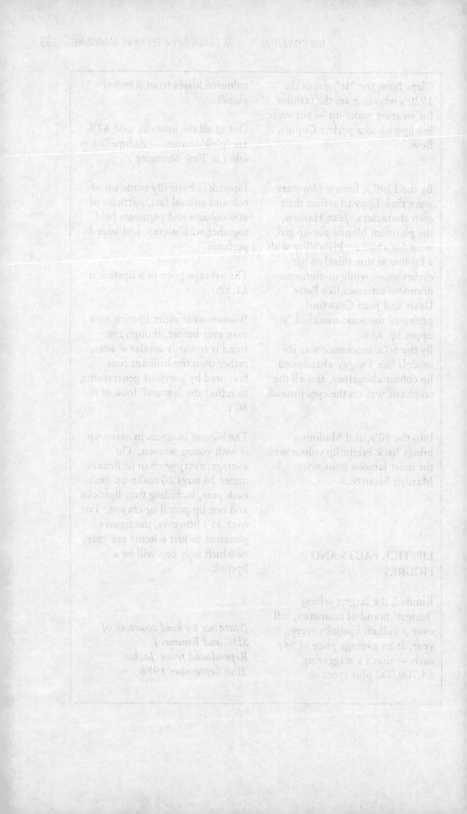

Part III

Critical Language Awareness in Schools

8 English Teaching, Information Technology and Critical Language Awareness

Michael Stubbs

> ... a technology that operates in a domain of language ... computers are machines for acting in language. (Winograd & Flores 1987: 7, 178)

> Round the city of Caxton, the electronic suburbs are rising. To the language of books is added the language of television and radio, ... the processed codes of the computer. As the shapes of literacy multiply, so our dependence on language increases. (DES 1988, 2.7)

Information technology (IT) has already been imposed on British education at a national policy level in various ways.[1]

However, what actually happens to such initiatives at school level can be very diverse. For example, the Cox Report (DES 1989) has a lot to say on knowledge about language in the school curriculum (chs 4 to 6), and it also discusses IT in some detail (ch. 9), arguing that most interactions with computers are language experiences.[2] But such reports require a great deal of interpretation before they can be turned into syllabuses and lesson plans by teachers and textbook writers.

This article gives examples of ways in which IT can provide a substantial area for work on critical language awareness. It discusses how syllabuses can be designed to develop children's awareness of:

(1) language and its interpretation
(2) new technological contexts in which language is used
(3) the social implications of these technologies.

The article therefore also discusses how English teaching should be developing to take account of major changes in the ways in which language is used in society, and therefore how work on language can fit into a wider programme of cultural analysis. (See Cox Report, DES 1989, 2.25.)

Within the next few years, micro-computers will be able to store more information more cheaply, and access and transmit it faster. But the main issues of principle are unlikely to change as fast. The technology will remain ahead of any sophisticated thought about its uses, and of the implications of storing, manipulating and transmitting information in this way. These are the topics for a language awareness course.

The Cox Report on IT

Information and communications technology have to do with the storage, retrieval, searching, processing and transmission of information, much of it linguistic. Therefore, as the Cox Report argues, this huge and expanding technology is of great importance to teachers of English.

The Report also argues that education itself deals centrally with information. Not exclusively, since information has little directly to do with forms of aesthetic or literary education. Furthermore, there are profound differences among information, knowledge and understanding. And, crucially, because of the power and limitations of computers, *information* itself comes to be defined in particular (sometimes narrow) ways.

One essential point made by the Report is that teaching about IT, and about media more generally, has to do with children's developing interpretations of language in use. This is something which English teachers have always had special responsibilities for: teaching children how to create and interpret different forms of information. So learning about such a technology can therefore be central to the traditional aims of English teaching.

This article therefore discusses what English teachers can contribute to children's understanding of this technology: the technology itself, the new uses of the term *information* to which it has led, and also the rhetoric and social attitudes surrounding its use. How can they help pupils to understand how language and communication are changing in society? Of course, all literate cultures use information technologies, including pens and paper, typewriters, printing presses, or whatever. More accurately, this article is restricted to computer-based IT and computer-driven peripherals, including printers, compact disks, electronic mail, etc. (Rymaszewski 1989: 5–6)

The Cox Report also argues that there are different general aims of the English curriculum: fitting children to the social order by preparing them for the world of work; but also developing their critical understanding of that society, and their ability to act on that understanding. It is probably now widely accepted that education should prepare children to live and work in an increasingly computer-oriented society. And it is easy enough to find examples of computer-assisted learning in many school subjects. As well as being built into attainment targets and programmes of study in the core subjects (English, maths and science) of the National Curriculum, business computer tools are used in business studies, databases for information retrieval are used in history projects, and so on. But thinking about what is involved in such a computer-oriented education is certainly underdeveloped: for example, as recently as 1985, the GCSE national criteria for English made no reference to new technologies.

The Cox Report deals with media education and information technology together in one chapter, arguing that it is increasingly difficult to distinguish between the newer technologies. (For example, video disk involves visual images under computer control.) Media education tends to be concerned with modern mass media such as television, cinema and radio, but it can logically be extended to all public forms of communication including printed materials (books as well as newspapers) and computerised sources of information such as databases.

Changing forms of literacy

The Cox Report places learning about IT under two main headings: study skills and cultural analysis.

IT extends literacy and therefore requires new study skills for school and work: the newer technologies can provide access to learning resources, such as documentary films and databases, and therefore lead to an increase in collections of authentic language products for teaching about the uses of language. The key question is therefore accessibility. The diversity of self-access teaching materials and study packages, and the increased availability of CD–ROM, video disk, satellite television, etc. will require an increase in study skills to access such materials.

In terms of cultural analysis, the study of IT can contribute to pupils' critical understanding of how messages are conveyed and interpreted in different media, such as some of the ways in which information can be manipulated (e.g. in databases and mail merge programs), and can therefore contribute to pupils' increasing discrimination in their interpretation of such information.

Technological developments always mean that the concept of literacy changes: see the quote at the beginning of this chapter from the Kingman Report. It is important therefore that pupils understand the general significance of the medium of communication, whether printed, visual and/or electronic. As literacy comes to be used in a wider range of contexts for a wider range of purposes, it may permit people to do things with literacy which they could not do before (e.g. have access to a large database which is physically distant from the user, or communicate via electronic mail with people who are physically distant). Literacy means particular ways of using language. As Olson (1987) argues, literacy does not directly cause new modes of thought, but it may augment the workings of language.

The common equation between information technology and word-processing (used, for example, in the Cox Report's terms of reference) is too narrow and reductionist. This is certainly one important application of IT: word processors can avoid much of the sheer physical tedium involved in redrafting pieces of writing. But, a word processor is not just a fancy typewriter: when linked to other machines, for example, it provides new possibilities, such as office automation or electronic mail. Software can be designed so that it can itself record the use that is being made of it. This can have potential educational value, for example in tracking a student's progress through a task. But such technology now allows management to record how fast and how accurately typists operate, by monitoring how many keystrokes they make per minute, and how many mistakes they make. It is now very easy to collect information of certain kinds: but what are the moral implications of doing so?

Winograd and Flores (1987: 174) point out that there are systematic domains (typically professional domains, such as creating and typing documents or accounting) which were not created by computers, but where computers can allow people to work more efficiently. But by thus reorganising a domain of human activity, they may also cause a shift in who does the work (e.g. journalists rather than specialist printers). Computers can therefore profoundly affect the social relations in the workplace and the social organisation of knowledge.

Generic, content-free software

I am not concerned in this article with software which has been specially written for pedagogic purposes (e.g. Developing Tray, a sophisticated gap-filling program which is well known to many English teachers), but with applications such as:

> desk tops, windows; word processors, desk-top publishing; outliners or ideas processors; spelling checkers, style checkers, thesauruses, dictionaries; mail mergers; concordances; spreadsheets; electronic mail.

None of these applications was originally created for educational purposes at all: the motivation was either commercial or academic.

The major use of computers in English teaching may turn out to be via such content-free software, which is not designed to teach any particular curricular content, but can give children access to a powerful tool which they can use for some purpose, to a new medium of communication, or to a new environment in which language can be used. Word processors have the ability to encourage the kind of learning which many English teachers favour: they encourage writing as a process, by making it much easier to edit and redraft a piece of writing. Word processors and desk-top publishing packages allow children to experiment easily with different forms of written text, before giving their writing a professional appearance. Along with access to electronic mail systems, this can encourage writing for real audiences.

The combination of software and hardware (e.g. word processor and printer) is providing a new kind of language environment for children. The technology can remove much of the tedium and physical frustrations of writing: revision of a text is easy, both at the level of individual words, and also in the way whole sections may be moved around; perfectly formed letters, evenly spaced words and impeccable print-outs are possible. Spelling checkers, thesauruses and style checkers (though primitive at present) can help children to experiment with form, and also to focus on content (since some superficial features of form are automatically taken care of).

Changing demands of literacy

However, it is simply not yet known what kinds of language awareness this will lead to, or what the general educational implications of such developments will be.

There are regular panics that standards of literacy are falling. However, the evidence (from APU 1988: 217–18, for example) is that standards are rising slightly, although arguably not fast enough to cope with the rapidly increasing demands on literacy. Various computer uses, such as databases, require new competence and great efficiency in searching, scanning and interpreting written language.

Computers are tools for working on texts. They provide rapid and powerful ways of changing texts. But it is not known what awareness this requires of children. For example, do uses of IT require new linguistic competences? Do they expand our concepts of literacy? Or do they simply provide a new medium for old behaviours? For example, given the very large amount of information potentially available via encyclopedic databases (e.g. on CD–ROM), what competence is required to select from it? Is this in principle different from selecting information in a library? What novel uses and representations of language and knowledge are brought about by computer systems?

Some aspects of computer use, likely to be much more wide-spread in the future, involve new uses of restricted language. For example, specialised languages may be required to interrogate on-line information sources, in banks, information offices, etc. Computers require precise and accurate instructions, and the production and interpretation of clear and precise information is an important goal of English teaching.

But IT can also support other traditional aspects of English teaching. Since the information on a computer screen is visible to several children at once, when children are using a word processor to write (or using a computer terminal for other purposes), this can often encourage group discussion, around the computer, of the language on the screen. Since such writing on a computer screen is public, it is likely to inhibit certain kinds of writing, and to encourage some kinds of collaborative, group discussions. Similarly, using computers requires children to understand systems of filing and classification, including alphabetic ordering, lists of contents, indices, symbols, etc. Knowledge of such systems is of wider use in information handling.

Other aspects are more novel. What happens, for example, to the concept of a *written text*, when it is represented on a screen eighty columns wide and twenty-five rows deep, and when it can be viewed, browsed through, searched for patterns, edited, sorted, merged with other texts, transmitted via electronic mail, and so on. Print in this medium is no longer permanent: it can be altered, transmitted or deleted in seconds. Any text is just one of a series of possible transformations. Alterations can be made without any trace of the change remaining in the original, and this ease of alteration has both advantages and dangers. Questions of authorship will also have to be rethought: not only due to forms of collaborative writing which are possible; but because access to on-line databases, etc. may allow pupils to import sections of text, with or without editing, into their own work (Rymaszewski 1989: 15).

Computer-constructed texts may be non-linear: windows may be opened on different texts at the same time; different degrees of detail may be hidden or revealed, according to the interests of the reader. Of course, conventional printed texts need not be read sequentially, from start to finish. But, via computers, written texts can also be merged with audio sequences and graphics. And different strategies are available for using such media to take account of their new ways of representing knowledge. Problems for writers of such texts include providing signposts so that readers do not get disoriented, and being unable to assume, in a browsing environment, that readers have read particular earlier sections of text (Rymaszewski 1989: 11). Relational databases are also non-linear and invite types of use not available with traditionally printed books.

Cognitive issues are also at stake. Technologies of writing always affect the ways of thinking of people who use them: different possibilities of communication are opened up by slates, printing presses, typewriters and word processors. For example, if children in classrooms write everything on a slate which is wiped clean at the end of a lesson, this is likely to encourage an emphasis on rote memory. It is widely thought that features of linear written texts have facilitated the development of particular kinds of logic and coherence in the presentation of arguments. It is not known what effect such non-linear written texts might have on such kinds of coherence. They might, for example, help children to make explicit a wider range of rhetorical structures.

These are not just technical but social issues. Such techniques of handling representations of written information make possible different relations between texts and people. People often attribute particular authority to information on the computer screen or print-out. Yet such information is by its very nature fugitive, and no-one may understand precisely how it was generated.

The communicative networks are certainly not stable. The really big changes are likely to come about when PCs are available throughout society in very large numbers. The same is true of any new communications technology. For example, telephones cannot affect a society profoundly when only a few people have telephones: but when most people have one, new types of communication become possible (Bolter 1984: 5).

Information technology and English teaching

The two-cultures view of intellectual life is often transferred to computers. It is often simply assumed that IT is the province of maths and science, and that English or modern language teachers could have nothing to contribute. In many schools computers are in the charge of maths or science departments. And as a recent major research funding initiative phrases it: 'mathematics and science are natural arenas for the deployment of the new technologies in education'. This is also a narrow assumption.

It is unfortunate if it restricts valuable cross-curricular collaboration in aspects of IT. Computers used to be convenient for number
crunching, but isolating IT in certain curriculum areas (e.g. science,
but not the humanities) may simply represent an out-of-date view
of the technology.

Equal opportunities

It is often supposed that computers have the power to break down
social divisions, by giving more people access to information.
However, a general finding is that the most active users of new
technologies are those who were most active users of the old
technologies, and there is considerable evidence that IT may be
preserving and deepening social divisions. (PCs are still, after all,
relatively expensive for a household budget.)

There are clear sex biases: boys, for various reasons, often have
easier access than girls to computers. Our culture often defines
machines as a male preserve, and girls may need encouragement
that they can be just as expert as boys in such areas. Hoyles
(1988: 32) reports that sex stereotyping of computers is found
at age 7. Similar stereotyping is found for science and technology,
but is potentially more serious with computers, given the cross-
curricular uses of IT which are now written into legislation for
the National Curriculum. New forms of technology often appear
to hold out the promise of increased access to knowledge, but
are then perceived in such a way as to reinforce traditional lines
of gender bias. Hoyles (1988: 8) points out three basic uses of
computers: games; the computer as an object in its own right (in
programming); and applications (e.g. word processing). It is only
in the third use that work by women is more frequent.

Similar points may also be made about the access of different
social groups to forms of educational technology. There is an
age bias: young people take easier than older people to new
technologies. And there are social class and cultural biases,
evident enough in general, but hardly researched. It is said that
95 per cent of adolescent bulletin board users in the USA are
white, male and upper-middle class (Rymaszewski 1989: 15).
Such group stereotyping can itself be a topic for explicit discussion
with pupils.

Types of usage and levels of understanding: concepts for a syllabus

It is possible to have very different levels of awareness and understanding of computers. For example, one might be able to use a computer by loading and playing a game, with very little understanding at all. Using a word processing package may similarly involve little understanding of the capabilities of the machine. Users often think that a machine on a desk is simply a word processor, rather than a general machine, which can do many things, but which is currently running word processing software. It is certainly possible to use computers in some ways, but still to regard them as sci-fi marvels, and to have no understanding of their limitations.

Many aspects of modern technology are, of course, just black boxes to their users. We operate many machines (cars, washing machines, pianos, etc.) in this way, by pressing buttons or throwing switches, with no idea of how they work internally. And it is not clear that understanding what goes on under the bonnet allows you to drive a car any better. Further, computers are always black boxes for almost everyone in the end: someone might be able to program commands in the operating system of their PC, but not know how the operating system itself works, or how the operating system controls the hardware.

However, the type of knowledge and level of understanding aimed at in work on IT and language awareness must be made explicit, if 'awareness' is not to remain a hopelessly vague concept. The conceptual basis of English teaching in general has often been unclear, in comparison, for example, with media studies, where concepts (audience, media agency, etc.) are often very explicit (Bazalgette 1989). Language awareness courses must be constructed in explicit and coherent ways: teachers have a responsibility to their pupils to be able to state the content and aims of the syllabus.

Often no new concepts at all are involved. Often English teachers will want to use computer-based IT to develop aspects of children's literacy which have long been recognised as central, for example:

- information handling strategies
- critical reading strategies
- drafting and presentation of final drafts.

And I have discussed above two ways of regarding IT (Rymaszewski 1989: 3). Though the two ways are not entirely distinct, IT provides both a support medium for existing language use (e.g. word processors), and a new medium for communication (e.g. electronic mail).

None of this, however, looks directly at computers in terms of their strengths and limitations. A syllabus on IT should be balanced between the linguistic and the social/cultural, but it should also look directly at the technology. And here there are central concepts, some quite traditional to English teachers, and some less familiar, which have to be tackled directly, if computers are not simply to maintain their unexplained mystique.

It is quite inadequate to discuss the social implications of new technologies without understanding what machines can and cannot do. As in other areas of language study, there is a tendency to discuss the social implications without any real basis in facts. It is only when children themselves use the technology to type in, file, alter, retrieve, transmit and print information, that they begin to have some feel for what such systems can and cannot do, and that the technology is demystified. They are then in a much better position to understand the merits and limitations of computers as tools.

So what are some of the basic, minimum concepts? I think the essential argument is as follows. If pupils are not able to program the computer in some way, then they have no real understanding of how it works, and therefore no power over it and no confidence in it (Hoyles 1988: 40). It is not the job of the English teacher to teach a programming language, but there are many language-related concepts which they could study with pupils. A computer program is a set of *instructions* which must be *explicit* and carried out in a particular *sequence*. Logic and programming are related in a particular, narrow, way. A computer will do what you *say*, and not what you *mean*. *Ambiguity* will not be tolerated.

These are all concepts which English teachers will naturally discuss in other contexts, whether in teaching about writing or poetry. They could lead here to discussion of fundamental issues of how humans and computers *interpret* language. What does this metaphor mean when applied to a computer? Computers are good at interpreting(?) certain kinds of logically sequenced language (if *a* and if *b* then *c* and therefore *d*), but not other types of sequence (e.g. which depend on common-sense knowledge). If pupils have not themselves constructed sequences of explicit instructions, this concept is very difficult to get across. And if they have not understood such concepts, it is doubtful that they have understood fundamental aspects of how computers work.

A crucial concept is the interaction of human decisions and machine processing. For example, people now carry increasing numbers of cards with machine-readable magnetic strips, which admit them to buildings (e.g. the London underground) or allow routine transactions (e.g. in banks) which used to be mediated by human beings. It is easy to forget that the information on such cards has been selected by human beings in the first place. Computer programmers themselves have a useful acronym GIGO: garbage in, garbage out. If what is put in (by a human being) is not reliable, what comes out cannot be reliable, no matter how good the program is.

Examples of teaching topics

These comments are about the overall design of a possible syllabus. In the next sections I will translate some of these ideas into a small selection of possible topics at the level of series of lessons.

Example 1: computer metaphors

I have already discussed the rhetoric surrounding computers. The metaphors go in two directions. First, human characteristics are used to describe machines. (A computer is *intelligent* or has a large *memory*.) And, second, computer terms spread into human domains. (Humans are *programmed* for a task.) Of course, all kinds of mechanistic ways of talking about human beings have been taken over from earlier technologies. (His behaviour is *as regular as clockwork*. She's so obsessed by work that she can't *switch off*. Don't be so boring, *put another record on*, etc.) But it is probable that computer metaphors are more pervasive. Children can study explicitly how computers are represented in words and pictures in magazines.

It is very difficult to separate the rhetoric from the reality. Computers do have a sci-fi image as strange, powerful, sinister machines. People fear and distrust them, are deferential to them, are fascinated or obsessed by them. Anthropomorphic metaphors abound of modern, super-human, intelligent beings. Any amount of material for classroom analysis could be found in the advertising in Sunday newspaper colour supplements or in many computer magazines. Or pupils could study how computers are represented in films: when are the representations plausible? And when do they just mean 'magic'? (Bazalgette 1989: 76.) But an awareness of precisely what is justified in such fear or enthusiasm is only possible if children actually understand something of the power and limitations of available hardware and software, because they have used them themselves.

The rhetoric, in phrases such as *the micro-chip is transforming society*, is probably true in a sense, though the ultimate impact is very far from clear. But the rhetoric must be analysed. It is a rhetoric of reliability, expertise, rationality, science and high-tech. The ways in which computers are represented often serve to mystify them, to make them objects of magical power. We might be told that they can transmit 50 million bits of information per second, or print several pages per minute. Typically, quantity, speed, accuracy and logic are emphasised. And, conceptually, the computer is often assimilated to maths/science/technology though this may be irrelevant to its use.

The social image of computers regularly involves the sex stereo-typing of their image. They are typically perceived as a male preserve. For example, the pictorial representation of males and females in computer magazines typically shows only women as computer-phobes (Hoyles 1988: 6, 10.) Just as happens in advertising more generally, discourse about computers reproduces other ideologies of gender, of expertise, etc.

Discussion of computers is part of a significant popular discourse in society, which is maintained by a large number of books and magazines. It draws heavily on the analogy between computers and human brains/minds, with talk of intelligent machines, and (a term used very loosely in artificial intelligence) *expert* systems. This discourse rests in turn on a more fundamental discourse about technology (Winograd & Flores 1987: 3ff).

Example 2: artificial intelligence, metaphor and reality

The validity of mental and psychological terms applied to computers is something that English teachers could pursue from a linguistic angle. Often the term *intelligent* is just an advertising slogan. But what does it imply to talk of humans and machines in the same terms? Can machines really have electronic brains or memories? (If they are like humans, do they also forget?) Can they *read* data or *recognise* characters? Why are those human-machine comparisons so irresistible?

The key test, according to a classic argument, of whether computers are really like humans, is whether they can carry on a conversation. Pupils could study software such as ELIZA[3], which simulates (or parodies?) a conversation between a non-directive psychotherapist and a patient. To what extent does the program really simulate conversation?

Example 3: data bank society

A central theme for a language awareness course could be Britain as a databank society. There must be few, if any, people in the UK who do not have information stored about them in computers. In fact, one estimate (*Personal Computer World*, October 1987, p. 142) is that the average British citizen has his or her name passed between computers five times daily. Different kinds of information are stored, for perfectly legitimate purposes, by banks, tax offices, the police, gas boards, etc. Information is transmitted across the country when you buy airline or ferry tickets. People access remote databases from cash dispensers.

The dangerous implications of such storage and transmission (and particularly merging) of information are, of course, widely debated. When is it legitimate? How can the accuracy and privacy of such information be maintained? How can out-of-date information be destroyed? And laws have been passed to require people storing such information to be registered. But alongside people's widespread perceptions of the authority of computers and the view that 'computers don't make mistakes', are experiences of inaccurate bank statements or out-of-date information. English teachers are likely to want to concentrate on the nature of the information. What categories of information are involved?

Such study could be part of a wider study in the sociology of knowledge: how information is transmitted in modern societies by radio, TV, films, libraries, telephone, mail, etc.; and part of a study of how other technologies have created new social relations between people. The typewriter, for example, was a major influence in the emancipation of women in early twentieth century Britain, since it created a particular type of job which they could respectably do outside the home. In turn, it created a particular type of social relation (boss–secretary) which is now deeply ingrained in our society, and perhaps now restricts the further emancipation of women.

Example 4: direct mail advertising

Here is a more specific example of what can be done with information about people which is stored on computers, and of how an understanding of facilities now available on many home computers can take the mystery out of a small, but important, part of the social and commercial world. Almost every household in Britain now receives direct advertising by mail, for large ranges of consumer products, foreign holidays and the like. This mail is not sent out at random: it would be prohibitively expensive and bring very small returns if it was. It is targeted and personalised in ways which are easy to understand by anyone who has access to word processing and database programs.

First, there are companies who maintain large lists of people who live in different areas. They may be linked to the electoral roll, but are also constructed from records of people who have purchased certain goods and services. These lists are big business and are rented out to retailers. *The Observer* (4 October 1987) reported that £500m a year is spent on direct mail advertising, and that the sales amount to 10 per cent of British retail spending.) An advertising letter can easily be personalised by using a mail merge program of the kind available on many word processors. Letters of the type:

Dear Mr Spooks,

I know you and the rest of the Spooks family – perhaps also your neighbours living in Ghastly Lane – will be unable to resist our latest offer . . .

If such a program has your address, it will also have your post code, which gives very accurate information about your housing:

and if you know the type of housing someone lives in, you can make a fair guess at their social class and income level.

Predictions about social class and age can also be made from someone's given name. A recent market survey analysed 43 million names to put a likely age to 13,000 first names (*The Observer*, 6 September 1987). (Names is a substantial topic in its own right for language awareness work.) An advertisement for one computer dating company uses photographs of couples, named *Carol and David, Leslie and Rita* and *Shirley and Ron*. Young, middle-aged and elderly respectively. It is easy to say which set of three people named below is likely to be younger:

Annie, Ethel, Percy;
Lynn, Lorraine, Daniel.

So, by combining a word-processing and printing program with a database containing knowledge about known interests, and likely correlations between post code, first name, age and social class, someone selling goods or services can accurately target their addressees. It is this ability of programs to cross-reference and interrelate information which gives much of the power to such systems. As *The Observer* (6 September 1987) put it, such systems ensure 'that a Florence isn't pestered in her retirement with a glossy hard sell aimed at a Sharon'.

Example 5: publishing students' work

Substantial claims have been made for the benefits of publishing pupils' writing. There is nothing original in that in itself. But a technology which allows the production of real print, at any stage in the acquisition of literacy, has great implications for real communication with real audiences. Desk-top publishing provides a new mode of production which is available to pupils, and which should lead to pupils understanding more about how texts are prepared, produced and disseminated to different audiences.

Kimberley (1989) discusses some of the issues concerned with community publishing. Such forms of local publishing can be much more responsive to local diversity. It is not mainstream publishing, and therefore potentially more open to a range of different ideas and different viewpoints. Combined with computer-assisted production methods, it should lead to a more active view of writing.

Conclusions

Technology is not just a set of inert things. It is also a set of social practices. It is represented to consumers in highly symbolic ways which convey messages about power and prestige, and the computer is one major symbol of progress in our times. There are commercial, industrial, governmental and national pressures on these representations, and on the ways in which technology is used to give some people rather than others access to the machines themselves and to an understanding of them. Like any other machines, computers can be used for good or bad. They are a vital part of our social world, and an analysis of how they define and handle information is an important part of a critical cultural analysis of society.

We just do not know the social effects of new technologies. It is dangerous to assume that they are too scientific for English teachers. And it is dangerous to have a generation of school-children who have only a superficial sci-fi view of IT. We need descriptions of what PCs can actually do, and theories of how the concepts of *information* and *communications* vary in IT and in other domains of human life. We need discussion of the institutions (e.g. commercial, industrial, governmental, educational) in which computers are used, and an understanding of the kinds of policy and planning decisions which have led to the present place of computers in our society. And we need to argue for educational uses of computers which are driven by educational and not purely technological arguments.

Such understandings should be part of every educated person's common knowledge, and therefore part of a curriculum on information handling in all its forms.

Research frameworks

As society moves from an industrial to an informational base, computers become more important in understanding how people interpret language. But it will be a long time before we know how to think coherently about the place of computer-based IT in education.

Van Peer (1988) analyses the uses of different media in society. He uses the term PRINT to refer to any kind of written language, and AV to refer to any electronic transmission of audio-visual material. He then points out that the central, typical uses of the media are different. The central function of PRINT is to provide information, and of AV to provide entertainment. In addition, PRINT includes more high prestige literature, whereas AV includes more low prestige products. Understanding the place of computers in society is complex, because they share features of both PRINT and AV: professional uses tend to share the features of PRINT, whereas domestic and other uses share the features of AV.

School subjects also have different relationships to PRINT, AV and computers, partly because they have different preferred styles of *explanation* and of *representation*. Traditionally, maths and science have been subjects which emphasise explicit and formal rules; whereas English has valued implicit forms of discourse. But, as I have argued throughout, this distinction may simply be based on out-of-date stereotypes.

The evaluation of educational change due to the new technologies involves the analysis of changed cognitive and social relations in the classroom. We therefore need simple but powerful concepts to study the *pedagogic and cognitive logic* of such situations. These are complex because several different factors interact:

- the students
- the teacher (who may intervene more or less directly)
- the machine (students may have perceptions of the hardware itself)
- the software (and therefore, indirectly, the programmer)

How, then, is the learning *regulated* by each of these relations? Is this regulation *implicit or explicit*? (See Bernstein 1975.) For example, the software *relays* a form of discourse with an explicit organisation (if it is not explicit, then it cannot be programmed). And it is *realised* as representations on the screen, which may either display or conceal this organisation.

Different aspects of student behaviour may be *regulated*: attitudes, interaction or cognition. Pupils' attitudes differ, for example, in what authority they attribute to screen representations. Different interactional skills are needed: for example, the hardware may require typing skills, and the software may require the manipulation of menus. And if pupils are writing on the screen, the public display may discourage some kinds of writing, but encourage some kinds of group collaboration and discussion. And cognitively, as I have discussed throughout, pupils may be encouraged or not to understand the effect of the technology on the information transmitted.

It is such relations between students, teachers, hardware and software which will have to be thoroughly investigated, before we have a systematic understanding of the educational implications of IT.

Notes

1. It is useful to remember that Kenneth Baker was Minister for Information Technology (and responsible for the policy of a micro-computer in every school) before he was Secretary of State for Education and Science (and responsible for the legislation on which the National Curriculum is based).
2. I was a member of the Cox Committee, and was responsible for drafting much of the material discussed here.
3. Weizenbaum (1976) provides a detailed discussion: he was the original author of the ELIZA program. The classic article on the computer intelligence problem is by Turing (1950): it is discussed by Hofstadter (1985). ELIZA is a feature of the plot in one of David Lodge's novels (Lodge 1984). One version of ELIZA is available as a demonstration program supplied with the version of SNOBOL4 by Catspaw Inc (PO Box 1123, Salida, Colorado 81201, USA). It runs on IBM-compatible machines. The program accepts any sentences typed into the machine and responds to them in a (partly!) conversation-like way.

Acknowledgements

I am grateful to Euan Reid, Norman Fairclough and Gabi Keck for useful critical comments on an earlier draft of this chapter. Several of the points in the final section derive from discussions with Basil Bernstein, Joan Bliss, Jon Ogborn and Peter Skehan.

References

APU (Assessment of Performance Unit) 1988 *Language performance in schools: review of APU monitoring 1979–83.* HMSO.

Bazalgette C 1989 *Primary media education.* London: British Film Institute, Education Department

Bernstein B B 1975 *Class, codes and control* Routledge & Kegan Paul

Bolter J D 1984 *Turing's man* Duckworth.

DES 1975 *A language for life.* (The Bullock Report) HMSO

DES 1988 *Report of the committee of enquiry into English language teaching.* (The Kingman Report) London: HMSO

DES 1989 *English for ages 5 to 16* (The Cox Report.) DES & Welsh Office

Hofstadter D R 1985 *Metamagical themas.* Basic Books

Hoyles C (ed) 1988 *Girls and computers.* Bedford Way Papers 34. University of London, Institute of Education

Kimberley K 1989 Community publishing. In De Castell S et al. (eds) *Language, Authority and Criticism.* Falmer

Lodge D 1984 *Small World.* Secker & Warburg

Olson D R 1987 An introduction to understanding literacy. *Interchange* 18 (1/2): 1–8

Rymaszewski R 1989 IT and language development. Occasional Paper, Inter/10/89. Economic and Social Research Council

Turing A M 1950 Computing machinery and intelligence. *Mind* LIX (236) Extract in Hofstadter, D R, Dennett D C 1981 (eds) *The Mind's I.* Basic Books

Van Peer W 1988 Reading, culture and modern mass media. *Journal of Information Science* 14 (5): 305–9

Weizenbaum J 1976 *Computer power and human reason.* Freeman

Winograd T, Flores F 1987 *Understanding computers and cognition.* Addison-Wesley

9 'What I've always known but never been told': euphemisms, school discourse and empowerment

Malcolm Mc Kenzie

The quotation which forms the first part of the title of this chapter was written by one of the students involved in the project which I am about to describe. To me, as to the rest of her class, it captured neatly a number of issues which our work on the nature and function of euphemisms in school reports had raised: that students generally know how their teachers feel about them; that teachers rarely inform students directly what their feelings about those students are; and, most importantly, that there might be a connection between the fact that students know and teachers don't tell which goes to the heart of power relations within many schools.

The purpose of this chapter is practical. I wish to describe a series of lessons generated by and shared between me and a class of 30 Form 4 students at Maru a Pula Secondary School in Gaborone, Botswana. This school is an independent institution with a total enrolment of just over 500 students. The exams which our students sit are the University of Cambridge Local Examinations Syndicate O and A level. Some of our students take their O levels at the end of Form 4, others at the end of Form 5. This particular class of Form 4 students wrote their O level exams about three months after the series of lessons described in this chapter. Most of the students in the group were either 15 or 16 years old at the time and their mother tongues were various: African, Asian and European. Almost all, however, had been educated through the medium of English since primary school and so were fluent in both spoken and written English. This fluency tended to manifest itself through a well-developed communicative competence which lacked almost entirely any awareness of language in either its descriptive or critical dimensions.

Learner-centredness

One of my starting points for the set of lessons that I am about to describe is my understanding of the notion of learner-centredness. The learning role of students in most schools in Southern Africa, even progressive ones, is essentially passive. Expressed in terms of the four traditional language skills, this passivity manifests itself through most of their tasks being receptive (listening and reading) rather than productive (speaking and writing). Despite what teachers in my particular school say about encouraging their students to talk and question, and I believe that our students are empowered in this regard more than students in most schools in the region, the fact remains that many of my colleagues (myself probably included) are compulsive talkers and their students compelled listeners. When it comes to writing, a skill which is practised a reasonable amount, much of this is dictated, either literally or by the demands of note-making from prescribed texts. Even when the writing is self-generated, this tends almost inevitably to be for corrective consumption by the teacher.

Although many teachers now pay lip-service to the fashion for learner-centred classrooms, their expressed intentions are often very different from what actually happens in those classrooms. I like Littlejohn's (1985, 255) summing up of this disjunction:

> The dangers that I have outlined in learner-centred syllabus design and learner-centred classroom activities all seem to derive from one basic fact: that in both cases it is the teacher or syllabus designer who has made all the decisions. In the first case, learners have no choice over *what* they will learn; in the second case they have no choice over *how* they will learn. The missing element for the learner in both can be expressed simply as *choice*.

The problem for Littlejohn boils down to a simple matter of

choice: who is given the choices and who makes the decisions? Traditionally, this is part of the job of teachers because they have been trained to regard themselves and be regarded by their students as authorities. How can teachers remain authoritative but at the same time become less authoritarian? Widdowson (1987, 87) puts the point well:

> The increase in learner-centred activity and collaborative work in the classroom does not mean that the teacher becomes less authoritative. He or she still has to contrive the enabling conditions for learning, has still to monitor and guide progress.

The combination of the guiding and monitoring role of the teacher with the sharing of choice suggested by Littlejohn is a difficult balance to discover and maintain. It must, however, be extremely important in the context of critical language teaching. For me, such language teaching is founded upon an attitude of critique towards and scrutiny of the meanings in language and discourse that are propagated by dominant groups and often accepted without question by subordinate groups. Institutions such as schools have easily observable hierarchies of administrative and pedagogic rank and power. They also possess and are possessed by what Pêcheux (1982) calls 'discursive formations', the less observable patterns and conventions of talk in and about the institution which reflect and recreate that social structure. The distribution of power within both school and classroom, and the discursive formations through which that distribution is expressed and reflected, must themselves become an object of language teaching and language study. This point has recently been made by David Corson (1990, 227): 'If schools and teachers are to implement "critical language study" a good starting point would be to implement a more critical approach to the exercise of discourse in their own institutional practices.'

Critical Language Teaching

I deliberately placed the section on learner-centredness (essentially Littlejohn's 'how') before this short outline of critical language teaching because I wanted to stress how vital to me the overlap is between practice and content in any teaching which claims to be critical. In the case of critical language teaching, precisely because of what it is that we are trying to teach, classroom practice and classroom content are like the two wings of a bird. It is simply not possible to take off on one.

What is it, then, that critical language teaching deals with? It is appropriate that I make some brief statement of intent at this stage. Critical linguistics and language teaching originate, for me, in the observations of Saussure (1959) about the arbitrary and conventional nature of the linguistic sign. One implication of this is the fact that the value or meaning of any linguistic sign is both socially determined and depends upon the relative positions within the language system of the people who use that system. Language is not neutral, it reflects and creates ideology, and language change is tied to social and political structures and their changes. At the same time, however, the conventions of language and discourse are often naturalised in the interest of dominant social groups. This suggests that the meanings they embody seem to be natural and inevitable, the only meanings possible. Because meaning is treated as absolute and given, the possibility of meaning shifts becomes disguised and opaque. Critical linguistics and language teaching attempt to denaturalise the givens of a language system, to problematise its conventions and to show how meaning, because it is socially constructed, can be deconstructed and reconstructed. It is often said by critical linguists that language is a site of struggle. Critical language teaching aims to bring students within sight of this site so that the view that they have of it will empower them to change aspects of their language, and consequently social, practice as people.

A crucial insight for the successful implementation of critical language teaching within a classroom is the perception by the teacher of students as social agents within the educational institution and not as isolated individuals. Kress (1985, 5) highlights some of the implications of this:

> For that social agent the grammar of a language, its syntax, phonology, and lexicon, has a very specific look, not 'language as such' but rather a particular set of potentials and possibilities within the whole language system. For her or him certain facets of the linguistic system are familiar, accessible, in constant use. Others will seem strange, used by speakers beyond the social grouping of this language user . . . or maybe differentiated by age or gender.

Social agents learn a language in order to have their access extended to the 'particular set of potentials and possibilities within the whole language system'. At the same time, as Kress states, certain aspects of the language system are familiar through constant use. A creative critical language-teaching programme should, in my opinion, attempt to tap areas of discourse within the school with which students are familiar through regular exposure and then make them appear strange by showing how and why only certain groups within the institution use them. Such an approach must rely heavily on the generative capacities of the students and not on texts which are 'imported' from outside the school either as textbooks or as worksheets. Textbook dependency is reduced and students learn to construct as well as deconstruct meaning. Becoming geographically specific for a moment, it must be admitted that in the Southern African region as a whole, as in many developing countries, a combination of large classes and less than adequate facilities has produced situations where teachers tend to fall back on non-productive methods of rote learning. Learner-centred critical language teaching, as I have tried to outline it in theory, can provide a way forward which does not ignore the realities of the present regional context.

Euphemism as Idiom

The title of this section suggests where my thinking on this topic began, at least from the pedagogic point of view. I had been looking through one of the language teaching books which we use as resource material in the school and had come across the following teaching definition of a euphemism (Jones 1980, 38): 'A euphemism is a figure of speech by which a harsh or unpleasant fact is given a milder or more gentle expression or is expressed in a more roundabout way.'

On any level other than that of the merely descriptive this statement seems to me to be wholly inadequate. In their studied attempts to be 'objective' and 'neutral' language textbook writers have often done their subject a disservice. I set about trying to think, therefore, of euphemisms in relation to school discourse, particularly in terms of their frequency and location of occurrence in my present school, Maru a Pula. In the area of report writing the variety of their use seemed unusually rich. On the basis of this

I made the choice of euphemisms as a focus for a series of lessons, and I determined to attempt to guide the class in the direction of their termly reports as a breeding ground for this 'figure of speech'. What happened after that was in large part a process of negotiation between certain members of the class and myself.

I began more or less with Jones's definition as a base and presented the class with a list of euphemisms which either have acquired or are acquiring the status of idiomatic expressions in English. In the first instance I wanted simply to find out about their familiarity with this 'particular set of potentials and possibilities'. However, as I shall show later, some of these phrases led easily into the beginnings of a 'critical' analysis and discussion. Here is the list:

> What do you understand the following phrases to mean?
> Genuine imitation leather
> Under the weather
> Senior citizen
> Learning resources centre
> A terminal disease
> Lady of the night
> Out to lunch
> To see a man about a dog
> Take appropriate cost reduction action
> Water closet
> Hard of hearing
> Sub-standard housing
> Light fingered
> To pass wind
> Separate development
> Asked to leave a school
> Pushing up the daisies
> Waste disposal unit
> They knew each other in the Biblical sense
> To call a spade a spade

I included the last example as a roundabout way of describing somebody who has decided to stop being roundabout! The average number that the students either knew or could work out was around ten. As one of my agenda items at this stage was to enable students to develop a sense of the deliberately concealed code of euphemisms, I asked them to generate as many euphemisms as they knew in the other languages that they spoke. In a multilingual classroom this works quickly and well. We focused on the three areas of sex, drunkenness and death. After a while I suggested that they try to invent some euphemisms of their own. The combination of trying to translate idiomatic euphemisms from one language to another so as to explain their meaning with attempting to invent new euphemisms, both difficult tasks, drove home the point about concealed meaning.

In the general discussion that ensued, questions such as the following were raised: Why is 'to kick the bucket' not a euphemism? To whom and of whom would you use the phrase 'pushing up the daisies'? Can a student ask to leave a school and what is the difference between this request being made by a student and by a principal? Why are there no 'gentlemen of the night' and if there were what would be a suitable phrase to describe them? Which political groups accept and which reject the description of apartheid as 'separate development'? What names are used by those who reject this term to describe the reality of apartheid as they see it? As I mentioned earlier, the discussion of some of these euphemisms moved easily into more 'critical' questions about context, register, access, speakers, audiences and possible alternative phrases.

This initial lesson filled a double period of eighty minutes. Towards the end of the session I posed the question about the use of euphemisms in the school and where they might be most likely to be found. It did not take long, and it required no prodding from me, for school reports to be identified, and this provided the springboard for the rest of the series of lessons. In describing these lessons, which were not planned by me, I shall use the students' own words in many places. Authorial comment, of course, is mine.

Dummy Reports

The next lesson began where we had left off at the end of the previous period with a shift in focus to a specific area of school discourse, namely reports. At Maru a Pula the students receive reports at the end of each term, that is 3 times per year, and these are written on separate slips of paper by every subject teacher, the form teacher, the boarding house warden, the director of studies and the principal. The idea of the separate slips, which allow for about six or seven lines of comment, is that teachers produce their impressions of students without recourse to or undue influence by the remarks of their colleagues. All of our students receive neatly stapled dossiers of report slips and these can contain up to fifteen different sets of comment. This means that after a few terms at the school our students become experts at decoding these regularly received and sometimes cryptic messages.

The first question raised in the class about reports was why teachers never or hardly ever write blunt, direct reports about bad students. One of my responses to this, only partly facetious, was that learning to read between the lines was an essential part of language education and that we as teachers were slyly creating an opportunity for the development of this skill through our style of report writing. On a more serious note, I asked the class whether they could imagine what a really outspoken report about a really bad student would look and sound like. At that point one of the students suggested that we all try to write exactly such a report about a fictional 'worst possible scenario' student. The idea for this exercise was enthusiastically adopted by the rest of the class, and the writing of the reports took the remainder of the forty-minute lesson. It led into a creative by-way where the students collaboratively generated their own data for critical analysis, the data being what I have called dummy reports. This data was produced in the following three stages.

To begin with, here is an example of one of the bad, blunt reports produced during class time:

> Tebogo is a lazy uncooperative child. He behaves extremely immaturely, and takes a vindictive pleasure in disrupting lessons whenever possible. His exam mark this term is a disgrace, and is full of thoughtless answers and careless mistakes. It is evident that he has made no attempt whatsoever to grasp the subject. He persistently defies the teachers, and pays scant attention to his punishments. To be very frank, Tebogo is the bane of my existence and should be expelled without any further ado.

The next two stages, which occurred during the following lesson, resulted from an idea hit upon by me through discussing these first dummy reports with the class. I collected each student's report and redistributed them randomly. The task now was for the original report to be rewritten, this time as euphemistically as possible. I asked the class to try to stick as closely as they could to the substance of the first report, and only to soften the expression. This is how the example above came out when it was reworked:

> Tebogo does not appear to be very keen on the subject but I think if he could cooperate a bit more with the class and behave a wee bit more maturely it would do him a great deal of good. His exam mark, though not unsatisfactory considering the work he put in, could have been better if he had directed more thought and care towards his exams. He must try a bit harder to understand and must seek my help when he can't. I hope he learns to work with his teachers better and keep out of trouble. I look forward to teaching a more hardworking student next term.

The final piece of data that we generated again came through random distribution. This time each student received a sheet of paper on which were the two versions of ostensibly the same report. The paper, however, was folded to conceal the first report, and the task for the students was to rewrite the euphemistic report in such a way that they tried to reflect directly what they perceived to be the real thoughts behind it. The example that I have been using was changed in the following way:

> Tebogo does not pay attention in class and will not do as he is told. In general he acts immaturely and this is a very bad influence on his work. His work is messy and not thought through properly. He needs to respect his teachers and ask them for help. I expect to see a marked overall improvement next term.

Each set of three reports was returned to the writer of the first stage of the exercise and I simply asked the students to compare and contrast the three different reports as a homework assignment. To me the three-stage process had seemed similar in some respects to that of a teacher starting to write a report with negative ideas about a particular student in her or his head, then softening those ideas in the actual report, and then having those euphemistic expressions decoded by the student or parent recipient. However, I did not know what the class would come up with and I did not try to push the students in any particular direction. Certain comments about euphemisms had already been made during class discussions, and I was quite content to let these be their guide.

Analysis of the Dummy Reports

In their analysis of these reports the students focused again and again on four main areas. These were disguise, politeness, ambiguity and generalised vagueness. I shall take disguise first. The following paragraph tries to describe this ability of euphemisms to hide the truth:

> When we compare versions one and three we come to realise how much of the truth is hidden through the use of euphemisms. Little details which would otherwise help in building up an impression are missed out by the euphemistic version and therefore were not available to the writer of the third version. The second version not only hides some of the facts but also twists some others. The process of writing these 3 versions reminds me of a sausage machine. We put in a straightforward report and the machine rewrites it in euphemisms and then rewrites the euphemistic copy back into a straightforward version without any reference to the original. Some facts come out straight and some are twisted. Some are missing and some are added.

Many interesting comments were made on the usefulness of such disguises to both speaker and audience, in this case writer and reader. Essentially, what was being discovered here were some features of the illocutionary and perlocutionary effects of euphemisms. As far as the teacher is concerned, one student saw this in terms of freedom: 'Euphemisms are very important socially, as they are often used by teachers when a taboo or sensitive issue is being discussed. They give the speaker freedom to talk about taboos without being looked down upon for using vulgar language or being insensitive.' Another student, however, saw this process more as a kind of absolution for the teacher: 'Teachers like using euphemisms in reports because then they don't have to feel bad about saying nasty things.'

When it came to perlocutionary force, the power of euphemisms to camouflage was seen most often to have the dual function of keeping parents at bay and encouraging weak students at the same time: 'If teachers always wrote blunt reports about unintelligent or badly behaved students, parents would probably object and students would not endeavour to try harder as they would lose confidence in themselves.' Politeness overlaps considerably with disguise, constituting probably the most obvious social function of disguise, something similar to the 'freedom to talk about taboos' mentioned above. It is in this context that Leech's (1983, 147) one mention of euphemism in his *Principles of Pragmatics* occurs. Many students picked up this point, and some expressed it in ways which showed considerable insight:

> In comparing the original version of the report and the euphemistic version I observe that many of the truths of the first are hidden in the flowery language of the second. It strikes me that some of the positive statements of the first version have been made into negative statements. To give an example, 'Tom is lazy' is turned into 'Tom does not always do his best'. In other words, while the first version gives us what Tom is doing wrong, the second gives us what Tom is not doing right. These sentences act as if they were complementing each other. This kind of use of euphemisms is extremely helpful when one is trying to be tactful.

I found it especially pleasing that some attention was being paid to the linguistic strategies used for expressing politeness. The student who wrote the first report of the series of three quoted in the previous section had this to say about the euphemistic softening of her bluntness: 'In the second report the complaints have been moderated by using phrases such as "cooperate a bit more" and "behave a wee bit more maturely". Double negatives such as "not unsatisfactory" seem to play a similar role.'

Her first comment is a self-discovery of exactly the point that Leech (1983, 147) makes: 'the "minimizing" adverbials of degree *a bit*, *a little*, and *a little bit* are specialized towards negatively evaluated terms'. Her second observation about double negatives points to an all too common politeness strategy in report writing. I have since become hypersensitive to the number of times I am tempted to use formulations such as 'not unintelligent' in my own reports!

Very often my first impression of students who commented on ambiguity was that they were disagreeing with those who stressed the disguising capability of euphemisms. In fact, however, what many of them were pointing to is the sophisticated way in which the disguise can often be deliberately partial. The student who said 'what I've always known but never been told' wrote in this regard:

> Euphemisms have a strange effect on people's minds because although what the euphemism actually means is known or can be deduced people generally seem to find the news far less shocking than if it had been told bluntly or directly.

This type of ambiguity, where the claim is that two distinct impressions are held simultaneously in the mind of the recipient, is clearly connected to generalised vagueness. One student made precisely this link:

> When a direct statement is euphemised it is made general and somewhat vague. Therefore, when a euphemised or moderated statement is converted back into a direct statement it can be given a very different meaning from what it was originally intended to mean.

To me these analyses showed that many students in the class were beginning to get to critical grips with how euphemisms work in this particular area of school discourse. We had moved a long way from the Jones definition. Despite this, many of the students' assumptions were still obviously uncritical, such as the almost Platonic view expressed above that there existed an absolute truth of which euphemistic expressions were simply a pale and disguised reflection. The value of the dummy reports had been that they had allowed the students to generate their own data. Their fault, on the other hand, was that blunt speech had been given a kind of 'unmarked' status because that was where we had begun. In an effort to move to data that was more authentic I asked the class to bring in to school some of their old reports. I was checked, however, by a request to move away from the reports themselves to the people who wrote them. One student suggested a class questionnaire to teachers asking them about the ways in which they wrote reports. This is exactly what we did for what turned out to be the final stage of the series of lessons.

The Questionnaire to Teachers

The questionnaire about the ways in which teachers in the school write and feel about reports was put together entirely by the students in the class. To begin with they worked in groups of four; then, in a plenary session, the various questions that had been generated were discussed and twenty were selected. I submitted these questions on behalf of the class to all the teachers in the school, about thirty-five, and received a response of nineteen, over 50 per cent. These answers were then returned to the class for analysis, and each student wrote an assignment describing what he or she had learnt from this final stage of the exercise.

Not all the questions focused on euphemism. The opportunity for asking questions of the people responsible for their reports was clearly relished by the students and so they included a number of questions of a general nature. The list that follows is a selection of those that seem to me to relate in one way or another to the work that we had already done on euphemisms:

> What does a teacher mean by saying that you are 'well liked by your friends'?
>
> Some teachers use euphemisms that are easily seen through and so make the truth even starker. Do they do this on purpose?
>
> Why are you not blunt when writing reports?
>
> What exactly do you mean when you say 'he or she can do better'?
>
> Can you honestly say that you are as truthful about the bad students as you are about the good ones?
>
> What exactly do you mean when you say that a student 'has potential'?
>
> Do you often use flowery language when describing a student's performance? If so, why?
>
> Do teachers often find themselves lying when writing reports?
>
> Would you ever write lies to gain the popularity of a class or student?
>
> When writing a report do you ever consider the questions you asked yourself as a student when reading your reports?
>
> Do you ever feel like being so direct that the student's parents would want to kill that student?

In the analyses of the teacher's answers many points that had been made when writing about the dummy reports were reiterated.

A number of new insights were gained, however, and these from a usefully different perspective. The more imaginative students managed, through their response to the questionnaire answers, to project themselves to some extent into the position of their teachers. I wish to focus briefly on the comments in this category.

A common observation from this viewpoint was that teachers use euphemisms in reports because they are concerned above all to maintain the status quo:

> I conclude from the way these questions are answered that teachers are sometimes so tactful and euphemistic that the truth is hidden quite effectively. They feel that this is necessary if good relations are to be maintained and good results to be achieved.

Another student put this point more starkly: 'Most of the teachers answering questions based on euphemisms agreed that they are a commonly used escape route to avoid rocking the boat.' In some cases, the teachers came across as being fallible and all too human. The following revelation strikes me as a healthy learning experience for an adolescent student:

> Generally teachers felt that when they said that a student is 'well liked by others' they mean that the student is popular although I'm inclined to believe the teacher who wrote that the comment means nothing but just shows that the teacher has run out of ideas or doesn't know much about the student.

Other students made similar judgements, but put them more kindly:

> The use of euphemisms by teachers who are not prepared to commit themselves to a definite and damning report is fully justified. Such teachers know the limitations of their judgement and do not want to condemn students falsely. This avoids the tendency of some teachers of trying to be too insightful.

To me, the insights produced by the students at this stage were not startling, and I do not wish to make any great claims for them. The really important point as far as I am concerned is that they felt, at the end of what one student referred to as a 'Great Trek through euphemisms', in a much better position to appropriate and make their own the reports that had often seemed alien to them. Many students commented on the fact that they now had access to a form of discourse that was no longer strange and unfamiliar. Reports and report writing had become contextualised and some of their forms of expression, if not quite laid bare, at least opened up. This for me is one kind of empowerment, the kind that critical language teaching at the secondary level should investigate further. I conclude with a student comment that makes the same point:

> On the whole, I am now in a much better position to interpret teachers' opinions or beliefs regarding any topic in general. I can now claim that experience enables me to be a better judge of teachers' verdicts. The possibility that we have discovered certain weaknesses in the response of our teachers also now exists . . . and we should look at other ways in which they talk about us and write about us.

References

Corson D 1990 *Language policy across the curriculum*. Multilingual Matters

Kress G 1985 *Linguistic processes in sociocultural practice*. Deakin University Press

Jones R 1980 *New English fourth*. Heinemann Educational

Leech GN 1983 *Principles of Pragmatics*. Longman

Littlejohn A 1985 Learner choice in language study. *ELT Journal* 39: 253–61

Pêcheux M 1982 *Language, semantics and ideology* Macmillan

Saussure F de 1959 *Course in general linguistics* Fontana/Collins

Widdowson H 1987 The roles of teacher and learner *ELT Journal* 41: 83–8

10 *Initial steps towards critical practice in primary schools*

Paul Clarke and Nick Smith

Our central concern as teachers is in exploring practical ways in which critical educators can start to address the issue of ownership of learning, particularly through getting learners to review their own work. We see this as one way in which learners can begin to engage in activities which lead to an emancipatory practice. From starting points as simple as asking the learner to reflect upon what they have done, learners begin to develop an awareness of the world in which they live, building an experience-based body of meanings which they own and have control over. This practice is an initial step towards a critical view of the world, one element of which is a critical language awareness (CLA).

In this chapter we will discuss practical steps for teacher/educators to begin to address some of the issues raised in the paper by Clark et al. (1988) on critical language awareness. We refer specifically to primary education. We feel there is a need to put CLA into the context of a broader debate already going on in schools, which is about what sort of curriculum will provide learners with the knowledge and skills necessary for their future lives. We believe that knowledge and skills are insufficient, there also needs to be an understanding of the derivation and application of such knowledge and skills through reflection on past practices, in order that the learner can make sense of and exercise control over that which they learn. We believe that critical practice will prove to be an important issue in enabling teachers and learners to achieve these goals, in what can be seen as an imposed and non-negotiable curriculum. What we propose, therefore, are starting points, ways in which teachers can plan activities which begin to make *critical learning* a possibility, following on from which CLA can be introduced. The relevance of this debate to CLA will be discussed, and two brief examples will be presented, one in which learners review the learning process, and the other in which children discuss language use in a multilingual classroom. We will consider some of the National Curriculum documents in the light of our discussion of critical learning and CLA, and ask the question, if there is room for CLA in the National Curriculum, how far can we go?

Critical learning

The purpose of this section is to explain one way in which critical learning could become a regular part of classroom practice. Having described one such approach we will then show how this creates a basic critical orientation onto which CLA can be built. In introducing this chapter, we touched upon the main motivation for our interest in critical learning, that of ownership and control of learning. In exploring the nature of power in educational practice we found that the critical perspective provided an avenue of enquiry which is deeply relevant to the educational debate in schools at the present time concerned with the National Curriculum. At a time when many teachers consider the ownership and control of their work to be challenged through the National Curriculum, it may seem incongruous that we are presenting a case for greater independence for learners. What we suggest, we believe, offers teachers a position from which they can begin to look again at the National Curriculum, where they can determine critical practices which focus teacher and learner attention to the content and contexts of learning in the classroom. In reflecting critically upon their work, they may regain control over learning and begin to offer deeper understanding of what learning means in the classroom. We believe that this critique, which teachers will need in order to meaningfully challenge the National Curriculum, will come from working with the National Curriculum and reflecting upon its contradictions and inconsistencies. We see critical learning as a way in which a learner uses a cyclical process of reflecting upon past experiences, planning from these past experiences ways of approaching new tasks, acting upon the plan made, and finally evaluating the outcomes of the activity. If this process is to involve critical practice, then it must take as a starting point that the 'order' of classroom life is socially created, is open to question and change, and cannot be accepted as a 'given' reality. This means that at any point within the critical learning process the learner can identify and act upon emancipatory choices. This practice is one which has been described in both theoretical and practical terms by many, but our points of reference include, Boud et al. (1985), Carr & Kemmis (1986) and Grundy (1987). As a process this is familiar to many teachers and learners in implicit form, that is, in working a cycle of planning some form of activity, doing the work associated with it, and considering how successful it was. What we wish to stress is that where a teacher identifies and draws the attention of the learner to the processes they go through as they do an activity, it raises the consciousness of the learner to that process. In classrooms, this consciousness-raising about process is not common, perhaps because when practised, it begins to challenge the given assumptions through which classroom life is driven, i.e. conventions of power and authority, who decides what is taught or learnt, and who assesses what is learnt. Consequently, we believe that learner attention is generally focused towards product – 'what is done', rather than to process – 'how it is achieved', and critical practice is limited.

In order to illustrate how we might see classroom practice beginning to use critical learning practices, we have outlined a series of steps which teachers could take. We have divided these into reflective and critical practices. Reflective practices may be concerned directly with learning processes, but may lack a critical stage, that of consciously selecting some form of action, based upon informed choice from the opportunities available, and awareness of the origins and influences of decisions. Reflective practices might include:

(1) a consideration of the availability of classroom resources to learners, so that they have ready access to materials they will need
(2) introduction of activities which demand that learners make their own choices about classroom materials
(3) introduction of activities which demand that learners decide

when they have completed the activity, and that they
demonstrate or explain how they came to that decision
(4) introduction of planning in activity design, and assessment of
the success or failure of plans
(5) introduction of regular reviewing sessions into classroom
operations, activities, organisation and management
(6) use of planning sessions as a sounding board for learners to
discuss taking their activities further

Critical practices might include:

(1) drawing learners' attention to the nature of the learning process
they are working in, by asking learners to give names to the
stages they identify within planning, working and reviewing
sessions; they can then describe technically the procedures for
learning, and thus have more control over their own learning,
and over the way they communicate their learning to others
(2) addressing the influences, limitations and opportunities within
the activity, so that a greater degree of awareness of learning in
a class and school environment is generated, and an awareness
of what can and cannot be changed.

We are under no illusions that a general practice of critical
learning would take time to be introduced. First, because learners
need to become familiar with the process, and second, if classrooms
are to become places which engage learners in critical practices,
then these critical practices must be consistent from class to class
across a school. This challenges the 'given' realities of what
constitutes school knowledge, because knowledge is no longer
assumed to be owned by any one, powerful group of teachers.
It is substituted therefore with 'created' or 'negotiated' knowledge,
arrived at by choice, created through a continual negotiation of
meaning. This negotiated approach to learning, which provides us
with a way to examine the link between critical learning and CLA,
is what Bruner (1986) describes as a 'forum', 'It follows from this
view of culture as a forum that induction into the culture through
education, if it is to prepare the young for life as lived, should also
partake of the spirit of a forum, of negotiation, of the recreation
of meaning' (Bruner 1986: 123).

Critical learning and critical language awareness

In our discussion of critical learning we have illustrated how necessary critical awareness is to process learning in developing a wider awareness of the world. From this awareness we have shown practices which raise awareness of the potential for change. In CLA we believe this same process operates, but its focus is upon language, and in particular, upon the social and political constraints of language. This issue, of the broader critical awareness of the world linking with the specific awareness of the world of language, is described by Clark et al. (1988).

In arguing for a critical LA, we are applying to language a general view of what the main objective of schooling ought to be: developing a critical awareness of the world, and of the possibilities for changing it. In the matter of language it is a matter of coming to see the existing practices of a given 'sociolinguistic order' as socially created within particular social relationships, and therefore socially changeable.

We have argued that the practices of reflection, plan, and action, form the consciousness-raising process by which inequalities are identified, and through which learners have the means of action – a framework on which to structure their arguments and justify the action which they have taken.

We see critical learning and CLA sharing common processes and practices, critical learning, however, being the enabling framework through which CLA can function. CLA is, though, an especially important element of this broader critical debate, because CLA is the basis for creating meanings, in the spirit of a 'forum.' If we engage in a practice which has an aim to recreate meaning, then we begin to draw into question the nature of the meanings with which we currently live and work. Such challenges to the 'given' meanings of our lives, form an important link between the initial critical practices we have described in the section on critical learning.

Critical practices: examples of school experiences

We will now go on to describe two projects which are motivated by teacher interest in introducing practices which initiate a critical perspective on learning. The examples use some simple child-centred principles which act as a starting point for consideration of learner ownership of the activity. These principles are:

a) What the learners do builds upon their existing body of knowledge.
b) Learners use their understanding of their action and what informs their action as a body of knowledge, which can be seen to be valid knowledge by the teacher and other learners. The teacher does not prescribe what is, or is not, acceptable knowledge, rather, through negotiation, the learners formulate knowledge collaboratively, drawing upon past experience.

Setting the scene

One of the greatest potential strengths of the National Curriculum lies in the importance attached to speaking and listening. For the first time these are officially recognised as crucial curricular areas and furthermore recognised as being within the 'responsibility' of all teachers across the curriculum (Cox 2, DES 1989: 2.23). Not that these are new recognitions, but they are now for the first time enshrined within educational legislation. The Bullock Report (DES 1975) recommends:

> Language has a unique role in developing human learning; the higher processes of thinking are normally achieved by the interaction of a child's language behaviour with his other mental and perceptual powers. (DES 1975: recommendation 36)

Acknowledging this role places a clear responsibility with teachers to maximise the linguistic potential of the children they work with. That language plays a significant part in learning and thinking is clearly recognised in the National Curriculum. Cox Report 2 recognises as one of the primary purposes in developing 'capabilities in speaking, listening, reading and writing' that:

> English contributes to the personal development of the individual child because of the cognitive functions of both spoken and written language in exploratory learning and in organising and making sense of experiences. (DES 1989: 2.14)

Although specifically addressing English, Cox is here referring back

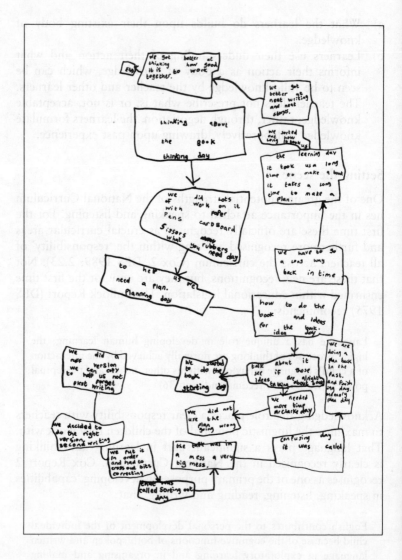

Figure 10.1

to the more general statements of both the Bullock Report (DES 1975) and the Kingman Report (DES 1988) the latter of which states that 'language is the instrument of intellectual development' (2.10).

The examples we now give draw upon these issues and attempt to exemplify them in practice.

Case study one: Learning processes within a storymaking project

Storymaking is something which happens all of the time in primary schools. We feel that it is an interesting point at which to begin to introduce critical practice as so many of the conventions of storymaking are taken as 'given'.

In this activity we worked with a group of 7 year-old learners for one hour each week for a duration of ten weeks. The activity was driven by the children's interest in producing a book. With this aim in mind we were particularly interested in looking at the ways in which the learners reflected upon their work and made decisions about where they would go next with it, at different stages of the book production. From this starting point we also explored with the group the ways in which stories could be changed, and how labelling particular parts of their work provided them with ways of describing how certain elements influenced others. We asked them to reflect upon the whole body of work and the learning processes they had been involved in, and to make recommendations regarding where they would like to go next with their learning. Figure 10.1 shows the children's flow diagram, which they completed at the end of the project as a part of the review activity. The diagram begins with the box called 'Thinking about the book', and can be followed by the arrows.

Our own plan of the activity concentrated upon the book production, contrasting with the flow diagram designed by the children, which considered the processes the children went through.

What we believe is important about the example is that it illustrates how a language of process, in this instance focused on the production of a book, enables learners to focus more clearly upon the way they did an activity. This is not a practice of CLA. It is, however, an example of learners beginning to explore ways in which they can explain rather than merely describe what they

Group are given a design brief, to gather together a selection of favourite books. From this selection they were asked to decide upon a target audience, and to collaboratively produce one book using the resources they had gathered as source material.

Looked at the source material.

Discussed why certain parts of the books were enjoyable.

Collected together the best sections.

Discussed how to use the material selected.

Made some plans from ideas generated.

Selected best plan.

Reviewed what had been achieved so far, gave each element of the work so far a name.

Considered audiences.

Drafting/redrafting.

Group reading and editing.

Re-planning to designate roles and to set timetables.

Final writing.

Collating and presentation to audience.

Final reviewing and recommendations for further action.

have done, a significant step towards critical practice. Looking at the group's flow diagram, each box is given a name, for example: planning day, starting day. These labels relate to specific elements in the process which the group considered as significant. The labels helped the group to put forward arguments about why one element was more enjoyable, or more successful, than another. This exemplifies a developing awareness of process, it also illustrates the idea expressed by Clark et al. (1988) that there are: 'radically different ways of wording the world according to the speaker's or writer's position or point of view' (Clark et al: 1988).

The group ownership of the activity validates their 'ownership' of the terminology used to describe the processes they went through. In order to make the link between CLA and critical learning real, the group might have gone on to discuss the nature of the labels, and consider in more detail the issue of the ownership of the language: who decided on the labels, what the labels meant to them and to other children with whom they talked, and how the labels enabled the children to discuss in more specific terms the different work they did on different occasions.

The last point we would like to make about this example concerns what is done next – the *action*. Earlier, we illustrated what we consider to be the basic critical processes which create action, which is derived from a critical awareness. The storymaking provided an opportunity for the group to develop a language to describe their work, and in creating a descriptive language they gained more insight and more control over that work. It enabled them to review over a long period of time the development of their ideas, and to put their learning into the context of the past – their previous experience of storymaking activities – and the future – the potential for further storymaking, with more awareness of its methods.

Again there is a common principle between the example and CLA. With young learners there is a danger that educators provide activities which lead to improved practice in learning, but which fail to provide a heightened awareness of that practice. The final element of the storymaking activity was to ask the group what they will now do, how they will act. They draw upon awareness and capability, reflect upon past experience and then determine where they want to go through 'informed committed action' (Carr & Kemmis 1986). This, we believe, is a practical way of including learners' experiences in learning; it says to the learner, what you propose is 'legitimate school knowledge' (Clark et al. 1988); furthermore, it is a 'potential basis for emancipation' (ibid).

Case study two: An oral storytelling project

This project grew out of an attempt to create a 'programme of study' for a class of top juniors who predominantly were bilingual in Punjabi and English. The work drew on the children's first language and was intended to raise the children's awareness of language generally and introduce them specifically to ways of reflecting critically upon their language use. This necessitated that the children should become more consciously aware of language in use, but also how the language used related to the social, historical and political environment within which we work at school. It was our aim that an outcome of the discussions would be some form of action.

Quite incidentally, we were presented with an excellent introduction for the project when two members of the class returned after playtime one day. They were arguing hard about whose fault it was that they had got into trouble with the teacher on playground duty. Their conflict was opened to a class discussion of the different versions of 'story'. In the course of discussion it became clear that many factors influenced both the generation and the reception of the different versions of stories about the same event: the two children's different perceptions and interpretations, their different wishes for particular outcomes, and their different roles in the event; all variables which also acted on the teacher on duty.

The class then considered stories that were well known, looking at different versions, how oral stories change and evolve over time, and some of the structural aspects of stories the children had enjoyed. For the following week it was decided to gather together as many stories from as many sources as possible.

The following week the question of who the stories were going to be for was raised. Several children thought they would like to take their stories to tell to the infants. This was adopted by the whole class as one of the easiest and most practical outcomes. Groups then worked on exchanging stories and ideas. Each group was asked to decide to prepare and practise one particular story suitable for telling a group of middle infant children. The children were encouraged to use whatever language they wanted in discussing their stories – all groups being fluent Mirpuri Punjabi speakers, including the infants.

Conferencing and reviewing discussions were lively discoursal events – made all the more so by a spokesperson from each group, other than the originator of the story, reporting back and telling the story. This approach meant that in the course of the telling lively interactive debate took place. Exchanges occurred in which issues such as intentions, meanings and interpretations were debated and negotiated. A major issue for all groups was the choice of, and justification for, the language variety to be used; particularly within the context of the prevailing ethnocentric and inhibiting ideology of 'school'.

A frequent concern was the suitability of the stories to the perceptions and interpretations of the infants who were to receive them:

- would the language be suitable?
- would the infants understand?
- would they be able to switch in and out of two languages?
- was the story suitable to the level of maturity of the listeners?

One group rejected a horror story on these grounds, saying that parents might be cross if their children had been upset by an unsuitable story.

- was the story suitable on cultural grounds?

Beyond this the stories were told, tape-recorded, re-interpreted in books and pictures by the infants; and the project and their contributions assessed by the juniors. By focusing on variables that affect the process of communication, and encouraging the use of a first language in a purposeful project, the children became involved, many of them closely, in critical language work. Their awareness of language, especially with regard to socio-cultural aspects, went 'critical'. They expressed understanding of the different language expectations of different groups of children and teachers, and were able to select what they considered an appropriate response related to the language expectations of the audience.

CLA and the National Curriculum

Having discussed some ways of introducing critical practices to the classroom, we would like to consider the context within which such practices are now placed. We will look at the possibilities that exist within the National Curriculum to develop a critical perspective on learning and language use. In discussing such possibilities we acknowledge that the current climate provides us with opportunities to introduce such measures only if we use the National Curriculum documents as the vehicle. We will argue that a critical understanding of the National Curriculum documents provides us with the basis from which we can argue for CLA. Without a critical framework which operates from within the National Curriculum, initially created through teacher reflection on curriculum product and process, we see little opportunity at present to take CLA beyond a marginal practice.

It may be that the National Curriculum will suffer from simplification in its translation to practice, due to its cumbersome nature. The focus within the National Curriculum documents on attainment targets, which children will be assessed against, and which relate to notional norms, has to a large extent obscured the ideals held by many teachers of child-centred learning which attaches far more closely to the processes of learning. Such an over-emphasis on attainment targets, is, we believe, at the expense of the development of worthwhile, individualised, child-centred programmes of study. The worst implication of a target-based approach to curriculum is that teachers will rely heavily on transmission models of teaching, where teacher knowledge becomes paramount, to be transferred to the child, negating the possibility for negotiation of learning. To put it crudely, 'what' to teach is redefined by teachers as 'how' to teach. This approach to teaching may in part be a consequence of the difficulties encountered in trying to identify any clearly stated aims for the National Curriculum. However, there would appear to be a substantial hidden agenda based around such aims as standardisation, conformity and centralised control. Cashdan (1990) identifies some of the ends served by centralised control of the curriculum: these can be summarised as ideological, to do with the prevailing political will for central control; economic, by virtue of centralised supervision; guarantee of standards, with options on greater ideological control;

and 'highly visible performance standards', necessarily facilitated by a 'specified, deliberately narrowed curriculum'.

The National Curriculum for English necessarily drew extensively on the model of the English language recommended by the Kingman committee. In doing so, the centralised and controlled view of the English language has become absurdly reductivist and reactionary. Commenting on the Kingman report Cameron & Bourne (1988) point out that: 'In its underlying attitudes of nationalism, ethnocentricism, an authoritarian impulse to unity in culture, Kingman is far more like Newbolt than it is like the more recent Bullock and Swann reports (DES 1975, 1985) where the model of culture was being reworked towards diversity and pluralism'.

The theme of 'entitlement' to Standard English which persists strongly in Cox Report 2 (DES 1989) contributes significantly to this view of English. The claims that Standard English is 'essential for many purposes', and that 'schools have the clear responsibility to ensure that all pupils become competent in Standard English' (4.36) are not acceptable. That Standard English is essential in any way or that competence in it is necessary are socially constructed notions which imply that other varieties are inadequate for these purposes. Within such a view the development of Standard English is seen as a necessary part of the development of a fuller competence in language use. Although they were referring to the American Headstart programme, it is pertinent to quote from Baratz and Baratz (1970) who observed that: 'Because of their ethnocentric bias both the social pathologists and the genetic racists have wrongly presumed that linguistic competence is synonymous with the development of Standard English.'

Compensatory programmes were proposed for the emancipation of the lower classes. However, their effect was to adapt and integrate the lower classes to a prevailing ideology. In much the same way notions of entitlement profess an aim to empower individuals through the National Curriculum. Their effect may well be either alienation or integration, not empowerment or emancipation.

The notion of entitlement could be more usefully applied to linguistic awareness rather than to Standard English. If individuals were seen to be entitled to an awareness of language that operated within a critical framework, then we would be moving towards a situation in which individuals were being genuinely empowered through their own language.

Nevertheless, there are elements in the National Curriculum that appear to make space for critical language studies. In its presentation of the 'Role of English in the Curriculum', Cox Report 2 identifies a cultural analysis view which:

> emphasises the role of English in helping children towards a critical understanding of the world and cultural environment in which they live. Children should know about the processes by which meanings are conveyed, and about the ways in which print and other media carry values.(2.25)

The language work implied here would clearly fall within the ambit of critical language studies.

Paragraph 2.19 in the Cox Report identifies two aspects of language development, the personal and the social which both 'contribute to giving pupils power over their own lives' (2.19). The paragraph suggests that people who have sufficient awareness of language can recognise when it is being used manipulatively and in turn can use their language more effectively to be 'freer and more independent'. Unfortunately the comparison here is with those who suffer from 'linguistic inadequacy', which smacks of compensatory programmes.

Although the National Curriculum may be able to accommodate critical language awareness work, a nationally prescribed curriculum with clearly defined attainment targets does not allow for many of the consequences of critical approaches to learning. At the heart of critical learning is the need to hear the voice of the learner, to hand over control of what is to be learned. Learners will need to be in a position to determine the current state of their knowledge, plan what they need to learn and how they can best achieve that learning. To do this they will need to be able to assess their own achievement so that they can act upon their current achievement in responsible and informed ways.

The Cox Report goes a small way towards this position in its chapter on assessment where it acknowledges a role for self-assessment:

> Self assessment by pupils themselves ... has a part to play by encouraging a clear understanding of what is expected of them,

motivation to reach it, a sense of pride in positive achievements, and a realistic appraisal of weaknesses that need to be tackled. It should be given due weight as part of the evidence towards a teacher's internal assessments. (14.16)

Certainly the National Curriculum already encourages individualised curricula for all pupils and appears to encourage the development of critical approaches to learning and the empowering of learners as well as a degree of self-assessment. However, it stops short of advocating the open approach to learning that would appear necessary to critical, action-led study. This may well be a function of a reluctance in teachers and government to accept the implicit yet radical shift of power necessary. For a curriculum founded on centralised control and reductivist notions of what should be taught, such a shift is difficult to accommodate, yet as Edwards (1988) points out: '[it] . . . may be worth considering if the early years of education are to provide an enabling environment for the responsible exercise of children's personal powers . . . to allow them to build personal theories of self effectiveness.' CLA and critical learning engage the child in such theory building, but take theory beyond the making meaning stage, into making action out of meaning.

Conclusion

What we have tried to illustrate in this chapter is that CLA is an important part of a wider view of what schooling and teaching ought to be. In practising a critical curriculum, advancing ideas through reflection, action and CLA, we challenge many of the 'given' realities of classroom and school life. Just how far we can pursue such practice is dependent upon two conditions:

(1) How aware the teacher is of the opportunities and limitations of critical practice within the institution she or he works in, that is how critically aware the teacher is.
(2) How far the institution is willing or able to accept the practice of critical educators that is, how critically aware the people who run the institution are.

Teachers interested in critical practice may find their efforts limited by a governing body of a school wholly at odds with such practices. Apart from trying to take a greater role in their institution's decision making, teachers in such a situation may also be able to use CLA as a vehicle for challenging assumptions about language and learning across the school and across the curriculum. We suggest that critical practitioners should adopt but also adapt the National Curriculum, drawing upon the limited openings for critical work that it provides. This at once restrains and liberates the teacher; *restrains* in that the teacher has to use the framework of the National Curriculum legally required; *liberates* in that this framework is open to broad interpretation and application, if interpreted carefully it gives critical practitioners a basis from which to argue for critical practices in classrooms *now*.

Such action could have the further effect of beginning to build a critical 'theory' of curriculum practice directly developed from within the National Curriculum, something which is currently lacking. It would then also begin to challenge some of the assumptions made within the National Curriculum, and be a means by which teachers could question and change them, through informed argument, and practical action in their classroom practice.

References

Baratz S, Baratz J 1970 Early childhood intervention: the social science base of institutional racism. *Harvard Educational Review* 40(1): 29–50

Boud D, Keogh R & Walker D (eds) 1985 *Reflection, turning experience into learning*. Kogan Page

Bruner J S 1986 *Actual minds, possible worlds*. Harvard University Press

Cameron D, Bourne J 1988 No common ground: Kingman, grammar and the nation. *Language and Education* 2(3): 147–60.

Carr W, Kemmis S 1986 *Becoming Critical – Education, Knowledge and Action Research*. The Falmer Press

Cashdan A 1990 Language, communication and reading. In Potter F (ed) *Reading, learning and media education*. Blackwell

Clark R, Fairclough N, Ivanic R, Martin-Jones M 1988 *Critical language awareness*. Centre for Language In Social Life, Lancaster University

DES (Department of Education and Science) 1975 *A language for life*. (The Bullock Report), HMSO

DES 1985 *Education for all* (The Swann Report) HMSO

DES 1988 Report of the committee of inquiry into the teaching of English language (The Kingman Report), HMSO

DES 1988 *English for ages 5–11*. (Cox Report 1) HMSO
DES 1989 *English for ages 5–16*. (Cox Report 2) HMSO
Edwards A 1988 Power games in early education. *Early Child Development and Care* 34: 143–9
Grundy S 1987 *Curriculum: product or praxis*. The Falmer Press

11 Critical Approaches to Language, Learning and Pedagogy: A Case Study

Lesley Lancaster and Rhiannan Taylor

In this chapter, we intend to describe and evaluate a language awareness course which took place in the Modern Languages Department of a Shropshire Secondary school, Madeley Court, during 1987/1988. First, however, we shall discuss the importance of a critical approach in the classroom, both at the level of developing students' understandings about language and at the level of the learning process itself. Then we shall review the history of language awareness/language study work in schools. Finally, before describing the Madeley Court work we shall look at the climate within the county at that time, with respect to language and consider its influence on the work at Madeley Court.

In our view, there are two tenets of a critical language study approach which are central to enabling all children to develop an *explicit* understanding of themselves as language users in the society in which they live. First, that a critical approach sets out to explain, not simply describe, the discourse of society. Second, that the child's own linguistic and other experiences are central to the learning process. The descriptive approach has predominated in language awareness work that has been taking place in schools. This offers to children a view of language as product, a matter largely of individual choice rather than of social determination. Although the intention might be to increase their knowledge and understanding about language, the effect is to disempower certain children. For example, children who speak non-standard forms of

English or whose home/first language is not English might be offered a view of their way of speaking as 'interesting' but 'inappropriate' in many circumstances. This suggests that their discourse is of less value than a more consistently standard form and its use a question of individual failure. A critical approach would consider the above issue in the context of examining the relationship between discourse, power and social context. This would entail an explanation of the different values attributed to certain dialects and varieties of language.

The second point as we have said, concerns the learning process itself. In Clark et al. (1987), the point is made that one of the major implications of a critical model for teaching and learning is that 'critical language awareness is built from the existing language capabilities and experience of the child'. The need to place the child's linguistic and other experiences at the centre of what is happening in the classroom means that a critical approach is also about how children learn at all ages and in all areas of the curriculum. It is about empowering all children as learners by giving them control over what they are doing. This can only be achieved as a result of greater understanding by both teachers and pupils of the relationship between language, learning and society. And it involves not just an examination of the discourse of the wider community, but of the classroom itself.

The Madeley Court work was not developed with a coherent critical language study approach in mind. Indeed this was not possible since papers about critical language study were being written at the same time as the work at Madeley Court was taking place. However, a critical language study view was very much part of the philosophy of language of most of those involved with the Madeley Court work and we attempted to reflect this in both the content of the course and in classroom practice. The degree to which we succeeded in achieving these ideals is discussed later in this chapter.

Language Awareness – the background

For many teachers, 'language awareness' is still not a familiar term. However, although not at the forefront of curriculum studies, work of this kind has been in existence for some years.

Language awareness or 'language study' as it can also be called, evolved in the 1960s with the development of Linguistics as a significant discipline and the demise of prescriptive grammar teaching based on an inappropriate Latinate model. For many teachers, this led to a rejection of anything that smacked of an analytical approach to language. For others though, it opened the doors to a much wider approach to the whole question of language. In 1964, there was a recommendation in the final report of the Secondary Schools Examination Council, 'The Examining of English Language', that as part of an A-Level Course, students should be involved in 'a study of the structure of language; the different types of English, the position of standard English, dialects and slang, and the relation of language to individual thought and behaviour and also its social implications'. In the same year the Nuffield programme in Linguistics and English Teaching was set up under the direction of Michael Halliday. The programme was a way of bringing together teachers and linguists to look at more effective ways of teaching language in schools. One product of this programme was Doughty et al. 1971. It consisted of a ring folder containing a vast range of language activities for secondary pupils under three broad headings, 'Language – its nature and function', 'Language and the individual' and 'Language and society'.

'The units', according to the authors, 'aim to develop in pupils and students awareness of what language is and how it is used and at the same time to extend their competence in handling the language' (Doughty et al., 1971: 8–9).

The very name of the book, *Language in Use*, showed it was a radical departure from anything done before. It also tried to steer a careful path between being aware of current trends in language research and not being seen as an exercise in applied linguistics.

'The Role of Language Study', as Doughty and Thornton (1973) said, 'is to act as a mediator between on the one hand, linguistics and related disciplines, and, on the other, the need of teachers and pupils to come to an understanding of the nature of language and its role and function in society'.

However, in spite of its theoretical and pedagogical excellence *Language in Use* was never really taken up. There were a number of practical difficulties in using the material. The folder was densely packed with information about language and suggestions for lessons. However, since the field was unfamiliar to many teachers they found it inaccessible and difficult to fit into English courses in any consistent way. Probably more significantly though, the early 1970s was a period which was largely unsympathetic to any attempt to look closely and analytically at the functions and structure of language.

In 1975, the last major report on the teaching of English, the Bullock Report, was produced but did little to change the situation. The Bullock report allocated only a small sub-section to the question of language study, concluding:

> We have advocated through this section that children should progressively gain control over language by using it in response to a variety of demands. They can be helped to do this by studying how it works in various situations, not in any sense of choosing models or opting between stereotypes but by insight into its richness and infinite possibilities. [Furthermore] Linguistics should not enter schools in the form of the teaching of descriptive grammar. (DES 1975: recommendation 133)

Multilingualism and bilingualism are very much the province of language awareness which can have a key role in supporting bilingual children in schools. The Bullock Report recognised the importance of bilingualism and of schools adopting a positive attitude to bilingual pupils. Awareness of these issues was growing by the late 1970s. In 1976, the National Congress on Languages in Education (NCLE) was set up to provide a forum where 'teachers, researchers, examiners, advisers, publishers and others interested in all aspects of language in education could meet and discuss their common problems'. A research proposal, written in 1982, 'Language Study in the Secondary School', follows in the *Language in Use* tradition but adds to its list of 'roles of language study' the task of helping pupils 'use this awareness to be interactive and responsible members of a mixed linguistic community'. Official thinking in the guise of the modern languages National Curriculum guidelines does not seem to have progressed from this view (though see now DES 1990).

During the early 1980s there was also increasing interest from modern language, EFL, ESL and community language teachers in work relating to all areas of language teaching. This led, in 1981, to a language awareness conference being called by National Congress on Languages in Education. A working group was given the task of establishing the state of the art as far as language awareness work went. Although there was some increase of interest it was still fairly marginal. In 1984 Eric Hawkins published a set of language awareness materials. This consisted of a theoretical introduction and a series of booklets on such topics as spoken and written language, learning languages and language variety, designed for 11–14 year olds.

These materials, and the NCLE approach had the advantage of being cross-curricular in intent and having a breadth of topic coverage. They were essentially descriptive in design and were seen as having a practical, even organisational purpose; '[Awareness of language] seeks to bridge the difficult transition from primary to secondary school language work, and especially to the start of foreign language studies and the explosion of concepts and language introduced by the specialist secondary school subjects' (Hawkins 1984: 4). Hawkins' aims were stated as: 'to challenge pupils to ask questions about language, which so many take for granted . . . to prepare the way for a language element in child care courses for fourth and fifth years . . . to challenge linguistic parochialism' (ibid.). However, the central question in our view is how to make children's knowledge and understanding of their language or languages explicit to them in ways that are meaningful, appropriate and empowering. These materials offered no kind of critical framework within which to answer this question. Indeed they seemed further away from any answer than Doughty and Thornton ten years earlier, in spite of considerable expansion of knowledge and insight from the field of linguistics.

In the later 1980s however, the question of what children need to know about language was once again being discussed. This was not least because discussions about an English National Curriculum led inevitably to a review of the relationship between 'standards' and 'grammar'. At the same time as papers about Critical Language Study were emerging from the Centre for Language in Social Life at Lancaster University, the Kingman Report and the first Cox report were published in 1988 and 1989 respectively. The suggestions in the Kingman Report were taken up by the LINC (Language in the National Curriculum) project which, at the time of writing, is still discussing and piloting materials.

The Cox documents discuss at length the issues concerning teaching pupils about language. Cox et al. conclude:

Two justifications for teaching pupils explicitly about language are, first, the positive effect on aspects of their use of language and second, the general value of such knowledge as an important part of their understanding of their social and cultural environment, since language has vital functions in the life of the individual and of society. (DES 1989: English five to sixteen)

This is a more expanded version of the Doughty and Thornton view and although it does not advocate a critical approach, it does not rule it out. However, further reading of the document suggests that the descriptive approach is the one which is followed. The question of standard English is discussed at some length and the equivalence of all language varieties and the need to value the language of all children is pointed out. However, the justification for teaching and using standard forms is again that of 'appropriateness'.

What is required is a way of discussing with children the contexts in which Standard English is obligatory, or appropriate for social reasons. (DES 1988: English five to eleven)

Like the Hawkins' materials the Cox document raises important questions but fails to answer them from a critical perspective. The contradiction is unresolved. On the one hand, we are told to value the language of all children but, on the other hand, we are told that the value is strictly limited.

For ages 11 to 16, the English National Curriculum encompasses a wide field of learning about language. It is not within the remit of this article to discuss the details of this. One of the main problems with the 'Knowledge about Language' strands within the English document is that they are tied into the assessment scheme (attainment targets) in a way which suggests that knowing about language involves learning a series of unrelated facts at particular stages. Hence at 11, pupils need to be able to talk about 'variations in vocabulary between different regional or social groups' but an understanding of 'some of the factors that influence people's attitudes to the way other people speak' is not assessable until age 16!

In spite of the contradictions which are contained within the English National Curriculum, it has raised awareness among teachers that knowledge about language is not a marginal issue. It is also the case, as we discuss in the introduction, that it is not just a question of the content of English lessons but most importantly a matter of language and learning across the whole curriculum. This question is discussed in the next section in relation to the view of language current in Shropshire at the time of the work at Madeley Court school.

The Shropshire Context

In a course held for all Shropshire Primary Language Coordinators during 1989/1990 a discussion was had as to whether or not there was a need to focus explicitly on language in the primary classroom. The case for this happening was made in the following terms. Unless we do provide an explicit focus on language we are failing to provide the kind of environment in which all children can develop as learners and language users. However, it is not just a question of enabling *pupils* to understand more, but also of *teachers* making their practice reflect an understanding of language and learning. The starting point needs to be 'what do children *know* about language' rather than 'what do they *not know* and how can this be remedied'. There is a need to redress this kind of deficit view not just through language study, but also through classroom organisation what we shall term a critical pedagogy.

The question of the relationship between language and learning is prominent in the Cox discussion papers and also in Primary and Secondary English Guidelines which were produced in Shropshire in 1988 and 1989.

> there is an intimate relationship between language and learning, in which learners get better at language (mainly but not entirely unconsciously) in using it to communicate and comprehend (mainly consciously) other things. (SED 1989)

Although these were guidelines for teaching English, their emphasis on language and learning was relevant across the whole curriculum.

> Because so much of children's learning occurs within the medium of language, the more we understand about the workings of language, the more likely it is that we will be able to provide circumstances in which children will learn successfully. (SED 1988)

Since most young children come to school as successful learners and users of language, we need to consider the qualities of the environment in which this learning takes place and to reflect these in the classroom. The first Cox document characterised this environment as providing:

A constant respect for the child's language.

A very high expectation of success.

An apprenticeship approach which offers successful models of spoken and written language and constant support while children learn.

Strong motivation to acquire control over language and understand the power which it can have.

As this implies, children's earliest experiences of language are not restricted to the spoken mode; all children whatever their background, live in a world full of print so that by the time they come to school at five, they all have some experience and implicit understanding of the written mode.

There are three fundamental points which can be drawn from these understandings of how children learn language:

(1) All children of normal brain function learn to speak and know about language without formal instruction.
(2) They come to school with a considerable amount of knowledge and understanding about language.
(3) They learn this in ways which are purposeful, meaningful and enjoyable.

If we acknowledge these points, they have serious implications for classroom practice at all levels. Let us take each point in turn.

The question of whether or not to teach children about language by means of structured, formalistic exercises, known commonly as *grammar* teaching, has been hotly debated by educationalists and politicians at key points over the years. The reason for its political significance has been interestingly discussed by Cameron and Bourne (1989). Most recently, with the introduction of a national curriculum, the question has been systematically considered by the authors of the Cox and Kingman reports and by those involved in the Language in the National Curriculum (LINC) project. The view taken by these reports was that there is little to be gained by teaching children about language by these means. Indeed such an approach can be positively harmful, particularly with respect to children's writing. It is also the case that presenting children with language in the form of a series of decontextualised exercises in no way reflects what we know about effective and meaningful language learning as exemplified by young children's earliest acquisition of language. And it in no way reflects the interactive nature of the language modes but rather presents a view of language as a set of discrete skills which can be acquired quite independently of each other. The guidelines and the Cox Report emphasise the importance of reflecting this interaction in the classroom; reading, writing and spoken language work together to create meaning; presenting language as non-interactive drills or routines obscures meaning.

> Writing is not something which can be taught as a sequence of steps, or of sub-divided parts to be put together later. Drawing on their experience of reading, talking, and listening, writers develop by composing whole texts of a wide variety of different kinds, for purposes they understand. (SED 1988)

The Secondary Guidelines talk about moving away from: 'the exercise of language as a set of drills and routines, divorced from real acts of communication and comprehension' (SED 1989).

The considerable degree to which children come to school at five with knowledge and understanding about language is something which some teachers find hard to accept. In spite of the fact that teachers are expected to know something about early acquisition of language, there is sometimes little or no recognition of the significance of this achievement for classroom practice. Implicit in this is frequently a deficit view of the language of certain children. Some infant teachers express this view in comments along the lines of 'most children in this school don't have any language when they first come', frequently qualified by statements to the effect that the school is fed by 'a large estate' or 'a farming community'. At Secondary level, similar qualifications are provided as explanations for poor results and even poor teaching. Such statements reflect a powerfully negative view of the language and culture of many children and a lack of understanding of how children learn and develop language. The effect of such attitudes on school performance are of course well documented.

Turning to our third point, when planning the work at Madeley Court we were conscious of the need to reflect the wider aims of the course (discussed in a following section) and our views of language and learning not just in the content of the course, but also in classroom organisation. There was a strong emphasis on collaborative group work, on discussion and active learning, and on letting students have control over what they were doing. There would have been a serious contradiction in, for example, our aim of 'exploring the way language is used in school' within the traditional discourse structures of the classroom. Such structures by their very nature are not open to discussion and criticism by students.

The extent to which this work involved a critical pedagogy will be discussed in greater detail, but some points are relevant at this stage. All good teachers attempt to provide a curriculum which is purposeful, meaningful and enjoyable. Unfortunately teachers frequently operate a set of premises which work well enough for them but do not have logic or coherence for all students. In spite of our desire to plan a course which had these qualities and looked critically at language, we didn't always succeed. This happened mainly where we failed to make the students' own experiences of language our starting point. We decided to plan the first unit according to chronological principles (the rationale for this is discussed in a later section). Although, at the time, this made sense to us, it did not on the whole make sense to the students. We did not set the activity up in such a way as to allow them to make links with their own experience, to interact with what Fairclough (1989) describes as *members resources* (MR). Interestingly however, because we had tried to change the discourse structures within the classroom it was easier to ascertain where we had gone wrong and to allow teachers and students to jointly renegotiate the direction of the work.

The decision of the Madeley Court Modern Languages Department to view its work in the wider context of the social role of language, happened at a time when the climate within the county as far as language and learning were concerned was dynamic. A number of factors had contributed to this: a succession of progressive English advisers, involvement with the National Writing Project, an active National Association of Teachers of

English group, an active language centre, a Talk project set up in 1987 and a number of primary and secondary teachers who were interested in such issues. It was an excellent context within which to tackle a language awareness project in school. We now go on to describe the school context at Madeley Court.

The School Context

Madeley Court School, in Telford, is a purpose-built comprehensive school that serves a predominantly working-class area in the south of the town. The majority of the pupils' families represented at the school are from the West Midlands conurbation and have settled in the area within the last fifteen years. Approximately 4 per cent of the school's population come from Ethnic Minority families, predominantly of Asian origin. As a community Telford has more in common with other urban areas in the West Midlands than with the Shire County in which it is situated. Shropshire is a predominantly rural 'all-white' county, with Shrewsbury as the major market town and administrative centre. As we have suggested, the Local Education Authority is encouraging change and development within the service, but progress is inevitably slow. This is not without some advantages, as the pace of change is such that teachers and parents feel in control of what is happening.

The school was one where the staff were not afraid to discuss and implement educational innovations where appropriate. In January 1987 the school was beginning to seriously address the issue of multicultural, anti-racist education, supported by the newly appointed Advisory teachers from the Education Support Grant (ESG) funded 'Education for a Multi-ethnic Society' (EMES) project.

The Modern Language Department at the school offered two European languages, French and German to A level. All pupils took French for the first three years, and able pupils studied German in the third year. The take-up rate at 14+ was average for the county at about 35–40 per cent with many more girls than boys opting for languages. The department was acutely aware of the failure of boys to continue to study languages and was working to change current attitudes to foreign language study.

The department had a policy of supporting bilingual pupils who wished to extend their 'mother tongue' or 'community language' skills. In practice this meant that an attempt was made to find people from the local community who would be able to teach and guide these pupils, who would then be entered for appropriate exams if they wished. The department realised, however, that support of this nature, voluntary and after school, did nothing to challenge the dominance of European languages in the school curriculum. In order to raise the status of bilingualism and to value the variety of languages that the pupils had at their disposal, the school and the department had to act more positively.

At the same time as the school was beginning to develop an awareness of issues relating to multicultural, anti-racist education, the Modern Language department was taking a fresh look at its aims and objectives. One of the five aims of the department was: 'to develop an awareness of the nature of language, its structure and the possibilities of its use.'

The department realised that while some pupils did develop this sort of awareness while they were learning French, it is doubtful that it came from the content of the lessons. Drawing pupils' attention to the similarities of the words 'château' and 'castle' and how the latter might have derived from the former does not contribute to the sort of awareness that had been nobly formulated in the above aim. 'language awareness' was not a totally new idea for the department, Some years previously, Eric Hawkins had been involved in a whole school Inset session, at which he had presented his ideas and developing work in this area. For a short time a cross curricular working party had met to look at the possibilities of introducing a language awareness course into the school. However, the school was subsequently involved in a major upheaval and the initiative came to nothing.

In 1987, when the idea re-emerged in the department, not only was the school more settled, but support also existed in the LEA, as we have outlined previously.

The Course and its aims

Detailed planning of the course was a collaboration between the three members of the Modern Languages Department at Madeley Court School and three members of the Talk project. However a great deal of thought had gone into the course long before specific planning took place. This had involved discussions within the department itself, with other departments, with the Head and with the Education for a Multi-ethnic Society project. The original aim was for the project to be cross-curricular, but for various reasons the other departments which were approached, were not able to involve themselves at this time.

In the initial planning stages the following four aims were formulated:

(1) To develop an awareness of the nature of language, its structure and the possibilities of its use.
(2) To help equip students to live in a multi-ethnic, multilingual society.
(3) To explore the way language is used in school, at home, in the street and in the community.
(4) To encourage students to explore attitudes to language and dialects.

As mentioned in the introduction, we adopted a chronological approach to implement the first aim. There is a progression from non-verbal communication, through sign language and spoken language to written language, as can be seen in the outline in Figure 11.1. By adopting this approach, we hoped that the pupils would develop for themselves an understanding of the historicity of language and its social construction. Hence, by placing an emphasis on how language has changed and is constantly changing over time, we intended that the pupils would come to see that language is not the fixed entity that it seems. At the same time, questions would be raised as to why language has changed in particular ways, who has determined those changes and how they have taken place. We were aware that not only lay people but many teachers too, hold the belief that language is in some way a body of 'knowledge', immutable and transferable as such to pupils by 'good' teachers and 'good' teaching. We wanted to challenge the view that discourse conventions exist in some natural way and to raise the children's awareness that language is socially produced and controlled.

We intended the children to apply the critical awareness created by this approach to present-day use of language and to begin to question and understand why some languages or varieties of language are more prestigious than others. Thus armed, we felt that the pupils would then be in a position to reflect on how society's

Topic	Starting points	Activities
Non-verbal Communication	Theatre in Education Presentation	Drama /Role-play
Animal Communication and its limitations	Tape of animal noises	Group discussion to identify animals and the emotions communicated.
Sign Language: its possibilities and uses	Film 'First Signs of Washoe' (a Horizon film showing attempts by a group of researchers to teach Chimpanzees to communicate using American sign language)	Questions, observations deductions in response to the film.
Spoken Language	1. Cartoons (showing a range of possibilities accounting for the origins of human language)	Group speculation based on Cartoons.
	2. Illustrations of specific environments e.g. an office, a kitchen, a space capsule	Creating/inventing a new language starting with words and building them into larger units of language based on the illustrations
Written Language How and Why it developed	1. Overhead Transparency of world Mao.	Group speculation as to why and where writing developed.
	2. Examples of Early Writing from picture writing to early symbolic writing.	Range of activities including designing pictograms.

Figure 11.1: Outline of the Course: Unit One – Beginnings of Language

devaluing of certain languages or varieties of language might affect themselves or others. This point will be developed below. But it is worth repeating that if we failed to realise this aim, it was because we did not make the students' experiences our starting point.

The first unit of the course was primarily directed towards encouraging the children to understand the nature of language, its structure and the possibilities of its use. We considered it important that each Unit should begin with a presentation that would create an impact on the children by inviting their active participation. Shropshire Theatre In Education (TIE) was asked to lead a workshop in mime and drama on the theme of non-verbal communication. From an initial input using a mimed interpretation of a love story, the TIE team led the students through a series of activities exploring the use of touch, gesture and facial expression as ways of conveying messages. We encouraged the children to comment on their experience of working with TIE:

> We thought it was expressing the full acting in all of us and words are not necessary. Hanif could join in and learn even though he can't speak English very well. (Lee, Hanif and Gary)

> We thought it helped us in co-operation and to get something through to somebody without using our mouths and voices. (Leighton, David, Philip and Lee)

> We think the work we did was very good and taught us how to work in group work without talking. It would be fun to do it again. (Sally, Alex, Joe, Prathiba and Shelley).

Having explored with the children the use of non-verbal communication, the course went on to consider sign language as an alternative means of communicating. We wanted the children to draw their own conclusions as to the ineffectiveness or limitations of this as a form of communication. One other section of this unit dealt with the development of writing. Using the Peter's projection world map, we invited the children to speculate where and why writing developed. We were surprised at how knowledgeable the children were and how confident they were at putting forward reasons for their hypotheses. This was obviously something they knew about and were able to show ownership of, in a way that had not happened with the previous sections. Some of the places that the children suggested were way out, being based more on their knowledge and understanding of twentieth century society, than on any understanding of the reasons for the development of writing. One pupil suggested that writing had started in Britain, because the British are hooligans and would have scrawled graffiti in stone!

The Unit ended with activities to involve the pupils in working out for themselves the significance of the development of symbolic writing. The children were given a series of pictures (shown in Figure 11.2) and in pairs they worked out a story and wrote it down. The children compared their stories and were able to see that more is needed than picture representation to convey meaning in any detail, particularly in our complex twentieth century society. Two of these stories are presented here:

> There was a man and a woman who lived in a house. It was sunny and they went on a donkey through the rain and cloud to a castle. At the castle they had wheat and grapes then they went back on the donkey to their house where the rest of the family were. Then night came and they went to sleep.

> The man and the woman went to a barn. The sun started shining so they went out and had a ride on the donkey. It clouded over and started to rain and they ran into a temple where they found corn and grapes. The donkey went into the barn and found three people in there. The moon came out and they went to sleep.

If the first unit attempted to encourage students to think about how language changes and develops through time. The second unit related more specifically to the other three aims, namely:

(1) To help equip students to live in a multi-ethnic, multilingual society.
(2) To explore the way language is used in school, at home, in the street and in the community.
(3) To encourage students to explore attitudes to language and dialects.

Aims (1) and (2) reflected our intention to explore with pupils the connection between the structure of society and the nature of discourse conventions allowed within that structure. We also hoped that the pupils would develop an understanding of the

Look at the sequence of pictures and make up the story they tell with your partner. When you have decided on a final version write it down.

Figure 11.2

social construction of language and of how and why language is constrained by social convention.

As we said in the introduction, there would have been a serious contradiction in our aim of 'exploring the way language is used in school', if our classroom practice did not also reflect this.

Hence we had to address the way that discourse is structured and determined by social relationships. But we needed to go further and to begin to identify the way that discourse can also determine social relationships, in the sense that it has an impact on them. In other words no participant in any discourse is passive, and it lies within the power of all of us to either reproduce or transform social relationships. So it was essential that not only the content of the course but also the way in which we worked should contribute to the process whereby the pupils would become conscious about themselves as language users and confident in their ability to be in control. At this point we added a fifth aim that had clearly been in our minds during the planning of the course, but had remained inarticulated until we became involved in the delivery of the second unit. This aim was:

5. To promote awareness among pupils of their own role as experts in the use of language.

We have chosen below some examples from the second unit of the course to show how the content and methods of working set out to support aims 1, 2 and 3 above. The second unit involved the pupils in an investigation of language variety and the grid represented in Figure 11.3 shows the sequence of work.

Precisely because we wanted to equip students to live in a multi-ethnic, multilingual society, we decided that the input for the second unit should come from members of the students' own communities. Staff and pupils took part in an assembly, either talking about themselves or reading something in their first languages.

The children were clearly impressed by the skills of their friends and peers and perhaps for the first time in their lives they had come face-to-face with 'real' people who were bilingual. They were fired up to find out more about their own language and that of other people they knew. At this stage we thought it would be appropriate to involve the pupils in reflecting on a wide variety of accents and dialects, their relative status in society and possible reasons for this difference in status. We began by asking the children to identify accents that they liked best and least, and to give possible reasons for their choices. We hoped to draw out of the discussion with the pupils the idea that prejudices about certain accents and dialects

Topic	Starting Points	Activities
Variety of language	Presentation in assembly. Pupils and staff talking and reading in their first language.	Pupil and staff participation.
Accents	Tape recording of 6 people using a range of British accents to describe their childhood.	Group work identifying accents. Individual ranking of preference and discussion of status of accents. Role-play using accents.
Dialects	Tape recording of 4 different dialects (Madeley, Telford, Afro-Caribbean, Geordie, Dublin Irish)	Group listening and interpreting the tape, identifying particular dialect words and meanings. Sharing dialect words.
Language in Britain	1. Introduction to Language Survey	Inquiry into how to say given words in as many 'community' languages as possible. Written forms as well.
	2. Languages around us.	Gathering written form of different languages e.g. food wrappers.
	3. Languages Survey	Presentation of findings in groups. Sharing written and spoken forms of numbers 1–10 in languages known within the class including Urdu and Gujarati.

Figure 11.3:   *Unit Two – The Variety of Language*

are not based on aesthetics or individual taste but are socially constructed. (We referred in this connection to research carried out into attitudes of non-British people to British accents that found a completely different hierarchy in terms of preference.) Exploring reasons for their own particular preferences and ours, the students were able to move from the personal to the general, and to begin to formulate ideas about social attitudes to language and social class, albeit at a very basic level.

Encouraging participation from teachers and students in this assembly (unfortunately not parents at this point) was very much in tune with the pedagogy that we had developed whereby we tried to involve students in their own learning. In addition the involvement of students and teachers allowed us to challenge the idea of the teacher as expert, since both groups appeared as learners and experts.

We now describe two activities from the second unit and, by focusing on one class in particular, we shall show how these activities contributed to a change in the pupils' attitudes towards language and dialect.

The pupils were asked to identify and then rank ten different accents that they listened to on a tape. They were at first unable to identify the local Madeley accent (remember that the majority of these children's families originated from other parts of the West Midlands and one or two had Black Country accents). They also ranked it towards the bottom of the ten accents in terms of liking it, on the basis that it was 'ugly' and 'they'd never heard it before'.

The next activity involved listening to a tape of four different dialects – Geordie, Afro-Caribbean (Jamaican), Southern Irish (Dublin) and Shropshire (Madeley). Again they listened in groups and had to try to identify differences in the use of vocabulary and syntax. This class enjoyed this exercise and went on to role-play situations using words and phrases in the dialects that they had been working with. It is interesting to note that the Madeley accent had been the least popular in the first activity, but by the second activity the Madeley dialect had become the children's most popular choice for these role-play activities. We discussed this change in attitude with the pupils.

By engaging in this way with these dialects, we were encouraging the students to see that there was no intrinsic barrier to communication inherent in any of them. They were able to experience for themselves that dialects are equal in terms of their ability to communicate, although by making connections between the two activities on accents and dialects the students understood that they may not be equal in terms of status and ability to command respect. We would suggest that the change in the pupils' attitudes to the Madeley accent and dialect came about as a result of the increased awareness the pupils had of issues to do with social attitudes and language.

To support and extend the classroom activities on language variety, the children were also involved in a language survey. The first part of this survey consisted of the children gathering and sharing examples of the written form of different languages found on artefacts collected at home. The results of the work done by one class are shown in Figure 11.4. The second part of the language survey involved the children collecting information under various headings by interviewing members of the school community. The actual survey is reproduced in Figure 11.5.

The pupils were encouraged to work in groups, to think about the skills involved in collecting the data and to share the work. Each group was given time to report back and the results were recorded on a large chart on the wall of the classroom as well as on video. Several pupils had learnt the numbers 1–10 in other languages, ranging from Urdu to German. Some pupils had learnt to say things in five different languages.

We encouraged the bilingual pupils to make their own presentation in this lesson. This involvement varied from an account of an event in their community language with a translation afterwards in English, to helping groups of pupils write the numbers they had learnt in that particular language (Gujarati and Urdu).

Thus far, we have concentrated on describing elements of the course which were obviously successful. But we need to attempt to identify why certain aspects of the course were successful while others were not.

We need to consider the use of advisory teacher support for curriculum development, and question how curriculum development can become embedded in the overall school curriculum. Finally, we must question what the whole experience meant for the pupils.

One overriding reason for the relative success of the second unit (and some parts of the first) was its capacity to *promote awareness*

Item	Language	Countries Where Language Spoken
Ice cream lids	French	Canada, Switzerland Africa, France,
Perfume box		Vietnam, Belgium
Perfume		
Cream bath		
Skin cream perfume		
Cheese spread		
Foam bath		
Newspaper	Italian	Italy, Yugoslavia, North Africa
Instructions for model men		
Game instructions		
Birthday cards	Flemish	Belgium, Holland
Caramel nuts	Arabic	Countries in North Africa
Plastic bag	Punjabi	Britain, India Pakistan
Instructions	Dutch	The Netherlands, South Africa
Bag	Spanish	Spain, countries in South America
Wine bottle	German	Germany, Austria, Switzerland
Instructions		

Figure 11.4: Results of survey of written forms of different languages found at home

4. During your survey see if you can find out how to say:
   HELLO
   GOODBYE
   WELCOME
   MOTHER
   FATHER in as many languages as possible.

5. How many languages are there in your school?
* Begin by asking your friends in your year.
   Present your work like this:

Name	Language	Understands	Speaks

6. How many languages are there on the staff?
* Ask your teachers what languages they know.
   Present your work like this:

Name	Language	Understands	Speaks

7. How many languages can you identify?
   Look around the school and make a list of the different
   languages you can find.
   Present your work like this:

PLACE	WORD	LANGUAGE	MEANING

* How many people will you interview?
   How will you present your results?
   Will you display your results?

Figure 11.5: Language Survey

among pupils of their own role as experts in the use of language – in other words, to achieve our fifth aim! Wherever the pupils saw themselves as experts (or to put it another way, were in control of their learning), then what happened in the classroom was meaningful and enjoyable and contributed to purposeful learning. However, where the work did not engage the pupils in this way, there was a noticeable lack of enthusiasm and motivation from the vast majority. The following examples will serve to illustrate the point.

We have already said, in relation to meaningful language learning that 'presenting children with language in the form of a series of decontextualised exercises in no way reflects that we know about effective and meaningful language learning as exemplified by young children learning to talk.'

This applies equally to learning *about* language. And it is, therefore, clear why the activity in which the students had to imagine a time before spoken communication, failed to engage the majority in the way that many of the other activities did. To us, the context for this activity as part of a chronological sequence had seemed perfectly clear. However, not only was the context unclear to our students, but the activity itself did little to increase their sense of control over what they were learning. Interestingly enough, the teachers too lacked confidence during the delivery of this activity. In many ways both teachers and students were asked to renounce the expertise that they had and place themselves in a situation that was not part of their experience and where they were not in control. (It is also possible that the pupils sensed the teachers' own insecurities at this point. We discuss the teachers' role below.)

In total contrast to this activity was the involvement of pupils in the language survey. One class became involved to a much greater degree in the survey than the other three. One possible reason for this is that this class had two bilingual pupils – one, a girl, who was literate in Gujarati and English, and the other, a boy who was literate in his mother tongue, Urdu and was developing oracy and literacy in English. These two pupils were able to act as experts to the rest of the class and their presence contributed to the engagement of the whole class in this exercise. All pupils had learned a few words in these two community languages and were proud to present their knowledge during the feedback lesson.

The two bilingual pupils each took charge of a group of pupils and taught them how to write the numbers from one to ten for a display in the classroom. Throughout this lesson and the process leading up to it, the pupils were in control of everything that they learned. It was they who decided who they would ask for information, how they would record it, who they would work with and how they would present what they had found. One pupil who had failed totally to learn to count in French succeeded in learning the numbers in Urdu in the space of three weeks. One of the bilingual students was his friend. This boy's growing acquisition of skills in English served as the trigger for a heightened awareness of the role and use of language for his friend and for the rest of the class.

It would be possible to quote other examples of successful and unsuccessful learning from the course. However, other aspects of the course require attention if we are to attempt to evaluate our success in terms of achieving the aims of the language project as a whole. We would like to turn now to the involvement of the Advisory Teachers from the Talk project and discuss their role in developing and implementing this course.

The teachers from the Talk project brought with them an expertise in terms of curriculum development and knowledge and understanding of language matters. It is probable that the course would have relied more heavily on published materials and would not have developed the critical aspect we have highlighted without the support of this team.

The Talk project also brought with it resources in terms of materials and relief cover to allow the Modern Language teachers time out of school to work as a team. Although most of the time was given over to preparing resources, some time was spent discussing pedagogy and the relationship between teaching and learning styles and how these would contribute to the successful achievement of the aims of the course.

Vitally, the involvement of the Talk project provided classroom support during the course. This allowed for the possibility of team teaching, that was very much in line with the philosophy of collaborative learning that underpinned the course. Given that most of the learning took place in pairs or small groups, the presence of an extra teacher was useful. But an extra teacher could have been put to better use if, in the planning process, we had properly taken this into account. Team teaching requires the classroom teacher to be prepared to relinquish some of her or his 'power' a potentially threatening situation if it has not been adequately discussed.

It seems appropriate at this stage to consider the experience of the Modern Language teachers in the implementation of this course. Most secondary school teachers consider themselves subject specialists and although falling roles have forced some teachers to take up subsidiary subjects or indeed entirely new ones, much else that is happening in education nationally reinforces this notion of specialist.

As a whole the experience was a positive one for these teachers and they learned a lot about curriculum development and ways of teaching and learning. There are two issues in particular that we would like to address here. The first concerns teachers' attitudes to students and the second considers issues to do with teachers working as a team.

As part of our aim of 'exploring the way language is used in school' we wanted to consider the teacher's role in creating and maintaining relationships of dominance and power with the pupils. As we suggested in the introduction, the traditional discourse structures of the classroom are not usually subject to examination and criticism by students. During the project, examples of teachers handing over control to their students did occur, for example when the teachers became learners of the students' community languages and the students became teachers.

However, for the teachers involved in this particular project, relinquishing the role and status of 'teacher' was in general difficult to achieve. The aims of the course were not sufficiently connected with how it was actually going to happen. Possibly if more time had been spent during the planning process on establishing a sound, clearly constructed theoretical base, we may not have experienced those insecurities that intruded at times during our delivery of the course.

We turn now to the second point about teachers working collaboratively. We must consider, first, the way the Modern Language teachers and advisory teachers from the Talk project worked together and second, the implications of what we were trying to do for relationships with colleagues in the school. We saw the idea of working collaboratively as important in our overall aim of challenging the dominant power of the teacher. The very fact that there was more than one teacher in the classroom meant that no one individual person could claim the traditional role of expert. We had also attempted to involve other departments in the planning and implementation of the course and we still feel this would have greatly improved the course. There were, however, tensions in the classroom that arose directly from this sharing. In spite of the collaborative approach the Modern Language teachers perceived the advisory teachers as 'experts' in matters to do with the English language, and during some of the activities in Unit One wanted to hand over responsibility. They did not, however, wish to relinquish control, because they saw themselves as ultimately responsible for their pupils' learning. Although the department had an 'open door' policy, very little team teaching took place because of lack of flexibility within the timetable.

It is also possible that there was some ambivalence about the students' reaction to having other adults in the classroom and this contributed to their feelings of insecurity.

The second problem in working collaboratively relates to the position of any initiative like this within a whole school context. If we attempt to challenge power relationships within our own classrooms by empowering our students, it is inevitable that this will spread beyond the classroom. We have mentioned several times that we were aware of the possible contradiction between our aims and the traditional discourse structures of the classroom. We did not want our course to offer illusory 'life' chances to children, while in reality legitimating dominant power structures. However issues to do with empowering our students and legitimising their experiences may not be part of our colleagues' agenda! We did explore this contradiction with our pupils when we attempted to relate the work done on accents and dialects to the school context. We could have done more and feel that this issue needs to be taken seriously at the highest level, if the aims of a course such as the one at Madeley Court are to be achieved.

In spite of these shortcomings in the teachers' role, it is important to say that the course was successful in much of what it set out to achieve. This was especially true in terms of the pupils' experience of the project and we hope we have shown the impact that the course made on many of them and their attitudes to language. The pupils enjoyed the course and felt they had something to contribute. They developed an increased level of awareness of languages other than English and ceased to refer to local community languages as 'speaking Indian'. They even became confident about giving the correct name to the languages they hear around them. Their attitudes to local accents and dialects also changed.

Other outcomes are less tangible. But relationships between students improved, and during the remainder of the year students often worked in mixed gender groups, which previously had been rare. There was also an atmosphere of collaboration in Modern Language lessons after the course.

We have tried in this chapter to describe a language awareness course in practice and to identify ways in which it took a critical approach. We have considered this in the wider context of developments in language awareness work over the last twenty years and the more specific context of development in the county. It has not always been easy to strike a balance between describing the course and discussing theory. However, the process of writing has helped us to identify the areas of the course where our theoretical base was insufficiently developed or where theory and practice failed to come together.

We have had to be selective in the activities we have described and we are aware that there are important issues that have not been fully addressed. One such is the idea that Critical Language Awareness is a whole school issue and should form part of any cross-curricular policies developed and that the development of a critical pedagogy is intrinsic to the successful outcome of such policies.

Since the introduction of the National Curriculum, many teachers have felt disempowered because both the curriculum and its assessment are being determined externally. It is also the case that the format of the National Curriculum could be seen to be strengthening subject boundaries. It is, therefore, more important than ever for teachers to work together and to hold on to key issues of language and learning. We hope we have made clear in this chapter our perception of the relationship between critical language awareness, learning and pedagogy.

References

Cameron D, Bourne J 1989 Kingman, grammar and the nation: Kingman in linguistic and historical perspective. In *Language and Education* 2 (3)/47–60

Clark R, Fairclough N, Ivanič R, Martin-Jones M 1987 *Critical language awareness*, Centre for Language in Social Life (CLSL), Lancaster University, Working Paper Series no 1

(DES) Department of Education and Science 1975 *A language for life.* (The Bullock Report) HMSO

DES 1988 *Report of the committee of inquiry into the teaching of English* (The Kingman Report). HMSO

DES 1988 *English for ages 5 to 11*, (The Cox Report, Preliminary Version). HMSO

DES 1989 *English for ages 5 to 16*, (The Cox Report, Final Version). HMSO

DES 1990 *Modern foreign languages for ages 11–16* (The Harris Report). HMSO

Doughty P, Pearce J, Thornton G 1971 *Language in use.* Edward Arnold

Doughty P, Thornton G (1973) *Language study, the teacher and the learner.* Edward Arnold.

Fairclough N 1989 *Language and power.* Longman.

Hawkins E 1984 *Awareness of Language: An Introduction*, Cambridge University Press.

Lancaster L 1982 *Language study in the secondary school*, a research proposal for NFER

Schools Council 1963 *Examinations Bulletin no 1 – the Certificate of Education.* HMSO

SED (Shropshire Education Department) 1988 *Curriculum handbook: the primary phase* SED

SED (Shropshire Education Department) 1989 *The making of meaning: guidelines for secondary English teaching in Shropshire.* SED

12 Whose Resource? Minority Languages, Bilingual Learners and Language Awareness

Arvind Bhatt and
Marilyn Martin-Jones

In most language-awareness materials currently being developed in Britain, some reference is made to minority community languages. This multilingual dimension of language awareness work is seen by educational practitioners as a means of responding to the presence of bilingual minority children in the classroom and a way of bringing languages such as Bengali, Chinese, Gujarati, Punjabi and Urdu onto the classroom agenda. It is also seen as one of the principal ways in which a pluralist perspective can be incorporated into the language curriculum for *all* children, bilingual and monolingual.

In this chapter, our focus is on this multilingual dimension of language-awareness work. In the first section, we give a brief historical account of the policy context in which this aspect of language awareness work has developed. We show how the home languages of minority children have come to be seen as a 'resource' in different areas of the curriculum: in multicultural education, in the teaching of modern foreign languages and in English teaching. We also show how the emergence of the minority-language-as-resource[1] theme coincided with the development of more general pluralist views on the relationship between dominant and minority groups, their languages and cultures. In this first section, we draw attention to: (1) the claims that have been made about the benefits that accrue to bilingual and monolingual learners when language awareness work is undertaken; (2) the endorsement given to the development of language awareness work of a multilingual nature in different educational policy documents since the Swann Report (DES 1985).

In the second section of the paper, we take a critical look at the approaches to the study of linguistic diversity adopted in some published language-awareness materials. We examine these approaches in the light of some of the claims that have been made about the benefits of undertaking language-awareness work in the multilingual classroom. We also give an account of the kinds of teaching/learning activities that are incorporated into these materials

In the third section, we outline what we see as a *critical* approach to the study of bilingualism and minority community languages. We argue that this approach is consonant with anti-racist work being developed in other areas of the curriculum. In our final section we highlight the importance of the links between critical approaches to language and the teaching of minority community languages as subjects in their own right in the modern languages curriculum.

Minority Language as Resource

There are now a number of detailed analyses of the ways in which the educational service has responded to the presence of linguistic minority children over the last few decades (Linguistic Minorities Project 1985; Tansley 1986; Verma 1987; Reid 1988, 1990; Bourne 1989; Martin-Jones 1989; Turner 1989). We focus here on the emergence of the minority-language-as-resource theme and on the different ways in which the term 'resource' has been employed in different areas of the curriculum.

Throughout most of the 1960s and early 1970s, the home languages of minority children were excluded from the curriculum of the local schools they attended. Assimilationist views pre-dominated during this period. The main preoccupation was with the teaching of English as a second language. The view of the British nation as a unitary whole with a homogeneous culture was implicit in most educational thinking at the time. Children with a different cultural and linguistic heritage were expected to accommodate to a 'British way of life'. In the educational discourse of this period, bilingualism was represented as a 'problem' and minority languages were seen as a source of interference in the learning of English.

In the mid-1970s there was a clear shift in thinking about the home languages of minority children. The publication of the Bullock Report (DES 1975) marked the turning point. The Bullock Committee espoused an explicitly pluralist view and insisted that schools should respect the linguistic and cultural heritage of children from minority groups. This principle is now familiar to most educational practitioners: 'No child should be expected to cast off the language and culture of the home as he crosses the school threshold and the curriculum should reflect those aspects of his life' (ch. 20: 5).

In the same chapter of the Bullock Report, a clear language-as-resource position is outlined. Minority languages are represented as a 'resource' for their speakers. It is argued that: 'In a linguistically conscious nation in the modern world, we should see mother tongue as an asset' (ch. 20: 17). However, the Bullock Committee did not give guidelines as to how they felt this principle should be translated into pedagogic practice.

The 'resource' argument and language awareness

Specific proposals were eventually put forward in the early 1980s by those who called for the development of language-awareness work as a distinct component in the language curriculum. Hawkins (1984) was prominent among the proponents of this approach to language-awareness work. He argued that a language-awareness component should be built into the curriculum in the later years of primary schooling and the first few years of secondary schooling so as to facilitate the transition from primary to secondary school language work. As a modern language specialist, Hawkins' particular concern was with making language learning more attractive to both bilingual and monolingual pupils and in 'bridging the space between L1 and L2' (1984: 40). In setting out his case for developing a separate component in the language curriculum, Hawkins cites examples of 'language foundation' and 'language taster' courses adopted in different schools as a prelude to or as a complement to the teaching of specific languages.

Hawkins advocated a multilingual approach to language-awareness work: one which would incorporate *both* minority community languages and foreign languages into the comparative study of human language. In presenting guidelines for teachers as to how you approach the study of language variation and change in Britain, he clearly articulated a language-as-resource position, though in contrast with Bullock the emphasis is on what all pupils can learn from the presence in their classroom of children who speak a language other than their own (ibid.: 171–2). This is linked to improving inter-ethnic communication and challenging 'linguistic prejudice and parochialism' (ibid.: 4), as aims of language awareness with a multilingual dimension. A similar position is taken in the Swann Report (DES 1985). By the mid-1980s, specific proposals had been made as to how a language-as-resource orientation might be incorporated into language-awareness courses.

In the period from the mid-1980s to the present, we have witnessed a retreat to a much more ethnocentric view of the curriculum, and, in particular, the English curriculum. The role of standard English as the emblem of a common national culture was reasserted in the Kingman Report on the teaching of English (DES 1988). It is quite remarkable that, in the model of language presented in the Kingman Report, virtually no reference is made to language variation along the lines of race or class. The main aspects of linguistic variation on the Kingman agenda were historical and geographical variation. As Cameron and Bourne (1988) have noted, the covert effect of the affirmation of the cultural authority of standard English is the containment of minority community languages and regional forms of English.

In the Cox Report (DES 1989), programmes of study based on the Kingman model of language were outlined in detail. More concessions were made to pluralist views and considerable attention was given to suggestions as to how minority community languages could be brought into play in language awareness work in the classroom. A whole chapter on 'Knowledge about Language' was included in this document (ch. 6). About a quarter of the chapter was devoted to a discussion of why and how the study of sociolinguistic variation might be undertaken in school. Bilingual minority pupils figure prominently in this discussion and the minority language-as-resource argument is clearly articulated:

> Many pupils in school are bilingual and sometimes biliterate, and, quite literally know more about language than their teachers, at least in some respects . . . This competence is a huge *resource* which should not be ignored but made explicit (6.11, our emphasis).

Here, the language-as-resource idea is extended so that children's knowledge of languages other than English is no longer a 'resource' for them and for other learners but also for monolingual teachers.

Predictably, the language-as-resource argument has surfaced again in the final report of the National Curriculum Working Group on Modern Foreign Languages (The Harris Report) (DES 1990). Our focus in this part of the chapter has so far been on the ways in which the language-as-resource argument has developed since the mid-1970s and, in particular, on the way the argument has been taken up by proponents of language awareness work. The pattern of curriculum development has been quite a variable one. In some local education authorities, language awareness work is primarily associated with multicultural education and builds on the ideas voiced in the Swann Report (DES 1985). In others, it is perceived primarily as a means of extending modern language teaching. In yet other contexts, particularly in schools with multilingual populations, language awareness work is being developed within the English curriculum. There is also evidence that, in some local authorities and schools, efforts are being made to develop language-awareness work across the language curriculum, involving teachers of minority community languages, modern languages and English teachers.

Since the language-as-resource argument is now quite frequently voiced in discussions about language-awareness work, we feel that it is important for those of us who are involved in these discussions to be quite clear about the way we are using the term 'resource' in referring to minority community languages. The kind of questions that will need to be asked are: Whose resource are we talking about? What educational purposes do we have in mind? How do the materials we employ and the teaching/learning activities we engage in reflect these purposes? Who will be the main beneficiaries of different types of language awareness work – monolingual or bilingual learners?

Current Language-Awareness Work: Approaches To Linguistic Diversity

In this section, we present a critical analysis of the approaches to the study of linguistic diversity adopted in some published language-awareness materials. These materials reflect well established practices in current language awareness work in schools. We have selected a sample of the kinds of topics and activities that are included in these materials. The three main aspects of the multilingual content of these materials that we want to comment on are: (1) the 'neutral' ahistorical way in which the 'facts' of linguistic diversity are represented and, in particular, the relationship between English, European Community languages and minority community languages; (2) the static and deterministic view of the uses of language among bilinguals from linguistic minority groups; (3) the preoccupation with the comparative study of language forms. Our focus is on the content of these materials, but we are well aware that there are teachers who are using them to undertake language awareness work of a more critical nature, along the lines suggested in our next section. We offer our critique of existing materials as a way of supporting their pedagogic practice. We are also aware that materials of a more critical kind are now being developed: take, for example, the materials produced by the Afro-Caribbean Language and Literacy Project in Further and Higher Education (1990). We see this as an encouraging development.

The representation of the 'facts' of linguistic diversity

A number of published language-awareness materials invite teachers and pupils to start out by documenting the linguistic diversity represented in their class, in their school or in their local neighbourhood. This is usually done by means of language surveys (Raleigh 1981; SCMTP and LINC 1984; Garson et al. 1989). This kind of exercise is also supposed to acquaint learners with ways of collecting and analysing language data in a systematic way. This idea was clearly endorsed in the Cox Report (DES 1989: 6.12): 'Work on knowledge about language can be based on pupils' own fieldwork, collecting and classifying their own data, learning about the methodology of observation, classification, description, hypothesis-making and explanation.

This kind of teaching/learning activity generally involves learners in a purely descriptive exercise. The languages spoken by different children in the classroom are referred to as if they were equal in status and inventories of different languages are drawn up. Sometimes, findings are presented in the form of graphs or bar charts (e.g. SCMTP and LINC 1984). We have found no materials which invite learners to discuss the significance of quantitative findings such as these. The focus is usually on the *what* rather than the *why* of linguistic diversity. In some materials (SCMTP and LINC 1984; Pomphrey 1985; Garson et al. 1989), learners are asked to indicate on a map where the languages are spoken outside Britain. But, learners are rarely invited to go beyond geography to consider social, political or historical issues. Most of the published language-awareness materials we have looked at specifically avoid the issue of linguistic inequality and the relationship between minority community languages and standard English.

One recently published set of materials typifies this neutral ahistorical approach (Garson et al. 1989). A map of the world is given with the areas of the world where English is spoken shaded in grey. No reference at all is made to British imperial expansion or to the processes which led to the imposition of English in many of the parts of Africa or Asia which are shaded in on the map. Learners are merely asked to make one list of countries where English is the 'official' or 'majority' language and, then, another list of countries where English is widely used. A label such as 'official language' has a common-sense neutrality which obscures the social and political processes involved in the selection and promotion of languages to 'official' status within a particular national arena. Similarly, the label 'majority language' obscures the power asymmetries that exist between speakers of the dominant language and speakers of minority languages.

Some teachers will, of course, use language-awareness materials such as these as a starting point for addressing language and power issues, but it is likely that most teachers will engage in these kinds of survey activities with their learners in the sincere belief that this will create an atmosphere of tolerance and 'civilised respect' in their class. Their confidence rests on the belief that learners will be well disposed to 'sharing' details of their language background with each other. However, languages which have been devalued as a result of social and historical processes cannot be revalued in the context of the classroom. Learners bring with them attitudes and values about different languages that they have acquired in their families and local communities.

We would argue that the neutral approach to language variation incorporated in many language-awareness materials is similar to colour blindness. When teachers claim to be colour blind, they deny the existence of structural and attitudinal barriers to equal opportunities for learners from minority groups. They are thus blind to the effects of institutional racism. We would urge teachers not to be blind to the realities of linguistic inequality or to the ideological processes that contribute to the devaluation of the languages of minority groups. If these crucial social dimensions of linguistic diversity are overlooked, children who are speakers of minority languages are more likely to be exposed to ridicule or scorn in the classroom context.

The static and deterministic view of uses of language among bilinguals

In the published materials we have read, rather little space is devoted to the *uses* of minority languages. Sometimes, in survey-type activities, bilingual learners are asked to document what language they speak to whom (SCMTP and LINC 1984). The focus seems to be on rules of appropriacy. The use of minority languages is only represented as being appropriate in certain community domains of interaction. This division of labour between minority languages and English is generally represented as a natural state of affairs. There is, of course, no discussion of the fact that there are no such constraints on the use of standard English. This variety of English can trespass on any domain.

Little or no attention appears to be given in existing language-awareness materials to the social and cultural meanings that bilinguals convey to each other through the language choices that they make in different communicative contexts. A diglossic view of bilingualism seems to predominate: one in which bilinguals are seen as passively observing rules of appropriacy for the allocation of languages to different domains. This is a static and rather deterministic view of language use. In real bilingual communities, patterns of language use are dynamic, unpredictable and capable of changing rapidly over time. In their day-to-day conversational interactions, bilinguals often switch from one language to another in *strategic* ways. Spontaneous language alternation, or code-switching, is a crucial resource for negotiating meaning in context and for conveying messages about the speaker's social and cultural identity. Given the prevalence of code-switching in bilingual communities, the absence of reference to it in language-awareness materials is puzzling. Neglecting this important dimension of bilingual discourse means missing an opportunity to make links with the communicative experience of bilingual learners.

The preoccupation with the forms of language.

The comparative study of linguistic structures appears to be the mainstay of language awareness courses. The first version of the Cox Report (DES 1988) which focused on the teaching of English in primary schools underscored the way in which the presence of bilingual learners could facilitate this aspect of language awareness work.

> Bilingual children should be considered an advantage in the classroom rather than a problem ... such children will make greater progress in English if they know that their knowledge of their mother tongue is valued and if it is recognised that their experience of language is likely to be greater than that of their monoglot peers, and indeed, if their knowledge and experience can be put to good use in the classroom to the benefit of all pupils to provide examples of the structure and syntax of different languages, to provide a focus for discussion about language forms and for contrast and comparison with the structure of the English language. (1988: 58–12.9)

We are, however, concerned about the way in which bilingual learners are expected to engage in this kind of comparative work. Particularly when the explicit goal is to compare and contrast their home and community languages with English. Often in this kind of classroom work, aspects of the structure of minority community languages are presented with no reference to contexts of use: as sets of facts about languages to be recorded and digested for their own sake. The same aspects of language form tend to show up in different published materials for language-awareness courses. These include: different writing systems and graphic symbols; word order; number systems; gender marking; plural marking; tense marking;

compound nouns; comparative inventories of phonemes; different ways of conveying politeness and non-verbal communication (Aplin et al. 1981; Raleigh 1981; Hawkins 1983; Pomphrey 1985; Garson et al. 1989).

The activities typically built around 'facts' such as these are: (1) reading of a passage providing information about features of different languages; (2) an exercise in which learners are required to confirm that they have absorbed the information: this might involve matching items, answering questions, making lists or tables to classify or build on information in the reading passage (ibid.).

Sometimes attention is drawn to similarities in the form of words or grammatical features from different languages. One common approach is to compare the forms of languages which can all be grouped into one language 'family', such as Indo-European languages. In one set of materials we have seen learners were asked to do a comparative exercise on number systems. Data from several Indo-European languages was given, including Bengali, French, Hindi and Urdu. The exercise consisted of spotting the similarities and differences in the phonological shape of numbers from one to ten (Aplin et al. 1981; Pomphrey 1985).

Another recurring theme in language-awareness materials is word borrowing (Aplin et al. 1981; Raleigh 1981). The focus is usually on words that have been borrowed into English from other languages. The examples that appear most frequently in different materials are words borrowed from South Asian languages. These include: *pukka, dekko, bungalow, khaki* and *dungaree*. This kind of exercise can provide a starting point for discussing the links between language change and socio-historical processes. Learners can be asked to find out what kinds of words have been borrowed and then to consider why. The Harris Report (DES 1990) underscores this point in the section devoted to the way in which language awareness can be fostered through modern language teaching (para. 8.18, vi, p. 50).

However, the potential of this area of language contact and change is not fully explored in the language-awareness materials we have seen so far. In one set of materials, there is no social or historical slant. The teaching/learning activity on word borrowing consists of a guessing game in which the 'donor' language has to be identified from a check-list (Garson et al. 1989). In another set, a historical dimension is introduced but only in a narrow etymological sense. Learners are merely asked to note *when* individual words were borrowed into English and to identify the 'donor' language (Pomphrey 1985).

The 'facts' about linguistic diversity are generally presented in a random and eclectic way in the language awareness materials we have seen so far. They are presented in *pot pourri* fashion with few opportunities for following through or seeking explanations for individual 'facts'. Learners are usually invited to treat these facts as 'data' to be examined or classified with a view to discovering general patterns in an inductive manner.

Sometimes pupils are invited to keep a record of language observations they make outside school. In one set of materials we looked at, primary school children were asked to note down where and when they had seen signs in languages other than English in a local street near the school (SCMTP and LINC 1984). The intention of those who write materials such as these is no doubt to bring community languages into the classroom. However, in this kind of activity, there is a danger that community languages can be merely represented as exotica, as decontextualised emblems of diversity.

When minority community languages are introduced in an eclectic and decontextualised way in teaching materials, this amounts to little more than the tokenism that has already been commented on in other areas of multicultural education. In the 1980s, tokenism was parodied in the well-known catch-phrase about 'the three Ss': saris, samosas and steel-bands. As we see it, 'the three Ss' of language awareness work are: surveys, scripts and sentence structures. The random inclusion of facts about minority community languages in the language curriculum does not constitute a genuinely pluralist agenda.

Minority Languages and Language Awareness: A Critical Approach

The aims of a critical pedagogy

In our view, the main aim of a critical pedagogy in multilingual classrooms in the British context should be to develop learners' understanding of the relationship between standard English and minority languages. This kind of work needs to incorporate a historical perspective. Learners have a right to know the history of their own languages. This needs to be set against the history of the rise and spread of standard English. And now, in the 1990s, some account also needs to be taken of the social and political history of some of the national languages of the other member states of the European Community.

A historical approach of this kind would also need to highlight the fact that values and attitudes about language are socially and politically generated. Particular attention should be given to: (1) the ways in which the values of dominant social groups are imposed and legitimised; (2) the ways in which minority languages and their speakers are represented. Different kinds of texts could be analysed: educational documents from the colonial era could be compared with contemporary policy documents. The connotations of terms such as 'modern languages', 'community languages', 'heritage languages' from contemporary documents could be discussed. The representation of minority languages and their speakers in different kinds of media discourse could also be investigated: in the popular press and in television and radio broadcasts.

These kinds of teaching/learning activities would provide a means of moving away from the neutral descriptive accounts of the 'facts' of linguistic diversity that are found in many language-awareness materials at present. They would also clear the ground for more critical work on the sociolinguistic realities of day-to-day life in bilingual families and communities. As we indicated in the previous section, this is one area that is currently neglected in existing language-awareness materials. If this area of language-awareness work is to be developed, the aim, as we see it, should be to highlight the ways in which day-to-day communicative practices are shaped by social conditions. The kinds of topics that could be covered include: inter-generational differences and struggles over language use; the social significance of code-switching as a communicative resource; the use of language alternation as a means of ethnic boundary marking or levelling; the lack of opportunities to use and develop the languages that form part of local community repertoires. These are topics that are likely to be of immediate relevance to the experience of bilingual learners. The emphasis should be on the links between culture and identity.

Another important step in developing a critical approach to language awareness work in multilingual classrooms is to address the options available for challenging existing conventions and making changes in one's own communicative practice. In our view, learners need to be given the opportunity to consider what alternatives there are to terms that are currently used in dominant institutional discourses to refer to minority community languages and their speakers. They should also be given the opportunity to think critically about notions such as language purity, correctness and appropriacy.

In addition, they should also be empowered to reflect on their own communicative practices and to consider the kinds of changes that they could make. Here is one example of how this could be achieved in a small way in a language class: Gujarati-speaking pupils sometimes use the English words *India* or *Indian* when speaking Gujarati. Gujarati teachers could simply introduce them to the equivalent terms in Gujarati: ભારત and ભારતીય[2] which are derived from Sanskrit. But they could also draw their attention to the etymology of the English terms *India* and *Indian*. They could show how they are derived from the Greek term meaning 'across the Indus river'. This could then lead to a discussion about consciously choosing between terms that express an Asian or a European perspective.

The link with anti-racist work

As we understand it, there are two main differences between pluralist and anti-racist views: first, those who have adopted an anti-racist stance see the pluralist conception of culture as a primarily static and apolitical one. Second, they argue that racism needs to be understood in terms of structural inequalities and dominant cultural values not just in terms of the attitudes and prejudices of individuals. One of the main aims of an anti-racist pedagogy is to enable learners to develop a critical perspective on a world characterised by structural inequalities between people of different races and between speakers of different languages; but, at the same time, to equip them with the means to challenge existing institutional structures and practices and to work for change. The aims of the critical language pedagogy that we have outlined above are clearly consonant with the aims of anti-racist work in education.

However, we are concerned about the way in which minority community languages have been neglected in the development of anti-racist perspectives across the curriculum. Educational practitioners continue to have a primarily monolingual outlook. They seem have a blind spot where language is concerned. Very little support is given to minority language teachers in their struggle to increase the status of minority community languages in the curriculum.

Critical Language Awareness and the Teaching of Minority Community Languages

The reason that we have undertaken to write this article is because we believe that there is a danger that provision for the teaching of minority community languages could be overshadowed by the development of language-awareness work. Schools where language-awareness programmes have been introduced could argue that they already have a multilingual component in their curriculum and that this obviates the need to make separate arrangements for the teaching of minority community languages.

In schools where language-awareness courses with a multilingual component have been introduced, speakers of minority community languages are unlikely to be the main beneficiaries. Their knowledge of languages other than English will serve primarily as a 'resource' for monolingual speakers of English. Rampton (1990) draws attention to the possible connotations of the use of the term 'resource' in discussions about language awareness programmes. He argues that:

> there is a risk that the much used word 'resource' will come to be most fittingly interpreted in terms of its mineral connotations, in a way that is actually rather reminiscent of traditional colonial exchange relationships ... the linguistic function of the school can only be *extractive*. (1990: 31)

Rampton points out, quite rightly, that it is important to be clear about what language-awareness programmes can and cannot do. It is sometimes claimed that language-awareness work can strengthen language proficiency. We would argue, from the point of view of bilingual learners, that the development of high levels of spoken and written proficiency in minority community languages requires substantial pedagogic support. We therefore believe that priority should be given to consolidating provision for the minority community language teaching within the mainstream curriculum.

The teaching of minority community languages already serves some of the educational purposes of critical language awareness work. It builds on the bilingual learners' existing knowledge and experience and it gives them a keener sense of the place of the language in their own culture and history. The development of a more explicitly critical pedagogy would therefore complement the work that some community language teachers are already doing. Because of the crucial links that can be made between community language teaching and critical language awareness, we would argue that bilingual learners can only fully benefit from language awareness work if there is provision available in their schools and colleges for the teaching of minority community languages as subjects in their own right.

Acknowledgements

Valuable comments on the first draft of this chapter were received from: Jill Bourne, John Broadbent, June Geach, Laurie Kershook and Norman Fairclough.

Notes

1. Ruiz (1984) first drew attention to the fact that language education policies reflect three main orientations to minority languages: (1) language-as-problem; (2) language-as-resource; (3) language-as-right. He was referring to language education provision for linguistic minority children in the USA.
2. Bhárat is the official name of India. Bháratiya is a citizen of India. Those who follow the Hindu religion are referred to as Hindus – a derivation of the word *Sindhu* (the river Indus).

References

Afro-Caribbean Language and Literacy Project in Further and Higher Education 1990 *Language and power* Harcourt Brace Jovanovich

Aplin T R N, Crawshaw J W, Roselman E A, Williams AL 1985 (Second edition) *Introduction to Language*. Hodder & Stoughton

Bourne J 1989 *Moving into the mainstream: LEA provision for bilingual pupils*. NFER-Nelson

Cameron D, Bourne J 1988 No common ground: Kingman, grammar and nation. *Language and Education* 2 (3): 147–60

Department of Education and Science (DES) 1975 *A language for life* (The Bullock Report). HMSO

Department of Education and Science (DES) 1985 Education for all (The Swann Report). HMSO.

Department of Education and Science (DES) 1988 Report of the committee of inquiry into the teaching of the English language (The Kingman Report). HMSO.

Department of Education and Science (DES) 1988 English for ages 5–11 (The first Cox Report). Department of Education and Science and the Welsh Office

Department of Education and Science (DES) 1989 English for ages 5–16 (The final Cox Report). Department of Education and Science and the Welsh Office

Department of Education and Science (DES) 1990 Modern foreign languages for ages 11–16. (The Harris Report). Department of Education and Science and the Welsh Office

Garson S et al. 1989 *World Languages project* (Student and Teacher's book). Hodder & Stoughton

Hawkins E 1983 *Spoken and written language.* (Awareness of Language Series.) Cambridge University Press.

Hawkins E 1984 *Awareness of language: an introduction.* Cambridge University Press

Linguistic Minorities Project 1985 *The other languages of England.* Routledge & Kegan Paul

Martin-Jones M 1989 Language education in the context of linguistic diversity: differing orientations in educational policy-making in Britain. In Esling J (ed) *Multicultural education and policy: ESL in the 1990s.* OISE Press

Pomphrey C 1985 *Language varieties and change.* (Awareness of Language Series.) Cambridge University Press

Raleigh M 1981 *The languages book.* The Inner London Education Authority English Centre

Rampton B 1990 Some unofficial perspectives on bilingualism and education for all. *Language Issues* 4 (3 2) 27–32.

Reid E 1988 Linguistic minorities and language education: The English experience. *Journal of Multilingual and Multicultural Development* 9 : 181–91.

Reid E 1990 Culture and language teaching: ESL in England. In B. Harrison (ed) *Culture and the language classroom.* Modern English publications and the British Council. ELT Document 132.

Ruiz R 1984 Orientations in language planning. *Journal of the National Association for Bilingual Education* 8 (2): 15–35. Reprinted in McKay S L and Wong S C (eds) 1988 *Language diversity: problem or resource?* Newbury House

The Schools Council Mother Tongue Project (SCMTP) and the Language

Information Network Co-ordination (LINC) project 1984 *The children's language project*. Institute of Education University of London

Tansley P 1986 *Community languages in primary education*. NFER-Nelson

Turner F 1989 'Community languages: the struggle for survival in D. Phillips (ed) *Which language? diversification and the National Curriculum*. Hodder & Stoughton

Verma M 1987 Issues of mother tongue maintenance. In Abudarham S. (ed) *Bilingualism and the bilingual*. NFER-Nelson

Part IV

Critical Language Awareness –
Perspectives for Emancipation

13 CLA and emancipatory discourse

Hilary Janks and Roz Ivanič

'Emancipatory discourse' is an integral part of emancipatory practice. It means using language, along with other aspects of social practice, in a way which works towards greater freedom and respect for all people, including ourselves. The term 'emancipatory discourse' implies that there are people or groups of people who need emancipation from someone or something. In this chapter we will consider who needs to be emancipated from what and how a critical language awareness (CLA) can contribute to the process of emancipation. It is a central tenet of this chapter that language 'awareness' or 'raised consciousness' is not liberatory enough. Only if CLA empowers people to successfully contest the practices which disempower them would we claim that it is emancipatory. Awareness needs to be turned into action.

Our central concern is with how practices which maintain and reproduce patterns of domination and subordination in society may be contested, especially language practices. We are concerned with the part people play in longer-term processes of change and struggle. By examining what it means to read and write from disempowered subject positions in educational institutions we hope to show that changing these language practices can be transformative. When discourse breaks the cycle of reproducing domination it becomes emancipatory.

First, we will set the scene for emancipatory discourse, explaining what we mean by power and asymmetrical power relations, and the relationship between subjection and language. We will then describe two dimensions of emancipatory discourse: discourse which does not disempower others, and discourse which resists disempowerment. Next we will outline some of the decisions and difficulties which face people as they contest conventional ways of using language. Finally, we will write about the practicalities of bringing emancipatory discourse into the classroom, with examples from our own and our students' experience – often painful experience – of contesting the conventions.

Power and asymmetrical power relations

In any asymmetrical relation of power there is a top dog and a person or persons below, the underdog. How people get to be on top in a society has to do with what that society values. It may be age or maleness or class or cleverness or a white skin. It is easier for those who have power to maintain it, if they can persuade everyone in the society that there is nothing unnatural about these arrangements. Things are this way because that is the way they are meant to be. We all know, because of the society we live in, that doctors know more about their patients' illnesses than the patients themselves do. We all know that teachers know what their students need. We all know that parents know better than their teenagers. Knowing these things we consent to the power that society accords to those with expertise and greater age and experience. And in using these examples we have not even attempted to address the problem of the continuing consent given to racist, sexist and class-based values in society. The more these values are seen as uncontestable givens, the less coercion is needed to maintain them. They work as the prevailing 'common sense' of a society, through what Gramsci (1971) calls 'hegemony'.

Our concern is with the underdogs who need emancipation. They may be patients whose doctors refuse to listen seriously to what they are saying; they may be students who are treated as empty vessels by teachers determined to fill them with expertise; they may be black people in South Africa denied their basic rights as human beings. However, it is not a question of clear-cut groups of top dogs and underdogs: most people are top dogs in some situations and underdogs in others. For example, a man who speaks Urdu may be subject to oppression on grounds of race, language, employment, and class. On the other hand, he may behave as a member of a dominant group on the grounds of gender, literacy, religion, sexuality and age. So he may be disempowered at work and in the streets, but he may be dominating his wife and children at home, and he may be treating gay people and members of other religions with disrespect in the community. We doubt that there is any group in any educational establishment which could be uniformly described as totally oppressed on all counts. Respect and emancipation are issues for all of us.

Consciousness raising, including CLA, is part of a process in which we learn how to emancipate ourselves and others. It is the first step in which we come to understand that underdogs need liberation. The second step is the 'emancipatory discourse' we are writing about in this chapter: when we decide to act so as to contest subjection, whether it be the subjection of ourselves or of others. In the next section we will outline how language contributes to this process of subjection, before describing two dimensions of emancipatory discourse in more detail.

Language and subjection

Meaning lies not simply in the text but in the social relations in which it is embedded. For example, after the release of Nelson Mandela different 'readers' responded differently to his first speech. According to who they were and how they were positioned they foregrounded and backgrounded different aspects of what he said. The Conservative Party in South Africa focused on his insistence on maintaining the armed struggle. The Nationalists focused on the understanding he showed for white fears and their need for the protection of their rights. Neil Kinnock in Britain foregrounded Mandela's statement that it was too early to lift sanctions.

This foregrounding is not an inherent part of the text available to text analysis. It is what happens when the speech enters into existing social relations and struggle; when the speech is seen as discourse rather than as text.

All texts work to 'anchor' some meanings in preference to others. Hall (1980: 7) calls this the 'preferred meaning'. It is easy to resist accepting the preferred meaning if one is positioned differently to start with. From that different position the reader is able to offer opposing content, other language and alternative emphases. (We will pick up this point in the section on the role of groups in CLA and emancipatory discourse, where we discuss how groups which represent a wide range of perspectives are best for developing CLA. Critical, or resistant (Kress 1985) reading is much more difficult if one is in agreement with the text. The ability to resist such texts is particularly important because the reader's agreement may stem from the text's successful 'interpellation' of him or her.

Althusser's (1970) concept of interpellation is an important one for this chapter. It can be understood as 'inter-appellation': naming that occurs between people. 'Sticks and stones may break my bones, but words can never harm me' is only true if we refuse to take the words on board. Interpellation occurs when we recognize the appellation, when we accept it, when we are subjected by it. This is rarely a conscious process and does not occur only in language. We do not need to be 'named' as patient when we enter the doctor's consulting rooms. A range of social practices, of which language is but one, construct this position for us. These practices include such things as patients having to wait, the keeping of files on patients to which they have no access, as well as the language of traditional doctor–patient interviews (Mischler 1985). We are interpellated when the construction, the 'appellation' seems to fit, but we rarely recognise that we have been called into a specific 'subject position' by the process. The act of accepting the subject position created by another's appellation results in a surrender of power to the interpellator. There is no ideological (as opposed to coercive) domination without this acceptance. Without the acceptance, it is just appellation: name calling.

> Ideology 'acts' or 'functions' in such a way that it 'recruits' subjects among the individuals, ... or 'transforms' the individuals into subjects ... by that very precise operation which I have called *interpellation* or hailing, and which can be imagined along the lines of the most commonplace everyday police (or other) hailing: 'Hey, you there!' ... the hailed individual will turn around. By this mere one hundred and eighty-degree physical conversion, he (sic) becomes a *subject*. Why? Because he has recognised that the hail was 'really' addressed to him, and that 'it was *really him* who was hailed' and not someone else. (Althusser 1970: 48)

The problem is something like this: if one has been interpellated, often below the level of consciousness, how does one step outside the interpellation to see one's own subjection? And, if one manages to see the subjection, how can one be sure that even while resisting one is not in fact acting in a subjected or subordinated way? Giroux (1983) makes a useful distinction between 'opposition' and 'resistance' which is worth mentioning here. Giroux uses the term 'accommodation' to refer to accepting the preferred meaning, or the subject position, as mentioned above. But he then distinguishes between 'opposition' and 'resistance'. 'Opposition' means thinking which goes against the existing ground-rules, negating them, valuing their opposite. This is opposition which stays within the existing framework. 'Resistance' means thinking differently, rejecting the ground rules and the premises on which they are based: actively participating in attempts to change the whole framework on which the ground rules depend. Emancipatory discourse is to do with opposition and resistance: recognising the forces which are leading you to fit in with the status quo and resisting them.

We want to try to bring these threads together in the story of a research student at a foreign university. The fact that the university was in a foreign country is important because it meant that the student did not experience a sense of 'fit'. The common sense of the institution was not his common sense. The experience he brought with him made practices in this new institution strange rather than natural. It made him less inclined to consent to them than native students.

At home he was himself a university teacher with his own research students. The institution registered him as a 'student' and assigned him a 'supervisor': interesting appellations, constructing subject positions for both of them. The same person might have come as a 'research fellow' or as a 'visiting lecturer', appellations more likely to encourage a reciprocal relationship of learning. As it turned out the 'student' found himself in a deeply contradictory position. Because he was a higher degree student he was expected to think independently, to read critically, to take responsibility for his own research. At the same time he was attending courses where old-style transmission teaching prevailed: students at the receiving end of lectures by experts.

The student felt angry and disaffected but for a long time was unable to articulate his sense of disempowerment even to himself. He believed that foreigners having chosen a foreign institution should learn to fit in. Academics having chosen to become students should accept the change in their status. Underdogs find many reasons to blame themselves for their subjection. In so doing they consent to it.

Only after a visit to another university where he was treated as a colleague with interesting ideas to share did he remember what it felt like to be taken seriously. Only then was he able to recognise that he had been interpellated as a 'student'. Only once he had recognised his need for liberation could he properly contest his subjection. Only then could he confront his supervisor with his sense of disempowerment. And she heard him. The next day, instead of giving him one of her papers to read for his course, his supervisor gave him a paper that she was still working on for his comments. In doing so she constructed a new subject position for them both: collaborative colleagues.

What follows is the reason for this story. What, you are probably wondering, has all this to do with language? We will ignore for the purposes of this story the fact that all the teaching interchanges (the supervision sessions, the lectures, the supervisor's handouts and academic papers) were in language. We cannot show whether or not the actual language reinforced the teacher's power *vis-à-vis* her students because we have no record of all that transpired. Instead we offer the experience of this student-turned-colleague.

He spent a morning working on his supervisor's (now colleague's) paper. He had read many of his supervisor's other papers. Only when he finished reading this one did he realise that he had read it in a very different way. The other papers he had read as her student, from what we will call a disempowered position. He had been given the papers because they would help him with his work: some because they would help him understand a particular theorist, some because they would show him how to do the kind of analysis he was trying to do. Constructed as the student needing help, he read them as students do: underlining the important bits, putting question marks next to the difficult bits, occasionally indicating disagreement.

This paper he read from a empowered position: now *he had been asked to help* the writer. This time instead of underlining the important bits, he focused on those parts of the paper that were not working well. Where he was not able to follow, he tried to suggest how the paper could be changed. From the empowered position, failure to comprehend was not assumed to be a weakness in him, the reader, but in the writing. He shifted from asking as a student, 'Can I understand this?' to asking as a colleague, 'Is this understandable and useful?' We would suggest that, subtle as the shift is, it is emancipatory for both the student and the supervisor, freeing both of them to learn from one another. It is also important to note that when teachers read students' work, they read from an empowered position.

There is a salutary lesson to be learnt from this story. All the time that this student was resisting being interpellated as a student, he was reading like one. He was only able to behave differently when he was no longer named as a student but as a colleague. The mechanisms of power and subjection are not in our conscious control. He had to experience reading differently to understand how he had been reading before. It is possibly easier for 'students' who are also 'teachers' to step out of their role as 'students'. But for all students to be similarly empowered involves reconstructing what it means to be students and teachers. This process of reconstruction can already be seen in the work of theorists such as Freire (1970, 1972), Giroux (1983, 1988), and Apple (1979, 1988). Old practices, however, die hard and those of us who would like to be progressive teachers need constantly to re-examine our own practices. Common sense is hard to shake. It is difficult to believe that very often our students really do have a better understanding of what they need than we do.

In this story two meanings of 'emancipatory discourse' were interacting. The supervisor changed her discourse in order to stop disempowering the student. The student took action to resist disempowerment. In the next two sections we will elaborate on these two meanings.

Discourse which does not disempower others

However lacking in confidence we may be ourselves, we can develop a sense of social responsibility towards others in our language use, both individually and collectively. There are two categories of 'others': the people we speak and write *about*, and the people we speak and write *to*. We'll write about each separately.

1. Responsibility towards the people we speak and write *about*

We need to become aware of how we subject other people: how the language we choose sets up (consciously or not) subject positions for others. CLA can make people conscious of how language can be patronising, demeaning, disrespectful, offensive, exclusive, or the opposite. This, of course, is a language development objective for everyone, including teachers.

Here is an example from our own experience. Recently one of us contributed to a staff development programme and said: 'if the students can't handle it'. A course participant, recognising that we would prefer to use language responsibly, pointed out that it is patronising to learners to make assumptions about what they can 'handle', and that the word 'handle' is a rather flippant way of describing the battles students often face. This represents a new development in our own awareness of the subject position that our choice of language constructs, and we will be trying to take account of it in the way we speak and write from now on.

Those who are trying to be socially responsible in their language use often become self-conscious at first, tongue-tied in their choice of words. It is common to hear people say, for example:

(1) 'When it comes to the . . . erm . . . ethnic minorities', or
(2) 'I'm working with . . . erm . . . people with reading and writing difficulties', or
(3) 'Shall we ask someone from the . . . erm . . . gay community', or
(4) 'So a doctor might tell . . . erm . . . her or his patient'

These are invented examples, but we think many of you reading this chapter will identify with this moment of hesitation, in your current and/or past language use. The words we choose reveal a great deal about our own positions. As social conditions change so do the possibilities for what can be said. We try to avoid words from an old common sense with which we no longer wish to identify. When these hesitations precede reference to groups of people who are powerless and/or or stigmatised, we suggest that it is a sign that people are attempting to put into operation their critical awareness of the power language has to label people. During the '. . . erm . . .' the speaker is hastily sifting everything she or he knows about which terms the people she or he is talking to or about might find offensive or demeaning, in order to avoid them.[1] In Example four the hesitation accompanies a search for a way to include women, to indicate clearly that they, too, are doctors.

People in relatively low-status positions have two sorts of battles to fight with the way they are referred to. First, some terms are inherently and intentionally offensive, such as 'kaffir', 'wog', 'queer', and others have offensive connotations, such as 'illiterate' which has acquired connotations of 'stupid'. Second, some terms take on pejorative connotations simply because they refer to stigmatised groups; for example, black people in North America once fought to be called 'negro', but later had to start a new battle to be called 'black'. A succession of names has been used to refer to black people in South Africa, all until the last two successively stigmatised: 'native', 'non-European', 'non-white', 'Bantu', 'African', 'black'.

Another sign that someone is trying to avoid disempowering others and positioning themselves is over-lexicalisation, that is using many ways of saying the same thing. People often cover their uncertainty about how to refer to people by providing a range of options, for example: 'the disadvantaged, disenfranchised and poor majority'. This is common in both speech and writing.

We see these tendencies as cases of emancipatory discourse at work: people in the process of searching for ways of referring to others which do not disempower them. We believe that one of the goals of critical educators should be to encourage learners to take these first steps in eradicating offensive and disempowering language from their own spontaneous use, and adopting language which recognises the identities and values of others. People sometimes object to this suggestion on the grounds that attitudes need changing and then language will look after itself. But educators cannot just sit back and wait for attitudes to change: they need to help learners to question their attitudes and to gain access to alternative perspectives. As we said right at the beginning of this chapter, emancipatory discourse is just one of many emancipatory practices. However, it is a particularly important practice, since language shapes attitudes and meanings and is in turn shaped by them.

2. Responsibility towards the people we speak and write *to*

Speakers and writers can use language to impose their points of view on the people they are speaking to: all other things being equal (which they never are, of course!) speakers and writers have the balance of power in their favour. They can command and persuade, politely or impolitely. They can also represent their views as if they were truth: the printed word can be especially persuasive. This exercise of power is not necessarily intentional: the very conventions of language, what is expected in the circumstances, often position speakers and writers into exerting power. (For a discussion of this issue see chapter 2.)

CLA can help learners recognise the power vested in the speaker or writer, but mere awareness is not enough. Learners need also to find for themselves ways of speaking and writing which impose less on the people they are speaking to, and to practise them in their everyday language use. If we tend to dominate conversations, action requires that we speak and interrupt less, allowing more turns and time for others to speak and be heard.

There is also a more positive way of showing respect to other people through language choice, actively empowering others, rather than merely avoiding disempowering them. This is learning, valuing and as often as possible using patterns of interaction which others identify with. For example, some people find written dialogue easier to understand and write than written monologue. Dialogue is not a generally accepted form of discourse in academic writing. The more people use dialogue in their academic writing, the wider the range of readers they are inviting in, at the same time validating a form in which more people might prefer to write. This is patently empowering for the people we speak and write *to*. Indirectly it also empowers all people who identify with the patterns of interaction in question – bringing them on to the scene by using their language.

The idea of 'responsible language use' is complicated by the fact that there is no consensus as to what our rights and responsibilities are. One group of people in a society may have quite different interests and values, and therefore quite different views as to what their rights and responsibilities are. Another complication is that we cannot assume that all language users have good intentions – that they are not consciously using language to impose and manipulate. CLA can show ill-intentioned people how they might use language to subject others more than they do already. This is a real dilemma which faces all educators: knowledge can be used destructively. Critical educators have to take account of the full complexity of the social context when introducing CLA. One approach is to focus on how disempowered people can resist imposition and manipulation – which is what we will write about in the next section.

Discourse which resists disempowerment

Whereas in the last section we focused on how speakers and writers represent and treat other people, in this section we will focus on the needs of language users themselves. It's difficult to find a name for this aspect of emancipatory discourse. 'Self-asserting' would seem too aggressive; 'self-empowering' is probably a bit optimistic; 'self-recognising' is rather cumbersome, although it captures the idea well. It's easier to explain what we mean with a negative: we are talking about not letting our own needs be neglected, not allowing ourselves to be effaced. Discourse which resists disempowerment means using language in a way which is true to ourselves and true to the group(s) we identify with.

We will outline here three ways in which relatively powerless groups can look after their own interests and maintain their identity through language use.

1. Through CLA learners can become conscious of the way in which one variety of English has become standardised. Turning awareness into action means finding ways of challenging the view that this standardised variety is inherently better than any other, by defending the value of one's own patterns of interaction, and insisting at times on one's right to use them. An example of this is working-class people publishing in their own vernacular.

2. Through CLA learners can become conscious of the way in which people from certain groups tend to dominate interactions. Turning awareness into action means having the self-assurance to get our say, even if we are feeling dominated. An example of this is women from linguistic minority groups having a voice in maternity units. CLA may introduce discussion about the way in which doctors frequently disempower women by talking as if they are the only ones who know anything about childbirth. Women from linguistic minority groups may bring onto the agenda the additional sense of powerlessness they experience because they don't

speak the dominant language fluently enough to have their say. The educational process becomes potentially emancipatory if it takes the additional step of exploring possibilities for contesting those practices which silence people and deny them a voice. One way of doing this might be through simulations in which students are given different roles. Some are given roles in which they have to bid for turns in a discussion or conversation and others are given roles in which they are instructed to deny the floor to others. This could be followed by analysing the different strategies which students used to maintain their antagonistic roles.

3. Through CLA learners can become conscious of the way in which language tends to impose the speaker's (or writer's) view of the world on us. Turning awareness into action means practising critical and oppositional reading, listening and viewing – of advertisements, for instance. This means not accepting automatically the role of 'ideal reader' which is constructed in the text, but questioning and if necessary rejecting the view of the world represented there.

People in positions of power usually find it harder to give up their patriarchal, racist, condescending, insulting uses of language, whereas disempowered people find it harder to stand up for their own rights. We believe that in a balanced language development programme learners (including ourselves) should discuss and identify what they consider to be their own rights and should find ways of maintaining them in discourse, without negating the rights of others. Many people who enrol for language classes belong to relatively powerless groups on the grounds of age, occupation and educational status if nothing else. Many are also fighting an uphill battle on the grounds of gender and/or race. Discourse which resists disempowerment is therefore particularly important and particularly difficult for them.

Participating in the struggle: pains and rewards

In the previous two sections we have described two complementary sides of emancipatory discourse: discourse which is concerned with freedom and power for others, and discourse which is concerned with freedom and power for ourselves. Both involve flying in the face of convention: using language differently from the norm.

This is not just a question of individual choice: people's options both contribute to and are constrained by their socio-historical context. It is only in particular historical circumstances that people *do* have particular rights, or sets of choices between conformist and emancipatory practices. For example, you can't talk about the gender-related choices available to women and men without taking account of the overall state of the 'order of discourse' in 1990 versus 1890. There is a time when the struggle has not yet begun, and the possibilities for action are extremely limited. There is a time when the struggle is at its height, and every individual choice helps to shape the future possibilities for others. There is a time when the struggle is all but over, when last year's emancipatory discourse is this year's conformism, this year's common sense.

CLA can show learners how the weight of conventional usage and the prevailing orders of discourse pressure people into speaking, writing, interacting and comprehending in particular ways. Learners need to understand that rules of accuracy and appropriacy are not fixed, but subject to social forces. Moving beyond passive awareness to action means learning to choose when to conform to the conventions as they are, or to challenge them, and so help to break new ground. Action involves knowing how to choose, when to choose and whether to choose. People have to choose between conventional language use on the one hand, and practising emancipatory discourse with its commitment to some sort of change on the other. The choice is not easy! However critically aware people may be of language, they may still have very strong reasons for choosing not to contest their subjection through language. (There is also a discourse which resists empowerment!) In this section we will focus on this moment of decision, and the part critical educators can play in helping learners face it with confidence.

Practising emancipatory discourse involves having some principle you want to uphold, deciding how important it is to you, knowing whether others are currently engaged in the same struggle, knowing how powerful the people are you are communicating with, knowing how sympathetic they may be to your resistance, and knowing what you have to lose if they aren't.

In certain socio-historical conditions we will choose to conform to the conventions, because opposing them is too demanding. For example, most people in the early 1990s will try very hard to use standardised English in an interview for an office job, will conform to the convention that the interviewers will decide on the topics for discussion, and will not complain if the interviewer says 'We will expect you to work a bit harder at your English.' It is not in their interest to be oppositional, the prevailing discourse for job interviews being as it is: they would not get the job! Any good communicative language teaching will show learners how to conform to the conventions. CLA additionally helps people to conform with open eyes, to identify their feelings about it, and to recognise the compromises they are making.

However, when the socio-historical conditions are stacked more in their favour, people may sometimes feel confident and safe enough to challenge the conventions. They may not accept it when someone doesn't attempt to pronounce their name properly; they may request certain information in a language other than English; they may code-switch with monolingual friends without feeling guilty; they may use non-standardised forms of English in writing and demand that they are recognised as acceptable. These are difficult social actions, because they are likely to be dismissed as self-important, inflexible, rude, ignorant, wrong. But if we don't try, just occasionally, to contribute to change, it may never happen.

The words 'contribute to' in the last sentence are important. It is unlikely that any individual alone will have any effect in establishing alternative conventions. Because top dogs rarely roll over and die without a fight, contestation is often more successful when a group of people, similarly disempowered, resist together. Contestation is painful and hard and it involves taking risks. Group solidarity is empowering.

A concrete example may make what we are saying clearer. A group of students is likely to have more success in getting a teacher to change the way she/he treats them than one student is likely to have. It is too easy to ignore, to discount, to co-opt or to victimise individuals. In addition, if the one student is successful, there is a danger that the teacher will simply change the way she/he behaves in relation to that student, without becoming sufficiently reflective about her or his practice in relation to all students.

Individuals can identify with a collective consciousness that change is needed, and contribute to collective action in order to bring it about. An individual's decision to change her/his discourse practices is likely to be strengthened by the knowledge that others are doing the same and that every little effort will contribute to gradual change. An example of this is our use of 'her/his' as a generic form in the last sentence. We are not making a unique challenge to conventions. We have seen others do it, and we want to identify with the process of redressing the balance in favour of women which it represents. We don't think our choice is going to have much effect on its own, but it will make its small contribution to the challenge being made by thousands of other women writers in the late twentieth century. You may also have noticed that we try to use 'we' not 'they' when referring to language learners: this is a choice which links us to the learners as well as to those other educators who also see themselves as learners, and not as superior 'knowers'.

CLA which includes a commitment to action can give language learners the self-assurance to make these choices. Self-assurance involves understanding social situations, knowing what the options are for action, and knowing the consequences. CLA shows the consequences of complying with 'rules of appropriacy', but it doesn't insist on opposing them. It helps people to recognise when they are being subjected by language, and it shows them when and how to wrest control. This is obviously essential when we want to resist being disempowered by language, but we believe it applies to times when we want to avoid disempowering others too. Attempting to use language responsibly in this way is in itself an act of identity, and people need self-assurance to carry it through.

Emancipatory discourse as part of language education

So far we have written about the sorts of changes CLA might make to learners' discourse practices. A small number of learners will apply what they have learnt automatically. We believe that critical educators should take the lead in showing all learners how to turn awareness into action, giving them opportunities for practice, and supporting them in their first efforts towards emancipatory discourse. In this section we will discuss some of the issues which will face educators when they attempt to put this principle into practice.

1.   Integrating CLA and language development

CLA should not be separated from the language development part of the curriculum. Published material under the general heading 'Language Awareness' in the United Kingdom usually appears to be self-standing, as if it were intended to be a separate lesson in the week. This attempt to make 'language awareness' a site for breaking down boundaries between school subjects is one of the positive tendencies in the language awareness movement. However, it has the negative spin-off of encouraging teachers to separate it from 'English' lessons. We think that this is a shame. Learners ought not to be left to work out for themselves how to apply what they have learnt about language to their own language practices. If educators are helping learners to become critically aware of how language works, they should build on this awareness to help them develop as responsible and empowered language users. Even if, for good cross-curricular reasons, language awareness is taught by a variety of subject specialists in a separate slot on the timetable, the language development staff should know exactly what is happening in this course. They should be involved in the planning of both courses, ensuring that the critical language awareness is relevant to whatever reading, writing and oral interaction the learners are engaged in.

2.   Learning emancipatory discourse

We believe that CLA should underlie all language teaching and learning. It need not necessarily be the focus of all lessons but should regularly be foregrounded. In our view critical educators should help learners to identify situations in their own lives in which they currently feel dominated, and recognise the role language plays in this domination. Then they can discuss what might be done about it, and plan projects which can realistically contribute to change. This discussion can include the obstacles and constraints which deter people from emancipatory discourse, possible alternatives to the conventions, and the consequences of contestation. The learners' experience becomes the content of learning – a process which is itself empowering for the learners.

As far as possible, critical educators should try to arrange for learners to read, write and talk for real purposes, with real interlocutors other than the teachers, and real outcomes other than mere assessment. It is impossible to weigh up whether to conform or resist if there are to be no consequences for the choice. People can only learn how to practise emancipatory discourse when faced with all the subtleties of a real social context in which to choose their words. Having said that, we have to acknowledge the reality that this is not always practical. Educators often have to resort to simulations, but these need to specify not only the content for communication but also the complexities of social relationships in which they are embedded.

Such experiences should be accompanied by further discussion of when the learners chose to practise emancipatory discourse, when they didn't, the reasons for those choices, and how they carried them out. In this way becoming a more confident, responsible language user interacts with becoming more critically aware of language.

Learners could also be encouraged to watch television interviews and to observe the power relations at work. Who speaks most often? Who interrupts? How do people get the floor? How are underdogs treated? How much of this treatment is via language? Is there any evidence of contestation?

3.   The role of groups in CLA and emancipatory discourse

It is easier for individuals to identify their own need for emancipation in groups. If, for example, one reads a text from a particular subject position, another reading may only be possible from another subject position. It is not always possible to put oneself into another subject position or sometimes even to conceive that other subject positions exist. Groups made up of people from different social backgrounds, who do not share the same 'common sense', are unlikely to have the same reading of a text. They can therefore learn from one another. The range of perspectives available in the group serves to de-naturalise all perspectives. Multilingual, multiracial, multicultural, mixed-gender classrooms provide an ideal environment in which people can test their own readings against those of others. If the group is socially heterogeneous enough then members of the group can be encouraged to articulate a range of meanings based on who they are and where they fit in to the whole social fabric. Almost any text would generate a range of responses like this. This is a good way of moving from the analysis of the text to its function as discourse: text embedded in social relations, as we described it on pp. 307, with the example of the Mandela speech.

Groups of learners can work together to develop their collective language capabilities, through what Freire calls the *conscientisation* of existing language abilities and what enables and constrains them. They can support each other in sustaining alternative discourse practices which do not disempower others, and in resisting disempowerment.

4. Who needs CLA and emancipation?

Many people object to work of this sort because they say disempowered people just need to develop competence in standardised English, and they don't want to waste time discussing it. Members of minority groups don't need anyone to tell them about the way social practices, including language, exclude them from power. Members of dominant groups may need CLA to avoid disempowering others, but disempowered people know all this without teachers. We think this view is misguided for two reasons. First, however critically aware learners are, it is important that this awareness is brought into the classroom. It is important that everyone knows what everyone thinks about language values and language use. If they are not discussed, the learners might assume, rightly or wrongly, that the teacher advocates the status quo – or vice versa. Second, each individual in a class has many identities, as our example of the man who speaks Urdu on p. 306 shows. In some subject positions she/he may be a member of a dominant group and in others she/he may be disempowered. This complexity is worth teasing out, and then the rights and responsibilities attaching to the different positions in different social contexts can be addressed.

Summing up, we would envisage a CLA being embedded within a programme of language education which focused upon developing the collective language capabilities of groups of learners, rather than just individual abilities. This will involve recognising their different positions as top dogs and underdogs in different social situations, and learning how to use others-empowering and self-empowering language accordingly. It will include understanding the socio-historical conditions and constraints within which they act, and recognising the contribution their actions can make to longer-term social and discoursal change.

In the following two sections we will suggest ways in which these principles work out in practice. We will give examples of activities designed to lead learners through CLA to emancipatory changes in their discourse practices as readers and writers.

CLA, learning to write and emancipatory discourse

In this section we will suggest how educators might help learners to move beyond CLA to learning how to practise emancipatory discourse as a part of learning to write. Learning to write involves not just learning the language forms and psycholinguistic processes of writing, but involves also becoming a writer in different social contexts. Learning to write is a particularly important part of the curriculum from the point of view of applying CLA. First, learners don't have to commit themselves to their words instantaneously, but can weigh and discuss values and consequences in the course of revising their writing. Second, writers are producers of discourse, not just receivers. In deciding what sort of identity to create as writers they are in a position to exercise social responsibility towards others as well as self-empowerment.

Critical awareness of writing might include discussion of the power relations we enter into as writers of different types of text: the way in which writers of some sorts of texts appear to be authorities, with relative power over readers, whereas writers of other types of texts are open to evaluation and devaluation by their readers. The discussion opens up issues such as the difference between types of writing done by learners for teachers and all other types of writing. There are very few cut-and-dried answers: discussion shows that where the balance of power lies depends on an interaction between the text type, the specific context and the status of the writer and the reader. Learner-writers also need to realise the effects of their language choices on other people and the way in which they are positioned as writers if they follow the conventions of appropriacy. (See Chapter 2.) All these discussions are valuable in their own right, but achieve little unless they are related to learners' own development as writers.

To achieve this a critical educator needs to encourage learners to take what they are learning into consideration when they are writing, to give them opportunities for this, to help them know what the options for emancipatory discourse are in particular writing events, to anticipate the risks, and help them face the consequences.

Lessons might include discussion of the occasions when learners write 'as themselves'. In most of what they write at home and school they are likely to write from a relatively powerless position. If they want to resist conventions they will be taking a risk: a bit of a risk in choosing discourse which avoids disempowering others; a considerable risk in choosing self-empowering discourse. Each learner will have to decide which risks to take: for example, in academic essays using 'I' is not much of a risk these days, but refusing to use the passive in a scientific report might be highly risky. However, critical awareness may have given her/him the consciousness that she/he no longer wants to be the sort of person who represents knowledge as objective and impersonal. (For detailed discussion and examples of these decisions in academic writing, see Chapter 6.)

To take another example, a learner of Afro-Caribbean language background in Britain may not be taking much of a risk to write a song using British Black English, but would be taking a big risk to use the same variety for a letter to a headteacher. The role of the educator here is to ensure that learners discuss these issues, and to help them weather the consequences of their 'live' experiments.

To supplement naturally arising writing experience, an educator might design a simulation in which learners have to take different roles, several of which require memo and letter writing.[2] Some of the roles can give the learners the experience of having relative power as writers, others can give them the experience of being powerless and/or in unfamiliar situations. A simulation of this sort can give learners the opportunity to decide what sort of language use would be consonant with particular role-holders' values, and to weigh the consequences for them of using non-conventional discourse in the particular context. Learners can experience how emancipatory it can be when people with power avoid disempowering discourse. For example, if managers consult the people who work for them instead of informing them it helps to equalise relationships in an office. They can also experience how difficult it is for someone in a relatively powerless position to challenge conventions, however much she/he may want to do so.

Simulations need to be followed by a discussion of the issues they raise, and of how these apply to the learners' own current or future writing. However, a simulation is never an alternative to 'real writing' because it doesn't fully engage the learner in establishing what sort of person she/he herself wants to be as a writer.

Another activity which helps people to establish their social identity as a writer is rewriting from an alternative subject position: rewriting sexist advertisements to make them non-sexist; rewriting racist letters to the press so that they do not offend any racial group; rewriting publicity material so that it takes account of the needs of disabled people; rewriting school history textbooks. Rewriting doubles as a critical writing activity and a critical reading activity – which brings us to our final section.

CLA, learning to read and emancipatory discourse

In this section we will outline what we mean by 'reading' and what sort of CLA learner-readers (including ourselves) need. We will then give an extended example of how a particular text could be used to help learners develop CLA and more control over our position as readers.

Language as a practice has to be produced and received. As we showed in the story of the student at the foreign university, the subject position of the receiver affects the way language is received. This is surely true if the message is spoken or written. We would like to use the word 'read' very broadly. One can read a film, a book, a discussion, a poster, an interaction. 'Read' in this broad sense means to hear or see and to interpret: to give a 'reading' of something.

Oppositional reading, reading which actively resists the 'preferred' reading, is helped by a CLA which can be raised by classroom activities. A central aim of CLA is to uncover the choices which have been made in the creation of a text. At a macro level this includes the selection of a particular language, a particular variety of that language, a particular genre or mixture of genres, and a particular register or mixture of registers. At a micro level this involves the selection of specific linguistic items and linguistic structures in a selected order. Because language is a system it can be seen as 'a network of interlocking options' (Halliday 1985). Choice of one option necessarily implies rejection of other options. Because any selection directs our attention 'to what is present . . . and away from what is no longer there' (Kress & Hodge 1979), it is useful to consider the range of options from which a linguistic feature has been selected, thus highlighting what might have been selected but was not. Attention to what was and was not selected is a useful starting point for resistance. The constructedness of texts becomes apparent and this de-naturalises them. It is possible to de-construct something that someone has constructed. It is difficult at first to know what to focus on in a text without guidance: we suggest that it is part of the responsibility of a critical educator to offer this guidance to learners.

Here is an example of critical language analysis and a role-play designed to help readers consciously establish a reading position. The article (Figure 13.1) for analysis appeared in *The Saturday Star*, a South African newspaper, on 23 December 1989.

In a paper entitled 'Two worlds in one country: 'First world' and 'third world' in South Africa', John Sharp (1988) provides a detailed analysis of the use of 'first world–third world' terminology in South Africa.

> In the first half of this century South Africa's population was seen to comprise different 'races'; thereafter, for the next thirty years, greater emphasis was placed on cultural differences, and 'ethnicity' as factors responsible for diversity in the country's population . . . In the 1980's, however, some of this former diversity is being subsumed within a dualist paradigm, which sees the main divide between a developed sector of the population and an undeveloped and undifferentiated one. (Sharp 1988: 117)

This changing terminology is related to changes in the policy of the ruling party: ' "Race" was the language of segregation and "ethnicity" the language of apartheid; "first world–third world" is . . . a suitable discourse for the politics of reform' (ibid.: 118–19). It is clear from the newspaper article that 'third world' is for many whites in South Africa simply a euphemism for racist terminology. That 'Third World drivers' refers to black drivers is made clear in paragraph 7.

The dualist paradigm created by 'first world–third world' terminology maintains a divide between 'us' and 'them'. 'First world' connotes hi-tech sophistication, efficiency and wealth. 'Third world' connotes primitive backwardness and poverty. The under-

Saturday Star December 23 1989

Ignore the Third World driver at your peril

SUE OLSWANG

1 Road accidents claim an average of 30 lives each day in South Africa. And a further 87 people are seriously injured every 24 hours.

2 "Many of those 87 seriously injured will become permanently disabled in some way - either suffering from partial or total paralysis, brain damage or the loss of a limb.

3 "Some accident victims recover but others find their lives permanently changed as a result of a road accident which lasted mere seconds," said Mr Eric Wise, deputy director of the National Road Safety Council (NRSC).

4 Mr Wise, commenting on the country's alarming road accident statistics, which invariably climb during holiday periods when motorists rush to reach their destinations, said South Africa had large numbers of Third World drivers who travel in First World vehicles on First World roads.

5 He said: "The warning to First World drivers in South Africa is to watch out and be careful of Third World drivers. Ignoring the dangers can be compared to blindly jumping into a pool full of sharks because you don't believe they will go for you.

6 "We cannot, however, blame Third World drivers for their poor driving abilities because most have not been exposed to First World driving until now.

7 "The recent scrapping of certain apartheid laws has resulted in more movement among blacks; but being able to move about freely does not make First World drivers.

8 "The fact is that most Third World drivers have limited driving experience and it is foolish to ignore this reality."

9 Apart from inexperience, sheer negligence and recklessness, among all types of drivers, were also to blame for accidents.

Figure 13.1

development of the 'third world' is rarely seen as a consequence of the development of the 'first' (Sharp 1988: 112).

In the newspaper article, Mr Wise, who is quoted, uses this terminology to construct 'them' as a threat to 'us'. 'First World drivers', to whom his words are addressed (para. 5), are imperilled (headline) by 'Third World drivers'. The injunction to 'watch out and be careful of Third World drivers' and not to 'ignore the dangers' (para. 5) constructs black drivers as potential killers on the road. This is made quite explicit in the comparison of these drivers to 'sharks' who 'go for you'.

The negation which opens para. 6 implies that 'we' *are* likely to 'blame Third World drivers for their poor driving abilities'. The 'first world–third world' paradigm rarely attributes blame for 'third world' underdevelopment to the 'first world'. 'Third world' drivers who have passed 'first world' driving tests cannot be assumed to be more inexperienced than white drivers who passed the same test. It is not their inexperience that is foregrounded. What is foregrounded is the contrast between 'third world' technical backwardness and first world roads and cars, implying that black people lack the intelligence and skill to cope with 'first world' technology. This is racist discourse wearing the guise of 'current international discourse about problems of development' (Sharp 1988: 114).

A critical language analysis of the passage needs also to look at the sequencing of information. The passage begins with statistics on road accident fatalities and injuries (paras 1 and 2). It then gives a disproportionately long quote which focuses on the dangers of 'Third World drivers'. 'The negligence and recklessness of all types of drivers' (para. 9) is briefly referred to in the last paragraph, which is the least likely to be read in a newspaper article. The deputy director's comments on 'Third World drivers' *follow* the information on serious injuries such as 'paralysis, brain damage or the loss of a limb', heightening the sense of threat to 'First World' (i.e. white) drivers.

We could no doubt take the analysis of the language of the article further but we feel that enough has been said to give a sense of what kinds of insights a critical examination of the language can reveal. We turn now to how this might be taken further by group reading, with the aim of helping learners re-examine their own reading positions through recognition of other positions, and change them if they so choose. One way of doing this might be through a role-play, in which learners assume the identity of particular people in order to read and discuss the article. Here are ten roles which are likely to create lively discussion:

1. Mr Eric Wise, deputy director of the National Road Safety Association, who is quoted in the article.

2. The President of the South African black Taxi Association.
3. A white woman driver recently qualified.
4. A white man convicted of drunken driving after an accident in which a black pedestrian was killed.
5. The grown-up daughter of the black pedestrian who was killed.
6. A man whose family was badly injured after an accident in which his car was hit by a black taxi driver.
7. A white traffic inspector.
8. A black traffic inspector.
9. A black bus driver.
10. Sue Olswang, a white woman who is probably also a driver. She wrote the article in question.

We have chosen these people because it is easy to imagine that they will bring to their reading a range of different knowledge and experience that will produce very different interpretations.[3] Learners should quite easily be able to construct positions for the people they are role-playing, and so highlight differences between them.

The role-play should be followed by carefully directed discussion, in which the learners come to understand the importance of the fact that there is more than one reading of a text. This should be followed by a discussion of which reading the learners themselves – individually and collectively – want to make of the article. This will involve perhaps identifying with one of the roles in the role-play, or spelling out their own reading positions according to their own allegiances and values.

Learners can work out what they think the 'preferred' reading of the text is and how the use of language in the text supports this. If they choose to contest the preferred reading, they need to discuss what sort of action this might lead to, and what the consequences might be. The advantage of role play is that it takes learners away from what might be quite limited experience of alternative reading positions. In this case, the role play would be particularly interesting in classrooms inside South Africa, but it would also introduce learners outside South Africa to ways of thinking about issues which they might otherwise dismiss as 'not to do with me'. However, role-plays alone are not enough. Even quite young learners do already have reading positions constructed for them by their social context, and critical educators need to find opportunities for them to examine *those* positions, by reading 'as themselves', for real.

Conclusion

We wish to conclude with some thoughts on taking seriously the notion of 'for real'. We see the use of language as a meaning-making process and we believe that language users have to resist subjection and take responsibility for the meanings they construct. In so doing they have to understand that they can contribute either to reproducing or to reshaping existing social relations. We do not believe that language can be taught apart from social involvement. Knowledge about emancipatory discourse has to be learnt in the front lines. People who work with oppressed communities or grassroots organisations learn from experience and contact which language forms demean or devalue the people they are interacting with. We can all learn to think and write without sexism by studying feminist writings. We can all come to understand gay issues by reading gay newspapers and magazines. There are no textbook recipes. There are no short cuts. Lessons in classrooms are not enough.

'Emancipation' and 'contestation' are not just words in an academic paper. People endanger themselves when they challenge the prevailing power structures. Sometimes they even die. Hegemony depends on the consent of the masses. It starts to break down when people refuse to conform. Groups of people stand a better chance of changing social practices, but the more people there are, the fiercer the battle is likely to be. There is more at stake when people flex their emancipatory muscles together. Learning emancipatory discourse is one way in which each of us, individually and collectively, can contribute to the struggle for a democratic and just society.

Notes

1. This process is obscured in writing, of course, because writers can weigh their words as long as they like without the readers knowing about it.
2. A simulation of this sort is described by Littlejohn 1988.

3. If as the reader of this chapter it is easy for you to provide an oppositional reading of this article because the position from which you start is in opposition anyhow, then you need to recognise that there are many white South Africans who would accept the article as common sense. Mr Eric Wise, for example, may need exposure to the other readings if his position is in any way to shift.

References

Althusser L 1970 Ideology and ideological state apparatuses. In *Essays on ideology*. Verso

Apple M W 1979 *Ideology and curriculum*. Routledge & Kegan Paul

Apple M W 1988 *Teachers and texts*. Routledge & Kegan Paul

Clark R, Fairclough N, Ivanič R. and Martin-Jones M 1987 Critical Language Awareness. *Centre for Language in Social Life Working Papers Series no 1*. Lancaster: Department of Linguistics

Fairclough N L 1989 *Language and power*. Longman

Freire P 1970 *Cultural action for freedom*. Penguin

Freire P 1972 *Pedagogy of the oppressed*. Penguin

Giroux H A 1983 *Theory and resistance in education: a pedagogy for the opposition*. Bergin & Garvey

Giroux H A 1988 *Teachers as intellectuals*. Bergin & Garvey,

Gramsci A 1971 Notebooks. In Hoare O & Smith G N (eds) *Selections from the prison notebooks of Antonio Gramsci*. Lawrence & Wishart

Hall S 1980 Encoding/Decoding. In *Culture, media, language*. Central Cultural Studies Unit, Hutchinson

Halliday M A K 1985 *An introduction to functional grammar*. Edward Arnold

Kress G 1985 *Linguistic processes as sociocultural practice*. Deakin Press

Kress G, Hodge R 1979 *Language as ideology*. Routledge & Kegan Paul

Littlejohn A 1988 *Company to company: a new approach to business correspondence in English*. Cambridge University Press

Mischler E 1985 *The discourse of medicine*. Ablex

Progressive Literacy Group 1986 *Writing on our side*. PLG

Sharp J 1988 Two worlds in one country: 'First world' and 'third world' in South Africa. In Boonzaaier E, Sharp J. *South African keywords: the uses and abuses of political concepts*. David Phillips

Index

Note. As most references are to critical language awareness, this has generally been omitted as a qualifier.

Abercrombie, N., 41
academic discourse community, 20, 117–19; entering as student, 119–21
academic writing, 20–1, 141–73; cast, 20–1, 145–52; critical language awareness, 169–70; dialogue in, 314; examples, 132, 139–40, 153–69, 172–3; personal see 'I'; see also university classroom
adolescent girls see gender construction
advertising, 5–6, 316, 325; direct mail and IT, 217–18; and teenage magazine, 175–6, 188, 192
age and IT, 211, 218
Alderson, C., 70
Allwright, J., 137
Althusser, L., 308
ambiguity in euphemisms, 233–4
Andersen, R., 60
Aplin, T. R. N., 294
Apple, M. W., 311
appropriateness, appropriacy of, 14, 17–18, 33–58; and critical language awareness, 53–4; as ideology, 47–53; and language awareness, 37–9; in language education, 34; normativeness and inappropriateness, 36–7; presupposed, 43–7; and skills, 39–43; see also models of language variation
artificial intelligence, 215–16
Asians, 266; see also black housing association
assertive readers, 60
assessment see attainment
assignment setters/readers of students' academic writing, 21, 146, 152, 156–9, 168–9
attainment/assessment and NC, 250, 252–3
Auerbach, E., 65
authorities, 225–7, 323
awareness see critical language awareness

Baker, K., 221
Baratz, J. and S., 251
Barnes, D., 5, 43
Bartholomae, D., 119, 125
Bazalgette, C., 212, 215
Berne, J., 101
Bernstein, B. B., 220

Bhatt, A., vii; on minority
languages and bilingualism, 25,
285–301
bilingualism and multilingualism,
23–4, 45; in secondary school,
266–7, 271, 276–80; seen
as problem, 93–7; *see also*
black housing association;
euphemisms; minority
languages
black housing association,
communication skills
training in, 19, 93–116;
correspondence, 96–112, 115;
spelling, 95, 112–14
Bolter, J. D., 210
Boorstin, 194
borrowed words, 294
Botswana *see* euphemisms
Boud, D., 240
Bourdieu, P., 7, 14, 19
Bourne, J., 251, 263, 286, 288
Bradford *see* black housing
association
Brice Heath, S., 64–5
bridging assumption, 195
Brooke, R., 171
Brown, G., 195
Bruner, J.S., 241
Bullock\Report on language for
life (1975), 243, 245, 251,
259, 287, 288
Butterfield, C., 161

Cameron, D., 251, 263, 288
Candlin, C. N., 42
capabilities *see* skills
Carr, W., 240, 247
Carter, R., 52, 63
Case studies *see* examples
Cashdan, A., 250
cast: and academic writing, 20–1,
145–52; in teenage magazine,
174, 176–80, 181–6, 194

Centre for Language in Social Life
(Lancaster), 260
Certificate of Pre-Vocational
Education, 33, 40, 41
characters in teenage magazine,
177, 178–9, 181–6, 194, 195;
see also cast
Chase, G., 117, 118
Chomsky, N., 42
CLA *see* critical language
awareness
Clark, H., 195
Clark, R., vii, 53, 248, 257; on
university classroom, 7, 10, 16,
19–20, 21, 117–40
Clarke, P., vii; on primary
schools, 23, 238–55
class *see* social structure
code-switching, 293, 296, 318
collaboration and collective
action: education as, 138;
and emancipatory discourse,
318–19, 321–2; and IT, 209,
211; in secondary schools, 265,
270, 280–3; and social change,
4; and spelling, 114
college classroom *see* EFL
classroom
'committed-I' in academic writing,
147–8
communication skills view of
language education, 33, 40; *see
also* black housing association
communicative approach concept,
42
communicative competence
concept, 42
community: consumption,
175–6, 194; interpretative,
64; languages *see* minority
languages; of readers, 63–4,
67, 175–6, 194
comparative linguistics, 290,
293–5

competence *see* skills
comprehensive school *see*
  secondary
computers *see* IT
consciousness-raising, 240, 307;
  and academic writing, 124–5,
  127–30, 142; *see also* critical
  language awareness
consumption community, 175–6,
  194
content of academic writing, 124,
  145, 156–8, 159–62, 164–7
conversational language *see*
  informal
correctness, doctrines of, 51
correspondence *see* mail
Corson, D., 225
counselling, 11, 45
Cox Reports on English for ages
  5 to 16 (DES, 1989), 1, 12, 14,
  27, 28; and appropriateness,
  18, 33, 34–9, 41, 43, 46,
  52–3; and IT, 24, 203–5, 206,
  221; and minority languages,
  288–90, 293; and primary
  schools, 243, 251–3; and
  secondary school, 260–4
critical discourse analysis, 2,
  10–12
critical language awareness,
  1–29; *see also* appropriateness;
  educational contexts;
  emancipatory discourse;
  schools
critical language study, 2, 7–12
critical learning, 239–40, 242
critical linguistics, 2, 7
critical reading *see* EFL classroom
Crowley, T., 53
cultural analysis and IT, 205–6

data bank society, 216–17
'deficit' model of language
  teaching, 95–7, 115

description of text, 10–11, 256
devalued languages *see* minority
  languages; variations
dialects *see* variations
dialogue in academic writing, 314
direct mail advertising, 217–18
discourse: academic *see* academic
  discourse; liberation *see*
  emancipatory discourse;
  reading in EFL classroom, 68,
  74–80; reconstructed from text,
  74–80; school *see* euphemisms;
  and society, 8–12, 28
discrimination and stereotyping,
  68, 130, 136, 211, 215,
  251; marginalisation, 62, 65;
  sexism, 68, 130, 136, 306; *see
  also* emancipatory discourse;
  gender; racism; variations
discursive formations, 225
disempowerment: by
  interpellation, 309–10; of
  others, avoiding, 26, 311–15;
  resisting, 26, 315–16; in
  secondary school, 256–7; *see
  also* power
disguise in euphemisms, 232
diversity, linguistic *see* variations
doctor and patient *see* medical
domination *see* power
Doughty, P., 1, 12, 22, 52, 258,
  260, 261
drama, 269–70

Eagleton, T., 68
Education for Multi-ethnic Society
  (EMES), 266, 268
educational context, 18–22; in
  climate of change, 3–6; *see
  also* academic writing; black
  housing association; EFL
  classroom; gender construction;
  schools; university classroom
Edwards, A., 253

EFL (English as a Foreign Language), 42, 259
EFL (English as a Foreign Language) classroom: critical language awareness in, 18–19, 59–92; *see also* bilingualism; reading in EFL classroom
'ego-I' in academic writing, 147–8
electronic mail, 206, 207, 213
ELIZA program, 221
emancipatory discourse, 10, 20, 25–6, 305–31; in academic writing, 118, 124, 136–7; language and subjection, 307–11; and learning to read, 325–30; and learning to write, 323–5; not disempowering others, 311–15; as part of language education, 319–23; participation in struggle, 316–19; power and assymetrical power relations, 306–7; resisting disempowerment, 315–16
emotive issue, spelling as, 112–13, 115
empowerment, 297; in academic writing, 118, 124, 130, 136–7; and discourse *see* euphemisms; after interpellation, 310–11; and NC, 252; in secondary school, 257; *see also* power
encyclopaedic databases, 208
Englehart, J., 160
English: as foreign language *see* EFL; as 'official language', 291; *see also* IT; non-English speakers; standard English; variations
entitlement and opportunity, 14, 28, 42–3, 251–2
equal opportunities and IT, 211
essays *see* writing

ethnic differences and speech, 38–9; *see also* bilingualism; minority languages; non-English speakers
ethnocentrism *see* racism
euphemisms: school discourse and empowerment, 22–3, 223–37, 313; critical language teaching, 225–7; idiom, euphemism as, 227–9; learner-centredness, 224–5; *see also* teachers' reports
examples: academic writing, 132, 139–40, 153–69, 172–3; correspondence in black housing association, 97–112; EFL classroom, 72–80; emancipatory discourse, 308–11, 327; IT teaching topics, 214–18; primary school, 245–9; reading texts in EFL classroom, 70, 82–92; teenage magazine text, 181–6, 197–9
existing language capabilities *see* expert linguists
experiential meanings, 77–9
expert linguists, children as, 256–7, 263–4, 273, 279
explanation of text, 10–11

Fairclough N., vii, 59, 61, 67, 69, 123–4, 175, 265; on appropriateness, 33–58; on critical language awareness, 1–29
femininity *see* gender construction
fetishism, linguistic, 51
field, 77–8
Fish, S., 63
Flores, F., 203, 207, 215
flow diagram, 244, 245
foregrounding, 307
foreign languages *see* bilingualism, modern languages

form, 124; preoccupation with, 290, 293–5
forum concept, 241
Foucault, M., 7, 50
Fowler, R., 7, 121, 122
Freire, P., 7, 13, 311, 322
friendly relationship between writers and readers, 180, 189–94, 196
further education see academic; EFL classroom; university

Garson, 290, 291, 294
gender, 317; construction in teenage magazine, 21–2, 174–99; and IT, 211, 215; and modern languages, 266; and speech style, 38–9, 44, 45; see also sexism
generalisation of competence models, 41–2
Giroux, H., 13, 309, 311
Graddol, D., 136
grammar, 27, 51, 113, 226; demise of, 258–9, 263–5; and EFL classroom, 69, 77
Gramsci, A., 49, 306
groups see collaboration
Grundy, S., 240

Habermas, J., 7
Hafstadter, D. R., 221
Hall, S., 121, 122, 307
Halliday, M. A. K., 8, 51, 69, 77, 80, 121, 195, 258, 325
Harris, J., 101
Harris Report on modern languages (1990), 289, 294
Hasan, R., 77
Haviland, S., 195
Hawkins, E., 1, 12–15, 260–1, 267, 287–8, 294
Hawkins, E., 34

hegemony and language standardisation, 43, 49–52, 54
Henriques, J., 7
Hewitt, 43
hidden agendas, 250–1, 288
histories of reading, 64–5
Hodge, R., 7, 138, 326
home language see bilingual; expert linguists; minority languages
housing association see black housing
Hoyles, C., 211, 213, 215
Hymes, D., 42, 52

'I' in academic writing, 20, 120, 130, 136, 142–8, 153–4, 163–8, 324
idealisation of sociolinguistic order, 51–3
ideational function of language, 8–9
identical function of language, 8–9
identity of readers constructed see gender construction
identity of writers: expressed see 'I'; submerged see objectivity
ideology: appropriateness as, 47–53; and discourse, 8–9; interpellation, 308–11; and language in academic writing, 121–2, 138; in texts in EFL classroom, 60–1, 69–71; see also power
idiom, euphemism as, 227–9
imitation, 171
impersonal writing see objectivity
inappropriateness, 36–7, 47
Industrial Language Training, 94
inferences, drawing see EFL classroom
informal language, 4–5, 11, 46; and appropriateness see variations; in teenage

magazine, 180, 192; *see also* naturalisation
information technology *see* IT
interaction: between readers and writers *see under* reading; writing; interactants in teenage magazine, 177, 178, 193
interpellation, 308–11
interpersonal function of language, 8, 10
interpersonal meanings, 78, 79
interpretation, 10–11; as aim of PVE, 40; interpretative community, 64; of IT, 213–14; in model of discourse, 123–4
intertextuality, 67–8
interviews, 4, 5, 9, 11, 44–6, 49–50, 306, 318, 321
introductions to academic writing, 162–3
invisibility of minorities in texts, 65
IT (information technology) and English teaching in schools, 24–5, 203–22; Cox Report on, 24, 203–5, 206, 221; equal opportunities; generic, content-free software, 207–8; literacy, changing demands of, 208–10; literacy, changing forms of, 205–7; research frameworks, 219–21; teaching topic examples, 214–18; type of usage and levels of understanding, 212–14
Ivanič, R., viii, 53, 127, 130, 137; on academic writing, 20, 21, 141–73; on emancipatory discourse, 10, 20, 21, 25–6, 305–31

Jackie see gender construction
Janks, H., viii; on emancipatory discourse, 10, 17, 20, 21, 25–6, 305–31
Jessop, R., 27
Jones, R., 227, 228, 234

Keat, R., 41
Kemmis, S., 240, 247
Kimberley, K., 218
Kingman Report on teaching of English language (DES, 1988), 1, 12, 14, 27, 28, 288; and appropriateness, 39, 53; and IT, 203, 206; and primary schools, 245, 251; and secondary schools, 260, 263
Kinnock, N., 307
Kress, G., 2, 7, 60, 71, 72, 138, 226–7, 308, 326

LA *see* language awareness
Lancaster, L., viii; on language awareness in secondary schools, 22, 256–84
Lancaster University, 260; *see also* academic writing; university classroom
language awareness, 1; with appropriateness, 37–9; and CLA compared, 12–17; critical *see* critical language awareness
Language Ideology and Power Group (Lancaster), 137
Language Information Network Co-ordination project, 290–2, 295
Language in National Curriculum, 260, 263–4
language use *see* discourse
learner-centredness and euphemisms, 23, 224–5
Leech, G. N., 223
Leiss, W., 194
Leonard, S. A., 51
Levinson, S., 47–8

LINC *see* Language Information Network Co-ordination; Language in National Curriculum

linguistic competence concept, 42

listening, 40, 243, 248–9

literacy: events, 64–5; IT and changes in, 203, 205–10; *see also* reading; writing

Littlejohn, A., 224–5, 330

Lodge, D., 221

McCormick, 160

McKenzie, M., viii–ix; on euphemisms, 22–3, 223–37

McRobbie, A., 180–1

Madeley Court School, 266–83

magazine, teenage *see* gender construction

mail: advertising, 217–18; dealing with, 75–6, 96–112, 115; electronic, 206, 207, 213

Mandela, N., 307, 322

Manningham Housing Association *see* black housing association

Mappes, A., 160–1

marginalisation *see* discrimination

Marshall-Lee, A., 137

Martin-Jones, M., viii; on minority languages and bilingualism, 25, 285–301

Maru a Pula Secondary School *see* euphemisms

Marx, K., 51

mass media, 5–6, 206; and adolescent girls *see* gender construction; and emancipatory discourse, 326–9; texts studied in EFL classroom, 61, 83–92; *see also* advertising

meanings: absolute, 226; experiential, 77–9; interpersonal, 78, 79; preferred, 307–9; search for *see* EFL classroom; textual, 78, 79–80; *see also* social meaning

media *see* mass media

medical situations, 4–5, 9, 11, 44–5, 49–50, 306, 308, 315–16

members resources (MR), 265

metalanguage, 69

metaphors: computer, 25, 214–16; grammatical, 51

Mey, J., 2, 7

minority languages, bilingual learners and language awareness, 25, 285–301; critical approach, 295–8; linguistic diversity, 290–5; minority language as resource, 285, 286–9, 298; teaching minority community languages, 298–9; *see also* bilingualism

Mischler, E., 45, 308

mode, 78

models of language variation, 34–43; critique of, 43–53

modern languages, 13, 287–8; *see also* Madeley Court

multilingualism *see* bilingualism

Munion, 155

National Association of Teachers of English, 265–6

National Congress on Language in Education, 13, 259–60

National Curriculum: and IT, 205, 211, 221; and minority languages, 289; in primary schools, 23, 239, 243, 250–3, 254; and secondary schools, 22, 259, 260–3, 283

naturalisation of language, 6, 9–10; in academic writing, 121–2, 124; *see also* 'I'; informal

NC *see* National Curriculum

NCLE *see* National Congress on Language in Education
neutral attitude to linguistic diversity 290–6
Newbolt Report, 251
newspapers *see* mass media
non-critical approach, 12–17
non-English speakers: in housing association *see* black housing association; in university *see* university classroom; *see also* EFL classroom; bilingualism
non-linear texts, 209–10
non-standard English *see* variations
non-verbal communication, 5, 269, 270
normalising nature of PVE, 40–1
normativeness and inappropriateness, 36–7
Nuffield Programme, 258, 259

objectivity in writing, 20, 119–20, 130, 227
obligations, 37, 134–7
Olson, D. R., 206
opportunity *see* entitlement
oppositional reading, 325–6
oracy: oral storytelling project example in primary school, 248–9; *see also* listening; speech
outsiders, readers as *see* EFL classroom
over-lexicalisation, 313

passivisation in academic writing, 119, *see also* objectivity
Pêcheux, M., 7, 225
pedagogic principles of academic writing, 123–5
people written about, 21, 151–2, 168, 311–13

people written to, 21, 146, 152, 156–9, 168–9, 313–15
Perera, K., 158
personal identity in writing *see* 'I'
personalization, synthetic *see* gender construction
Pilger, J., 59, 66
politeness in euphemisms, 232–3
politics and international relations students *see* university classroom
Pomphrey, C., 291, 294, 295
population *see* cast; test population
post-reading procedures in EFL classroom, 18, 71, 74
power: assymetrical power relations, 306–7; and discourse, 8–9; and emancipation *see* emancipatory; and production of texts, 66; and social change, 3, 6; and standardisation of language, 43, 49–52, 54; *see also* disempowerment; empowerment; teachers
pre-reading procedures in EFL classroom, 18, 71, 72–3
pre-vocational education and appropriateness, 18, 33, 39–41
preference for standard English, 37
preferred meaning, 307–9
prescriptiveness and appropriateness, 36–7
presuppositions: of appropriateness, 43–7; ideological, in academic writing, 122–3; in teenage magazine, 179, 183–4, 190–1
primary schools, 23–4, 238–55; critical language awareness and NC, 242, 250–3; critical learning, 239–40, 242; critical practices, 242; storymaking

and storytelling project
examples, 245–9
problematisation of language, 6,
11, 63, 95–7, 113, 287, 299
production (publishing) of texts,
10, 63, 65–6, 123–4; and IT,
207, 209, 218; students' work,
66, 218
professional-client interaction *see*
interviews; medical
programming, computer, 213–14
Progressive Literacy Group, 141
prohibition, 50
projection of texts, 195
publishing *see* production
Pugh, A. K., 161
purposeful language learning, 16
PVE *see* pre-vocational education

questionnaire to teachers about
reports and euphemisms, 234–7

racism and ethnocentrism, 68,
130, 136, 211, 251; and
emancipatory discourse, 306,
326–9; and minority languages,
288, 291–2, 297–8
Raleigh, M., 290, 294
Rampton, B., 298
reader-friendliness in academic
writing, 139–40
readers and writers: in EFL
classroom, 60–1; and teenage
magazine, 175–6, 180, 187–93,
194, 196; in university, 146–8,
151–2, 159–64, 166–7
reading: as aim of PVE, 40;
between lines *see* euphemisms
and reading in EFL classroom;
and emancipatory discourse,
325–30; histories, 64–5;
learning and emancipatory
discourse, 325–30; magazines
see gender construction; *see*

also reading in EFL classroom;
reading in university; readers
and writers
reading in EFL classroom: aims
and procedures, 63; critical,
61–2, 69–70; discourse, 68;
interaction between reader
and text, 60–1; intertextuality,
67–8; methodology, 70–80;
practices, 63–5; processes,
66–7; production and
consumption of material, 65–6;
students and data, 62; texts,
70, 82–92
reading in university: of
assignments *see* assignment
setters; students as readers,
145, 149–50, 151–2; writers of
books read by students, 146–8,
151–2, 159–64, 166–7
real language *see* naturalisation
reality and IT, 215–16
Reid, E., 286
relational function of language,
8–9
reports, school *see* teachers,
reports
resistant reading, 308
resource, minority languages as,
285, 286–9, 298
responsibility: in academic
writing, 130, 164; and EFL
classroom, 312, 314–15
rhetoric *see* metaphors
rights and obligations in academic
writing, tension between,
134–7
Rimmershaw, R., 137
Roach, D., 171
Rogers, J., 162
role: identification in PVE, 40; of
people in university writing *see*
academic writing; simulations,
315, 324–6, 328–9

Rose, N., 41
rote learning, 227
Ruiz, R., 299
Rymaszewski, R., 205, 209, 210, 211, 213

Saussure, F. de, 226
Sayers, P., ix; on communication in black housing association, 19, 93–116
Scholes, R., 61, 67
Schools Council Mother Tongue project, 290–2, 295
schools, critical language awareness in, 22–6; *see also* euphemisms; IT; minority languages; primary; secondary
SCMTP *see* Schools Council Mother Tongue Project
secondary schools, language awareness in, 22, 256–84; background, 257–62; in Shropshire, 262–83; *see also* euphemisms
sexism, 68, 130, 136, 306; *see also* gender
Sharp, J., 326, 327, 328
Shearer, A., 161
Shropshire *see* secondary schools
sign: language, 269, 270; linguistic, 226
Simpson, J., ix, 130; on academic writing, 17, 20, 21, 141–73
sisterhood, false *see* friendly relationship
skills (capabilities and competence), 5, 15–16; and appropriateness, 18, 39–43; communication *see* black housing association; computer, 205–6, 220–1; study for students of politics and international relations, 125–6
Smith, F., 62

Smith, N., ix; on primary schools, 23, 238–55
social action, 10–11
social agents, teachers as, 226–7
social change, 3–6, 27, 312
social dimension of academic writing, 117–18, 123–4
social effects on discourse, 8–12, 28
social history and appropriateness, 48–9
social identity *see* identity
social image *see* discrimination
social meaning of language: ignored *see* neutral; natural, 121–2
social process, reading as, 67
social relations and emancipatory discourse, 307
social structure and class, 14, 19, 306; and appropriateness, 48–9; and discourse, 68; and IT, 211, 218; and NC, 251; and secondary school, 264; and spelling, 113
social subject of academic writing, 124
software, 206, 220; generic content-free, 207–8
specialised IT languages, 208–9
speech, 5; as aim of PVE, 40; people spoken about, 311–13; in primary schools, 243, 248–9; *see also* appropriateness; Talk project
spelling problems, 19, 95, 112–14
spoken word *see* speech
standard English, 8, 261; and appropriateness, 34–7, 42–3, 46, 51, 54; and emancipatory discourse, 315, 318; and LA, 13–15; and minority languages, 288, 292, 296; and opportunity, 42–3, 251–2

standardisation of language: and power, 43, 49–52, 54; see also standard English

static and deterministic attitude to minority languages, 290, 292–3

stereotypes see discrimination

storytelling and storymaking project examples in primary school, 245–9

Stubbs, M., ix–x; on IT, 24–5, 203–22

Study Skills: IT, 205–6; programme see university classroom

style in academic writing, 145, 158–9, 162–4, 167–8, 171

subject: positions in teenage magazine, 177, 179–80, 194; social, 124

subjection and language, 307–11

submissive reader, 60–1

survey, language, 276–9

Swann, J., 136

Swann Report on Education for all (DES, 1985), 251, 286, 288, 289

synthesised reader see gender construction

Talbot, M., x, 171; on gender construction in magazine, 20, 21, 174–99

Talk project, 266, 267–8, 280–1

Tansley, P., 286

targeting: language as target for change, 3, 5; readership see gender construction

Taylor, R., x; on language awareness in secondary schools, 22, 256–84

teachers: as authorities, 225–7; university see assignment setters; university classroom; see also primary schools;

secondary schools; teachers' reports

teachers' reports and euphemisms, 229–37; analysis of, 232–4; questionnaire to teachers, 234–7

Teaching of Writing Research Group (Lancaster), 137, 138

Tebbit, N., 77

technologisation, 5; see also IT

teenage magazine see gender construction

ten Have, 45

tenor, 78

tension and conflict in speech, 45

test population in teenage magazine, 174, 176–80, 181–6, 194

textual examples see under examples

Thatcher, M., 75

Thompson, J. B., 3

Thornton, G., 258, 260, 261

tokenism, 295

training: distinct from education, 39; see also education

Trew, T., 69

Tristram, H., 160

Turing, A. M., 221

Turner, F., 286

understanding levels and IT, 212–4

university classroom, critical language awareness in, 19–20, 117–40; academic discourse model, 123–5; course procedures, 126–34; good essay, characteristics of, 139–40; pedagogic principles, 123–5; tension between rights and obligations, 134–7; theoretical assumptions, 121–3;

see also academic discourse community; academic writing
Urbanak, S., 59
Urquhart, S., 70

vagueness in euphemisms, 234
Van Peer, W., 219
variations, linguistic, 5, 8–9, 25, 290–5; and appropriateness, 35–6, 37, 42, 44, 46, 48; and LA, 12–15; in secondary school, 256–7, 264–7, 271, 273–6, 283; *see also* bilingualism; informal language; minority languages; models of language variation
Verma, M., 286
visual images, 5–6
Volkman, C., 161
Voloshinov, V. I., 7, 50

Walker, R., 63
Wallace, C., x; on EFL classroom, 18, 59–92
we and you in magazine *see* friendly
Weizenbaum, J., 221
Wells, G., 148

while-reading procedures in EFL classroom, 18, 71, 73–4
White, C., 195
Widdowson, H., 60, 225
Winograd, T., 203, 207, 215
women *see* EFL classroom; gender
word processing, 206–8, 212–13
workplace, change in, 4
writing: academic *see* academic writing; as aim of PVE, 40; learning and emancipatory discourse, 323–5; and readers *see* readers and writers; writers as authorities, 323; *see also* writing in university
writing in university: characteristics of good essay, 132, 139–40; people written about, 151–2, 168; students as writers, 150–1, 164–8; *see also* academic writing; university classroom

Young, Lord (of Graffham), 39
Yule, G., 195

Zamel, V., 134
Zembaty, J., 160–1